ENGLISH
SUBJECT
EDUCOLOGY

英语学科教育学

主 编：秦 杰 田金平

外语教学与研究出版社
FOREIGN LANGUAGE TEACHING AND RESEARCH PRESS
北京 BEIJING

图书在版编目（CIP）数据

英语学科教育学／秦杰，田金平主编 . -- 北京：外语教学与研究出版社，2008.08
（2022.8 重印）
ISBN 978-7-5600-7744-4

Ⅰ . ①英…　Ⅱ . ①秦…　②田…　Ⅲ . ①英语－教学法－高等学校－教材　Ⅳ . ①H319.3

中国版本图书馆 CIP 数据核字（2008）第 128387 号

出 版 人　王　芳
责任编辑　李婉婧
责任校对　孔乃卓
封面设计　孙莉明
出版发行　外语教学与研究出版社
社　　址　北京市西三环北路 19 号（100089）
网　　址　http://www.fltrp.com
印　　刷　北京虎彩文化传播有限公司
开　　本　787×1092　1/16
印　　张　22.25
版　　次　2008 年 8 月第 1 版 2022 年 8 月第 17 次印刷
书　　号　ISBN 978-7-5600-7744-4
定　　价　68.90 元

购书咨询：（010）88819926　电子邮箱：club@fltrp.com
外研书店：https://waiyants.tmall.com
凡印刷、装订质量问题，请联系我社印制部
联系电话：（010）61207896　电子邮箱：zhijian@fltrp.com
凡侵权、盗版书籍线索，请联系我社法律事务部
举报电话：（010）88817519　电子邮箱：banquan@fltrp.com
物料号：177440101

记载人类文明
沟通世界文化
www.fltrp.com

前　言

21世纪是英语教育不断创新的时代。

21世纪是英语教育面临新机遇、应对新挑战的时代。

21世纪是英语教育进一步实现本土化和国际化的时代。

随着信息技术、多媒体和网络技术的迅猛发展，新的教学资源和教学手段不断涌现，如何有效地利用各种教学资源和方法培养具有创新意识和创造能力的英语人才是英语教师面临的新课题。从传统教学法的教师中心说到现在的学生中心说，从传统的单一的语法翻译法到现在各种各样的交际法语言教学，从教师培训(training)到教师教育(education)到教师发展(development)再到教师的自我强化(self-empowerment)，教师的创新能力在时代的变迁中不断得到锤炼。教师作为培养人才的人才，其创新意识越来越成为衡量教学水平的重要标准。

在21世纪，"网络教学"、"自主学习"、"以人为本"、"终身学习"等教育理念不断深入人心。面对门类众多的教学法、种类繁多的教学材料、需求各异的课程、不断变化的教学对象，如何把握标准、因地制宜地开展教学活动是广大英语教师面临的挑战。同时，日新月异的教学平台的建构也为教师的自我发展和价值实现提供了前所未有的机遇。

21世纪也是英语教育本土化和国际化同时发展、交叉融合的时期。当今的英语已经不再是单纯的American English或British English，而是World Englishes。对于英语语言使用的评判也不再是简单的"对与错"，而更多的是"能否接受"和在怎样的情形下可以接受的问题。英语交流的本土化和国际化发展趋势为英语教育提出了一系列崭新的命题，比如说世界英语对口语教学的影响问题等等。

基于以上对于时代赋予英语教育的特征和使命的认识，我们认为21世纪的英语教育具有全方位创新的需求。教师不能局限于传授英语知识，而是要培养学生寻求知识、整合知识、并且创造性地应用知识的能力和素养。在这个过程中，学科教育所起的作用是显而易见的。而学校教育在很大程度上可归结为学科教育。

英语学科教育学是研究英语教育的客观规律的科学，是研究英语教学过程以及影响英语教学的诸多因素，揭示英语教学的性质和规律的科学。英语教育学是英语教学法的提升和发展。它是以教育学、心理学、英语语言学、课程论等学科为理论基础的一门交叉应用学科。所谓"应用性"是一个相对的概念。它仅仅是和宏观的教育科学中的"理论"相对而言的。就英语教育本身而言，它有自己的理论和实践。而且英语教学实践是教学理论的源泉。英语教育学从英语教学的实践中研究英语教育现象，探讨提高英语教育质量的规律，反过来它又应用从实践中升华出来的规律指导英语教学实践。

　　本书作为英语学科教育的一本入门书既涉及宏观的与英语教育学相关的学科理论知识，也涉及英语教育学理论与英语体系，继而聚焦在英语教学的课程论、学习论、教学论、评价理论和课堂实践。本书共分九章。第一章作为全书的总括，介绍了英语教学论的基本范畴和概念，并且简述了英语学习理论和教学模式。第二章详细回顾了中外英语教学的历史、教学法的流派、英语教学发展的现状和任务型语言教学。第三章具体介绍了英语课程教学大纲的评价、选择和设计等知识。第四章是本书最长的一章。本章包括了英语听力、口语、阅读、写作、词汇以及语法教学的理论与实践知识。作为例释，每个部分都提供了课堂教学设计的案例。第五章介绍了英语语言教学中的学习者因素，具体分为学习者的个体差异、情感因素、认知因素、学习风格和策略。第六章探讨了英语教学中的文化意识。第七章集中在英语课堂教学的操控和管理，提供了英语教案的设计和课堂组织方面的知识。第八章介绍了英语语言测试的理论，调查了中国英语教学中测试的现状，并且针对中国英语测试的改革提出了一些建议。第九章讨论了英语教师的培训和发展的问题。

　　全书用英语编写，可作为英语专业教学法教材，其读者对象主要为英语专业的本科生和研究生，此外也可供英语教师以及对英语教学感兴趣的各界人士使用。本书如作为英语教育专业主干课的教材，我们建议课程设置一个学期（通常为第七学期），共十八周，原则上每周两课时，每两周（四课时）完成一个章节的学习。鉴于章节长短不一，老师们使用时可以酌情灵活调整。同时，理论课程可以与实践相结合，在每周讲授理论课的过程中适当安排学生进行实践活动，如：围绕课后练习，以小组为单位，设计课堂教学活动、设计测试题目、设计关于学习者因素的调查问卷等等。对于课堂时间内无法完成的任务或活动，授课老师可以安排课后作业，作为学生巩固知识和内化知识的延伸。由于本书比较全面地概括了英语教学领域所涉及的因素、对这些材料的学习有助于学生更好地掌握理论知识，为自己的进一步学习和实践工作打下基础。

　　本书参考了许多有关外语教学的著作和文章，其主要内容曾在山西师范大学的本科生和研究生中使用，并且得到部分教师和学生的宝贵意见和建议，在此一并表示感谢。书中出现的问题皆因作者水平有限所致，希望读者不吝赐教，提出宝贵意见。

秦　杰　　田金平

2007年8月于山西师范大学外国语学院

Contents

Acknowledgements

A number of the chapters of this book have developed from presentations at conferences, published papers, books and online resources.

English subject educology involves a legion of issues. In order to make the contents of this book as representative as possible, and meanwhile to keep up with the tide of English language teaching (ELT) development in the world, we made a wide scope of survey and quoted abundantly. Chapter 1 borrowed ideas from online *Educational Resources Information Center (ERIC)* and *Subject Educology* (Chinese version) edited by Prof. Tao Benyi of Shanghai Normal University. Chapter 2 followed Richards' study and classification on English teaching schools. Chapter 3 quoted Nunan's, Willis', Crookes', Dubin & Olshtain's study on syllabus and related studies; as for the studies on English syllabus evolvement in China, this chapter borrowed some Chinese scholars —Lu Zhongshe's, Huang Yuan-yuan & Xu Hua-li's research achievements. In Chapter 4, the ideas of scholars of the *British Council* enlightened us a lot, and we excerpted as exemplification and illustration some of their teaching models. Chapter 5 borrowed Carroll's, Arnold & Brown's research on learner factors. In Chapter 6, Peterson & Coltrane's (2003) viewpoints on cultural awareness in language teaching were quoted; Buttjes' (1990) contribution on culture teaching in language syllabi was referred to; Chris Rose's (2001) notion of intercultural communicative competence was also quoted. In Chapter 7, we followed and adapted Brown's (2001) ideas on lesson planning and classroom management. In Chapter 8, we quoted Carsten Roever's (2001) research on web-based language testing; in China this is still a weak area of study among researchers and scholars on ELT and language testing. In the last chapter, Chapter 9, we referred to Curtis (1999) on reflective teaching.

We are deeply indebted to all the above-mentioned (and those not mentioned here but mentioned in the other parts of this book) authors and resources for making our book available. We are also grateful to all those people who have given us the opportunity to make our thoughts public.

CHAPTER 1

Basic Concepts of English Language Educology

As the beginning and pavement of the whole book, this chapter focuses on the following major issues:

1. Introduction to English language educology;
2. The study of education and its relation to language educology;
3. Language acquisition/learning theories;
4. A brief survey of English teaching models.

In so doing, we put forward the paramount factors in educology—teaching, learning, and the interactive theories guiding practices in English language education.

1.   Introduction to English language educology

1.1   Why educology

With the modernization and globalization of the world, studies on English language teaching have become increasingly vigorous in recent years. So far various terms have been applied to the field: English teaching, English education, English pedagogy and English educology. While they roughly refer to similar practice guided by similar theories, English educology, as we observed, is more theory-oriented, which is in line with our purpose of writing this book—providing a theoretical basis of studies in ELT and ushering English teachers and student teachers into further theoretical and practical studies. It is, therefore, necessary for us to understand the term educology and subject educology as a first step.

The term "educology" refers to the entire fund of recorded knowledge about the entire educational process. It has been in use since the seminal work in educology by L. W. Harding in the 1950s. This fund of knowledge can be extended through three types of disciplined inquiry: *empirical*, focusing on scientific knowledge; *normative*, focusing on the intrinsic value of aspects of education; and *analytical*, focusing on the analytic philosophy of education, the history of education, and the jurisprudence of education. Like anthropology, sociology, and psychology, educology refers to the effects of variables on its central subject (ERIC)[1].

Subject educology is a discipline with the school subject education as its focus of study. Its final purpose is to completely realize the educational aims. The theoretical basis is taken from research achievements of relevant disciplines, studying the whole process of aim-making, course-setting, syllabus-designing, teaching, learning and evaluation of teaching programs. The development of subject educology has roughly experienced three stages—teaching methods and teaching materials; teaching theories; and branched educology (Tao, 2001)[2]. As for English language educology, the research objects and significance are illustrated as follows.

---

[1] ERIC: http://eric.ed.gov/ERICWebPortal/Home.portal, retrieved March 25, 2006.
[2] Translated from 陶本一．《学科教育学》．人民教育出版社．2001

1.2 Research objects of English subject educology

In the process of education and training, general education that is realized through curricula and teaching programs is generally oriented towards three directions: the development of cognitive competence, the development of the personal and social, as well as professional competence. While it is fundamental to strive to achieve the goals of general education in English language education, educology of English has its specific objects of study.

1.2.1 English subject curriculum

Since the birth of modern science, a close science system has been established. The way of resolution and specialization lays the foundation of modern scientific research, which helps the exploration of human race go from integration and roughness to differentiation and fineness. However, in the process, the inner link between different areas of knowledge has been broken, thus creating separations and limitations. In the case of English subject educology, especially as foreign or second language, there has been the long practice of dividing the process into various language skills like listening, speaking, reading, writing, etc. This arrangement has contributed a lot to the setting of English teaching **curricula**. However, with time going on, a complementary voice has already been heard: In the age of knowledge economy, the knowledge system of schools needs reconstruction while the main basis is the basic personal qualifications. The knowledge system should be characterized by integration, comprehension and openness. It should be noted that there is a phenomenon of discipline in the knowledge system. The construction of the knowledge system, as embodied in teaching **curricula**, requires the resolution of dialectical relations between consistency and difference, stability and deviancy, resolution and integration, as well as limitation and selection. The basic principles for the construction of the knowledge system include: to place emphasis on the fosterage of integrated personality, to establish a **curriculum** system balancing consistency and difference, to realize the integration of the knowledge system and to carry out multi-cultural education (Tao, 2001: 82). The past few years has seen the trial of integrated course books in the EFL (English as foreign language) field in China.

1.2.2 English subject learning

The research on learning in subject educology is first of all, directed towards the study of learning effect and learner factors. But it is not only engaged in the traditional research on learning behavior of people, but also involves research on learning as an important means of fitting into the society, seeking self-actualization and striving for self-perfection. Nowadays the conception of "live and learn" has penetrated into people's lives. "An integrated person" can be realized only through lifelong learning (Tao, 2001: 128). This is not only an opportunity but also a big challenge faced by the modern "individual being" during the process of seeking self-realization. Therefore, as an important element of subject learning, new and ample contents have been added to the connotations of modern English learning, especially some breakthroughs in English language learning theory. This book will expound learners' variables as well as some learning problems within the domain of subject education and review some researchers' achievements of study in such aspects of students' learning subjects as meta-cognition in English learning, strategies of English learning and case study of English learning.

1.2.3 English subject teaching

The ultimate goal of subject teaching is to promote and facilitate the production and growth of knowledge in learners to realize their overall development. The development of contemporary society makes the function of subject teaching in educational institutions continuously expand. Under the idea of lifelong, autonomous and integrated learning, the role of subject teachers in the communication of knowledge is also continuously changing. In today's English teaching field, while more and more emphasis is being laid on individualized learning, English teaching researchers and teachers spare no efforts in activating students' positive thoughts on teaching practice. The aim is that general students can be guided and helped to positively, actively and independently gain knowledge and to form a knowledge structure with their own individualized characters (Tao, 2001: 170).

And in the process of English teaching, the advantages of various teaching methods and approaches should be taken into consideration. Decisions should be made according to the practical conditions of teaching environment and students being taught. English teachers should advocate and improve the spirit of democracy in the process of English instruction and establish good relationships with their students through joint participation and collaboration. They should also create a teaching environment that is harmonious and beneficial to the production and growth of knowledge so that the classroom subject teaching activities may become invigorating. In such an environment, the skillful instruction of English teachers will deeply influence students' learning activities while the level of teachers' teaching arts will be continuously enhanced in the process of the teachers' subjective and initiative efforts; then the style of teaching arts with individualized characteristics will gradually be formed.

1.2.4 Contemporary educational technology in English subject educology

Teaching aids have long been a focus of study for teaching researchers and curricula developers. The impact of modern educational technologies on English language teaching is too big and strong to be neglected. Contemporary educational technology makes use of contemporary information technology in language teaching in order to promote the teaching reforms and students' learning achievements. Generally speaking, the function of the application of contemporary educational technology in English language teaching has experienced a gradual process of cognition:

Media——▶Tools——▶Resources——▶Environment

In the present digital and information age, contemporary educational technology has been becoming one of the basic means, resources and environment for acquisition and growth of knowledge. It is apparent that with the rapid development of multimedia technology and the Internet, great changes have taken place in school teaching activities such as curriculum and teaching materials, teaching models, different roles of teachers and students, etc. For instance, multimedia equipment like computer, DVD, EVD, MP4, etc. has enriched and freshened the meaning of audio-lingual and communicative approaches. The use of digital information in English teaching will become an important challenge in our nation's next major education paradigm and will trigger a revolution in all educational and learning approaches. However, regarding the flexibility of the role of technology in English teaching and learning, the discussion of educational technology is penetrated into various parts of this book.

1.2.5 Teacher training in English subject educology

Compelling evidence and various studies show us that the quality of a teacher is one of the most critical components of how well his/her students can achieve. In most cases we can even say teachers are the single biggest influence on how well students learn. So it's no surprise the discussion and debate about English subject educology also zeroing in on the quality of teaching in the classrooms. There are now many loud voices with differing opinions talking about teacher quality in the ELT world. And in many countries, teacher training has become established routine work.

The need to improve teacher quality and enhance the teaching profession is very urgent for China with regard to its vast area and large population. The challenge of improving English teachers' quality in China involves the following aspects:

Teacher preparation: Many new English teachers do not feel ready for the challenges of today's classrooms.

Teacher retention: English teachers are often left to "sink" or "swim," not receiving the nurturing they deserve and support they need.

Mastery of professional knowledge: English teachers in many areas lack opportunities to receive in-service training, resulting in an out-of-date, stereotyped knowledge system.

Teacher recruitment: English education faces the challenge of attracting a greater quantity of people to the teaching profession while also enhancing teacher quality.

Of course, as Parrot (1993) points out, whether someone can become a good foreign language teacher does not solely depend on his/her command of the language. There are a variety of elements that contribute to the qualities of a good teacher. These elements can be categorized into such groups as ethic devotion, professional qualities and personal styles.

With all these factors taken into consideration, the task of teacher training in China becomes more arduous.

1.2.6 Assessment in English subject educology

Assessment has a direct influence on the entire process of the development of education. When we are trying to inspect and study subject educology, it is necessary for us to study and explore the assessment system. For many people, assessment is solely associated with testing. Many EFL teachers would immediately think of tests when speaking of assessment methods.

However, testing is only one of the various means of assessment, which is a broader term. It is conclusion/judgment based on information collected about the learners' current situation, while testing is a way to collect information through formal and standardized form. In this book, both the formal and informal ways to gather information will be discussed. And the influence of social reforms and industrial social ideology over the assessment in subject educology will be touched upon. This influence, along with globalization, is having great effects on English subject assessment. Only after we know the social ideology behind educational assessment and the social function that appears after its effects are left on the assessment system, can we have deeper considerations for the problems and contradictions that exist in the current assessment system of English education. In the 21st century, social and cultural reforms not only bring about changes in the assessment functions of English educology, but also surface the disadvantages in the traditional English testing system. There has been an urgent call to construct a new, open and balanced English assessment system in China.

Above listed are the major issues within the framework of English subject educology. Besides these, language educology necessarily involves such topics as cultural awareness in language acquisition/learning. We will also dwell on cultural issues in detail in Chapter 6.

1.3   The importance of English subject educology

Most people would agree that we are moving into the "computer future," a future where everything will be different because of the presence of computers and other new technologies. In many walks of life, the dominance of computer is already visible and becoming necessary. Under the new socio-economical situation, it is important to develop new thinking in the field of ELT. The traditional methodology for studying innovation in education may have been adequate at a time when only small changes were possible. But we need a different methodology altogether when we envisage radical changes in education.

Generally speaking, there are two sides of English subject educology: one side facing towards society, the other facing the individual. The fundamental importance for learning English subject educology includes at least the following aspects:

To enable us to systematically master the general laws of English education;

To enable us to solve the problems which are difficulties for English education at special levels;

To explore and promote the theory of English curriculum and teaching;

To enable us to identify the difficult nature of English subject education.

In the following parts of Chapter 1, we will deal with more aspects concerning English educology: the relationship between education and language educology; main schools of language learning/acquisition theories; related practices in real language teaching domain and innovations.

2. The study of education and its relation to language educology

Among various disciplines, the study of education (educational science, educational theory) is one of the closest to language educology. Yet, it is probably the least recognized and the most neglected (Stern, 1983: 420). Language teaching in its most widespread forms occurs in educational settings: schools, universities, adult classes, and so on. Usually it forms part of a curriculum of studies and is meant to make an educational contribution to this curriculum. Concepts of education are applied as a matter of course in language teaching just as much as in other subjects of the curriculum. The language teacher almost inevitably operates with some notion of what teaching involves and how language teaching fits into the educational enterprises of which it customarily forms a part.

As a professional field of study, education draws on a number of other studies, such as philosophy, psychology, or sociology, as source disciplines. To be specific, education as a discipline is commonly divided into such sub-disciplines: (1) philosophy of education, (2) history of education, (3) educational psychology, (4) educational sociology, and so on (Stern, 1983: 425). In the following discussion, several sub-disciplines will be illustrated to show the importance of education to language educology as a whole.

2.1   Educational philosophy

Educational philosophy has bearing on any and every aspect of the study and practice of education, and language educology is no exception.

Language educology has operated, more or less consciously, with the notion of a defined curriculum (syllabus, program, or method) and has, in recent years, attempted to distinguish between the ends—purposes of language teaching (goals, aims, or objectives) and means of language teaching to achieve these purposes. It is therefore valuable to recognize that the ends/means model has been put into discussion by educational philosophers. In recent years the relationship between language teachers and language learners, implicit in this model, has also been seriously called into question. Educational philosophy can thus help in clarifying unstated assumptions. In similar ways, it can throw light on such key concepts as are often used far too lightly as discovery learning, individualization, interest, motivation, teaching, skill, and evaluation.

Moreover, the act of foreign language learning, moving from first language to second language, is an expression of ethnic value judgments. Even the desired degree of bilingual competence to be achieved by the student is ultimately a value question. The teacher's treatment of the language learners and of the learning process also indicates philosophical values. Are learners participants in the teaching-learning process, or are they passive recipients of pre-arranged mechanical activities?

These indications are sufficient to suggest the merit of a philosophical perspective for language pedagogy.

2.2   History of education

The importance of a historical approach to language teaching theory has already made itself clear. What is necessary to add in the present context is a reminder that the history of language education forms part of the history of education which provides the wider context, and in most respects the history of language teaching can be better understood in the framework of educational history. Language educology as part of educational history can be illustrated by an example.

In the second half of the nineteenth century modern languages took their place besides other "modern" subjects such as history and the natural sciences. Similarly, throughout the first half of the twentieth century languages were thought of as belonging to the curriculum of secondary education because the curriculum conventions dictated that primary education was vernacular schooling in which foreign languages had no place. It was only during the last decades of years that the primary curriculum has become sufficiently flexible to tolerate or welcome second language learning. Language teaching has also in many respects been subject to the same influences of educational thought that have affected other curriculum subjects and indeed the entire curriculum: psychology, testing, educational research, and educational reform movements. By recognizing these broad trends influencing education the language educational theorists can appreciate better common educational assumptions (Stern, 1983: 442-444).

2.3 Educational psychology

Since educational psychology covers every aspect of education from a psychological angle, it is central to educational theory. Take behaviorist theory as an example. The behaviorist theory of language learning was initiated by behavioral psychologist Skinner, who applied Watson and Raynor's theory of conditioning to the way humans acquire language. Based on their experiments, Watson and Raynor formulated an S-R (stimulus-response) theory of psychology. They claimed that emotional reactions are learned in much the same way as other skills. Skinner further suggested language is also a form of behavior. It can be learned the same way as animals are trained to respond to stimuli. This theory of learning is referred to as behaviorism, marked by Skinner's *Verbal Behavior*. Since the advent of Skinner's theory, it has been adopted for some time by the language teaching profession, particularly in the United States of America. One influential result is the oral-aural (audio-lingual) method, which involves endless drilling patterns of listening and repeating. The core idea of this method is that language is learned by constant repetition and reinforcement of the teacher to form habits in language learners. Mistakes were not tolerated and were immediately corrected, and correct utterances were immediately praised. Today, this method is still widely used and practiced in the world at large.

2.4 Educational sociology

As a branch of sociology, educational sociology places education as an activity and institution into a social context. It recognizes schools and other educational institutions as agencies within a society. Schools may be viewed as part of a society, reflecting the existing social structure. Writings in educational sociology have demonstrated how in many societies the composition of school populations inevitably reflects the divisions in society, and to what extent school systems are openly divided according to the major social strata in that society. Languages have played their part in this class division of education. Until recently, learning foreign languages was regarded as a mark of an "elitist" education; and in some school settings languages are taught not so much for their intrinsic merit but mainly because they give social prestige to the learner (Stern, 1987: 445-447).

Educational sociology also recognizes that schools have been created as agencies of social change through which the society may deliberately strive to modify its internal social structure. Education has been used in some societies as a means of breaking down class barriers, and thus creating equality of opportunity and increasing social mobility. Languages have sometimes been introduced into schools and colleges as a move towards more democratic education.

Besides these macro-sociological factors, education also offers opportunities for "micro-sociological" studies. In the past the teacher's role as the unquestioned director of all activities at all times and a class following the teacher's directions in a uniform way were accepted as the right and normal pattern of teacher-student relations. Today teachers are frequently encouraged to cultivate a more fluid and more flexible classroom organization and not to view themselves exclusively in the role of class instructor.

For language educology, as a result, education itself can be regarded as a multidisciplinary source discipline. By treating it as such, educational assumptions in language teaching can be brought to light, and language teaching can be viewed more clearly in relation to other educational activities. In the field of educology research, teaching and learning play central roles. This makes it necessary to look at them timely.

3. Language acquisition/learning theories

A great many theories regarding language development in human beings have been proposed so far and are continuously being proposed. Such theories have generally arisen out of related disciplines such as psychology and linguistics. Psychological and linguistic thinking have profoundly influenced one another and the outcome of language acquisition/learning theories.

3.1 Nurture vs. Nature

Until today, language acquisition theories have basically centered around **"nurture"** and **"nature"** distinction or on **"empiricism"** and **"nativism"**. The motif of empiricism is that all knowledge comes from experience and practice, ultimately from our interaction with the environment through our reasoning or senses. On the other hand, nativism holds that at least some knowledge is not acquired through interaction with the environment, but is genetically transmitted and innate. In simple words, some theoreticians have based their theories on environmental factors while others believed that it is the innate factors that determine the acquisition of language. However, it should be borne in mind that neither side totally disagrees with the ideas of the other side. What counts is the relatively little or more weight they lay on the environmental or innate factors.

Environmentalist theories of language acquisition generally hold that an organism's nurture, or experience, is of more significance to development than its nature or inborn contributions. The neo-behaviorist stimulus-response (S-R) learning theory is the case in point. Today in both cognitive science and language teaching theories, cognitive approach is regarded as an offshoot of behaviorism.

The nativist theories, however, maintain that human being is the product of biology and that much of the capacity for language learning in human is "inborn" (innate). It is part of the genetic makeup of human species and is nearly independent of any particular experience which may occur after birth. Thus, the nativists claim that language acquisition is innately determined and that we are born with a built-in device which predisposes us to acquire language and predisposes us to a systematic perception of language around us. Chomsky's innatist language acquisition theory is the case in point. Although most nativists do not deny the importance of environmental stimuli, they claim that language acquisition cannot be accounted for on the basis of environmental factors only and there must be some innate guide to achieve this end. The following table is a classification around the nurture/nature distinction[1].

FIGURE 1.1 Classification of language acquisition theories around "Nurture and Nature Distinction"

Nurture/Nature	Theories of language acquisition	Some Resulting F/S Language Teaching/ Learning Methods
Theories based on "nurture" (Environmental factors are believed to be more dominant in language acquisition.)	- Bakhtin's Theory of Polyphony - Bruner's Discovery Learning Theory - Vygotsky's Zone of Proximal Development - Skinner's Verbal Behavior - Piaget's View of Language Acquisition - The Competition Model - Cognitive Theory: Language Acquisition View - The Discourse Theory - The Speech Act Theory - The Acculturation Model - The Accommodation Theory - The Interactionist View of Language Acquisition	- Audiolingual Method - Community Language Learning - Communicative Approach - Task-based Language Teaching
Theories based on "nature" (Innate factors are believed to be more dominant in language acquisition.)	- A Neuro-functional Theory of Language Acquisition - The Universal Grammar Theory - Fodor's Modular Approach - The Monitor Model	- Winitz's Comprehension Approach - The Natural Approach

The next section lists the most important ones of language acquisition theories resulting from the two opposing views mentioned above.

3.2   Theories of language acquisition

As mentioned, language acquisition theories have been influenced especially by linguistic and psychological schools of thought. Nine different views of language acquisition will be discussed here.

---

[1] Adapted from Rod Ellis (2004), retrieved online Nov. 23, 2004. http://maxpages.com.

3.2.1 Bruner's discovery learning theory

Discovery learning is "an approach to instruction through which students interact with their environment—by exploring and manipulating objects, wrestling with questions and controversies, or performing experiments" (Ormrod, 1995: 442). The basic idea is that students are more likely to remember concepts they discover on their own in the process of inquiring and exploring. To Bruner, the main purpose of learning a course is not to remember textbook knowledge, but to involve oneself in the process of setting up the knowledge system of this course. Students should be active and, initiative inquirers of knowledge. Discovery learning takes place most notably in problem solving situations where the learner draws on his/her own experience and prior knowledge to discover the truths that are to be learned. Bruner wrote "Emphasis on discovery in learning has precisely the effect on the learner of leading him to be a constructionist, to organize what he is encountering in a manner not only designed to discover regularity and relatedness, but also to avoid the kind of information drift that fails to keep account of the uses to which information might have to be put" (Bruner, 1961).

3.2.2 Vygotsky's social constructivist theory and zone of proximal development

Lev Vygotsky is most often associated with the social constructivist theory. He emphasizes the influences of cultural and social contexts in learning and supports a discovery model of learning. The main theme of his theoretical framework is that social interaction plays a fundamental role in the development of cognition. According to Vygotsky (1978: 57), "Every function in the child's cultural development appears twice: first, on the social level, and later, on the individual level—first, between people (inter-psychological) and then inside the child (intra-psychological). ... All the higher functions originate as actual relationships between individuals". Another important aspect of Vygotsky's theory is the idea that the potential for cognitive development depends upon the "zone of proximal development" (ZPD): a level of development attained when children engage in social behavior. In a society, parents, teachers and peers etc. can function as the mediation and thus play a very important role in the students' cognitive development. Full development of the ZPD depends upon full social interaction. The range of skill that can be developed with adult guidance or peer collaboration exceeds what can be attained alone.

Vygotsky places an emphasis on the role of "shared language" in the development of thought and language, which "shared" refers to social interaction and can be best elucidated through the notion of ZPD. According to him, two developmental levels determine the learning process: egocentricity and interaction. This can be illustrated by looking at what children do on their own and what they can do while working with others. They mostly choose to remain silent or speak less on their own when they are alone. However, they prefer to speak to other children when they play games with them. The difference between these two types of development forms is "Zone of Proximal Development". In other words, this zone refers to the distance between the actual developmental level as determined by independent problem solving and the level of potential development as determined through problem solving under adult guidance or in cooperation with more capable friends of the child. In language learning and problem solving, the most important thing that children do is to develop concepts by talking to adults and then solve the problems they face on their own.

Vygotsky contends that language is the key to all development and words play a central part not only in the development of thought but in the growth of cognition as a whole. Within this framework, child language development can be viewed as the result of social interaction.

3.2.3 Skinner's verbal behavior

Behavioristic view of language acquisition claims that language development is the process of habit formation, and the result of a set of habits. This view has normally been influenced by the general theory of learning described by the psychologist John B. Watson in 1923, and termed behaviorism. Behaviorism believes knowledge is the product of interaction with the environment through stimulus-response (S-R) conditioning.

Stimulus(S)-response(R) learning works as follows. An event in the environment (the unconditioned stimulus, or US) brings out an unconditioned response (UR) from an organism capable of learning. That response is then followed by another event (reinforcement) appealing to the organism. That is, the organism's response is positively reinforced (PRE). If the sequence US──▶UR──▶PRE recurs a sufficient number of times, the organism will learn how to associate its response to the stimulus with the reinforcement. This will consequently cause the organism to give the same response when it confronts with the same stimulus. In this way, the response becomes a conditioned response (CR).

The most risky part of the behaviorist view is perhaps the idea that all learning, whether verbal (language) or non-verbal (general learning) takes place by means of the same underlying process, that is via forming habits. In 1957, the psychologist B. F. Skinner produced a behaviorist account of language acquisition in which he maintains that language development is the result of a set of habits.

When language acquisition is taken into consideration, the theory claims that both L1 and L2 acquirers receive linguistic input from speakers in their environment, and positive reinforcement for their correct repetitions and imitations. As mentioned above, when language learners' responses are reinforced positively, they acquire the language relatively easily.

These claims are strictly criticized in Chomsky's "A Review of B. F. Skinner's Verbal Behavior". Chomsky (1959) asserts that there is neither empirical evidence nor any known argument to support any specific claim about the relative importance of feedback from the environment. Therefore, it would be unwise to claim that the sequence US——▶UR——▶PRE and imitation can account for the process of language acquisition. What is more, the theory overlooks the speaker (internal) factors in this process.

The behaviorists see errors as first language habits interfering with the acquisition of second language habits. If there are similarities between the two languages, the language learners will acquire the target structures easily. If there are differences, acquisition will be more difficult. This approach is known as the contrastive analysis hypothesis (CAH). According to the hypothesis, the differences between languages can be used to reveal and predict all errors and the data obtained can be used in foreign/second language teaching for promoting a better acquisition environment.

However, the mother tongue interference cannot entirely explain difficulties that an L2 learner may face. It is true that there might be some influences resulting from L1, but research (Ellis, 1985) has shown that not all errors predicted by CAH are actually made.

Skinner's view of language acquisition is a popular example of the nurturist ideas. Behaviorism has been generally accepted by the influential Bloomfieldian structuralist school of linguistics and produced some well-known applications in the field of foreign/second language teaching and learning—for instance, the Audiolingual

Method. The theory sees the language learning as a process of accumulation with no built-in knowledge inside the learner.

3.2.4 Piaget's view of language acquisition

Piaget[1] was a biologist and a psychologist, but his ideas have been influential in the field of L1 and L2 acquisition studies. His theory of development in children has striking implications as regards language acquisition. Piaget views language acquisition as a case of general human learning. According to him, the course of intellectual development is as follows:

  • The sensory-motor stage from ages 0 to 2 (understanding the environment)

  • The preoperational stage from ages 2 to 7 (understanding the symbols)

  • The concrete operational stage from ages 7 to 11 (mental tasks and language use)

  • The formal operational stage from the age 11 onwards (dealing with abstraction)

Piaget observes, for instance, that the pre-linguistic stage (birth to one year) is a determining period in the development of sensory-motor intelligence, when children are forming a sense of their physical identity in relation to the environment. Piaget, unlike Vygotsky, believes that egocentric speech on its own serves no function in language development.

3.2.5 The cognitive language acquisition view

1) Ausubel's meaningful learning theory

David Ausubel is a psychologist who advanced a theory which contrasted meaningful learning from rote learning. In his view, to learn meaningfully, students must relate new knowledge (concepts and propositions) to what they already know. He proposed the notion of an "advance organizer" as a way to help students link their ideas with new materials or concepts. An advance organizer helps to organize new material by outlining, arranging and sequencing the main idea of the new material based on what the learner already knows. Advance organizers use familiar terms and concepts to link what the students already know to the new information that will be presented in the lesson, which aids in the process of transforming

---

[1] Amazon.com: *Fifty Modern Thinkers on Education: From Piaget to the Present Day* (Fifty Key Thinkers) (Routledge Key Guides) by Joy Palmer & David E. Cooper.

knowledge and creatively applying it in new situations. This process helps to embed the new information into long term memory. Advance organizers can be verbal phrases (e.g. the paragraph you are about to read is about Albert Einstein), a definition, a graphic, etc. In any case, the advance organizer is designed to provide, what cognitive psychologists call, the "mental scaffolding", to learn new information. The following FIGURE (FIGURE 1.2) summarizes Ausubel's Model of Learning.

When proposing meaningful learning, Ausubel criticized the popular Audio-lingual method for its theory based on reinforcement and conditioning; he stated that adults learning a second language could profit from certain grammatical explanations. Whether adults do profit from such explanations depends on (1) the suitability and efficiency of the explanation, (2) the teacher, (3) the context, and (4) other pedagogical variables.

FIGURE 1.2 Ausubel's Model of Learning

Phase One: Advance Organizer	Phase Two: Presentation of Learning Task or Material	Phase Three: Strengthening Cognitive Organization
Activities: Clarify aim of the lesson Present the organizer Relate organizer to students' knowledge	Activities: Make the organization of the new material explicit. Make logical order of learning material explicit. Present material and engage students in meaningful learning activities.	Activities: Relate new information to advance organizer. Promote active reception learning.

2) Cognitive theory

Cognitive theory is based on the work of a number of psychologists. Piaget's work, which dwells on the idea that students can learn things when they are developmentally ready to do so since learning follows development, can be regarded as a starting point of the cognitivist ideas. Cognitive psychologists emphasize the importance of meaning, knowing and understanding. According to them, "meaning" plays an important role in human learning. Learning is a meaningful process of relating new events or items to already existing cognitive concepts; and it is thought to involve internal representations that guide performance. In the case of language acquisition, these representations are based on language system and involve procedures for selecting appropriate vocabulary, grammatical rules, and pragmatic conventions governing language use.

Cognitive psychologists see second language acquisition as the constructing process of knowledge systems that can eventually be called automatically for speaking and understanding. Language learning, in this sense, has some Gestalt characteristics in that language learning is a holistic process and not analyzable as stimulus-response associations. Language learners pay attention to any aspect of the language that they are attempting to understand and produce. Then, gradually, they become able to use certain parts of their knowledge through experience and practice.

In general, the cognitivists claim that language acquisition can be automatically attained.

3.2.6 The discourse theory

The Discourse Theory results from a theory of language use. The theory emphasizes that language development be viewed within the framework of how learners discover the meaning capacity of language by taking part in communication. Brown's description of communicative competence (1987), for instance, reflects the principles of the Discourse Theory. Communicative competence includes knowledge of grammar and vocabulary, knowledge of rules of speaking, knowledge of how to use and respond to different types of speech acts and social conventions, and knowledge of how to use language appropriately.

According to discourse theorists, language acquisition will successfully take place when language learners "know" how and when to use the language in various settings and when they have successfully "cognized" various forms of competence such as grammatical competence (e.g. lexis, morphology, syntax and phonology) and pragmatic competence (e.g. speech acts). A language learner needs to "know" conversational strategies to acquire the language.

The early stage of Communicative Language Teaching (CLT) is the best-known example of such a theory. In the communicative classes, students are expected to learn by doing and expected to acquire the language through the presentation-practice-and-production principle.

The Discourse Theory has a number of drawbacks. It overemphasizes the role of external factors in the process of language acquisition and gives little importance to internal learner strategies (i.e. innate processes). The Discourse Theory is similar to the behaviorist view of language acquisition in that environmental factors and input (or positive stimulus) are at the very center in attempting to explicate the acquisition process. The Discourse Theory is of course more sophisticated than the Skinner's views in accounting for the complex structure of communication. Yet it overstresses the role of "knowledge of competence and functions" in acquiring a language, and hence fails to notice universal principles that guide language acquisition.

3.2.7 The speech act theory

That uses of language not only can, but even normally do have the character of actions was a fact largely neglected by those engaged in the study of language before the 20th century. Where the action-character of linguistic phenomena was acknowledged, it was normally regarded as a peripheral matter, relating to derivative or non-standard aspects of language which could afford to be ignored. With the rise of pragmatics, the 1960s saw the development of the Speech Act Theory.

This theory was originated by Austin (1962) and developed further by Searle (1969). It holds that saying something is a way of doing something. In speech act theory, two kinds of meaning are seen in utterances. The first is the propositional meaning and the second is the illocutionary meaning. The former refers to the basic literal meaning of the utterance conveyed by the particular words or structures. The latter refers to the "effect" the spoken or written text has on the listener or reader. For instance: Getting a cup of tea is an act. Asking someone else to get you one is also an act.

When we speak, our words do not have meaning in and of themselves. They are very much affected by the situation, the speaker and the listener. Thus words alone do not have a simple fixed meaning. This theory distinguishes three types of acts:

- *Locutionary act*: saying something with a certain meaning in traditional sense.
- *Illocutionary act*: having a certain "force", e.g. informing, ordering, warning, undertaking.
- *Perlocutionary act*: bringing about or achieving something, e.g. convincing, persuading, deterring.

Searle (1969) identifies five illocutionary/perlocutionary points:

1. *Assertives*: statements that may be judged true or false because they aim to describe a state of affairs in the world.
2. *Directives*: statements that attempt to make the other person's actions fit the propositional content.
3. *Commissives*: statements which commit the speaker to a

course of action as described by the propositional content.

4. *Expressives*: statements that express the "sincerity condition of the speech act".

5. *Declaratives*: statements that attempt to change the world by "representing it as having been changed".

It is, of course, normal for someone to use these utterances in his native language. The problem is how propositions and implicatures are acquired in first and second language. Does a formal instruction environment help the learners acquire them?

3.2.8 The universal grammar theory

Among theories of language acquisition, Universal Grammar (UG) has also gained wide acceptance and popularity. However, UG is more of an L1 acquisition theory rather than L2. It attempts to clarify the relatively quick acquisition of L1s on the basis of "minimum exposure" to external input. The "logical problem" of language acquisition, according to UG proponents, is that language learning would be impossible without "universal language-specific knowledge". The main reason behind this argument is the input data:

Language input is the evidence out of which the learner constructs knowledge of language—what goes into the brain. Such evidence can be either positive or negative. ... The positive evidence of the position of words in a few sentences the learner hears is sufficient to show (him) the rules of (a language). (Cook, 1991)

This view supports the idea that the external input per se may not account for language acquisition. Similarly, the Chomskyan view holds that the input is poor and deficient in two ways. First, the input is claimed to be "degenerate" because it is damaged by performance features such as slips, hesitations or false starts. Accordingly, it is suggested that the input is not an adequate base for language learning. Second, the input is devoid of grammar corrections. This means that the input does not normally contain "negative evidence," the knowledge from which the learner could exercise what is "not" possible in a given language.

As for L2 acquisition, however, the above question is not usually asked largely because of the frequent failure of L2 learners, who happen to be generally cognitively mature adults, in attaining native-like proficiency. But why can't adults who have already acquired an L1, acquire an L2 thoroughly? Don't they have any help from UG? Or if they do, how much of UG is accessible in SLA? These and similar questions have divided researchers into four basic camps with respect to their approach to the problem (Cook, 1991):

Direct access—L2 acquisition is just like L1 acquisition. Language acquisition device (LAD) is involved.

Indirect access—L2 acquisition utilizes LAD via L1 mechanism.

Partial access—Only that part of UG which has been used in L1 acquisition is used in L2 acquisition.

No access—L2 learners use their general learning capacity rather than LAD.

Proponents of UG believe that both children and adults utilize similar universal principles when acquiring a language; and LAD is still involved in the acquisition process. Advocates of UG approach working on second-language learning argue that there is no reason to assume that language faculty atrophies with age. Most second-language researchers who adopt the UG perspective assume that the principles and parameters of UG are still accessible to the adult learners (McLaughlin, 1987: 96).

Fodor's view has some parallels with the UG Theory. Jerry Fodor (1975) studied the relationship between language and mind and his view that language is a modular process has important implications for a theory of language acquisition. The term modular is used to indicate that the brain is seen to be organized with many modules of cells for a particular ability (for instance, the visual module). These modules operate in isolation from other modules that they are not directly connected with. Modules are domain specific. Basically, Fodor's arguments are similar to that of Chomsky or the proponents of UG Theory in that the external input per se may not account for language acquisition and that language acquisition is genetically predetermined.

As for the pitfalls with Universal Grammar, it can be said that UG's particular aim is to account for how language works. Yet UG proponents had to deal with acquisition to account for the language itself. "Acquisition part" is thus of secondary importance. A second drawback is that Chomsky studied only the core grammar of the English language (syntax) and investigated a number of linguistic universals, neglecting the peripheral grammar, that is, language specific rules (i.e. rules of specific languages which cannot be generalized). Thirdly, the primary function of language is communication, but it is discarded. The final and the most significant problem is a methodological one. Due to the fact that Chomsky is concerned only with describing and explaining "competence", there can be little likelihood of SLA researchers carrying out empirical research.

3.2.9 The monitor model

Krashen's Monitor Model is another example of the nativist theories. The model forms the basis of the Natural Approach, which is a comprehension-based approach to foreign and second language teaching. The model includes five hypotheses[1].

1) The acquisition-learning hypothesis

Krashen (1985), in his theory of second language acquisition (SLA) suggests that adults have two different ways of developing competence in second languages: acquisition and learning. "There are two independent ways of developing ability in second languages. 'Acquisition' is a subconscious process identical in all important ways to the process children utilize in acquiring their first language, ... and 'learning'..., is a conscious process that results in 'knowing about' the rules of language" (Krashen, 1985: 1).

Krashen believes that the result of learning, learned competence (LC) functions as a monitor or editor. That is, while "acquired competence" is responsible for our fluent production of sentences, LC makes correction on these sentences either before or after their production. This kind of conscious grammar correction, "monitoring", occurs most typically in a grammar exam where the learner has enough time to focus on form and to make use of his conscious knowledge of grammar rules (LC) as an aid to acquired competence. The way to develop learned competence is fairly easy: analyzing the grammar rules consciously and practicing them through exercises. But what Acquisition/Learning Distinction Hypothesis predicts is that learning the grammar rules of a foreign/second language does not result in subconscious acquisition.

2) The natural order hypothesis

According to this hypothesis, the acquisition of grammatical structures proceeds in a predicted progression. Certain grammatical structures or morphemes are acquired before others in first language acquisition and there is a similar natural order in SLA. The implication of natural order is not that second or foreign language teaching materials must be arranged in accordance with this sequence but that acquisition is subconscious and free from conscious intervention.

---

[1] The explanations of the hypotheses below are based on an article entitled *"A Promising Approach to Second Language Acquisition"* (Kiymazarslan, 2000: 72-82).

3) The input hypothesis

This hypothesis relates to acquisition, not to learning. Krashen claims that people acquire language best by understanding input that is a little beyond their present level of competence. Consequently, Krashen believes that "comprehensible input" (that is, i+1) should be provided. The "input" should be relevant and "not grammatically sequenced". The foreign/second language teacher should always send meaningful messages, which are roughly tuned, and "must" create opportunities for students to access "i+1" structures to understand and express meaning. For instance, the teacher can lay more emphasis on listening and reading comprehension activities.

4) The monitor hypothesis

As mentioned before, adult second language learners have two means for internalizing the target language. The first is "acquisition" which is a subconscious and intuitive process of constructing the system of a language. The second means is a conscious learning process in which learners attend to form, figure out rules and are generally aware of their own process. The "monitor" is an aspect of this second process. It edits and makes alterations or corrections as they are consciously perceived. Krashen believes that "fluency" in second language performance is due to "what we have acquired", not "what we have learned": Adults should do as much acquiring as possible for the purpose of achieving communicative fluency. Therefore, the monitor should have only a minor role in the process of gaining communicative competence. Similarly, Krashen suggests three conditions for its use: (1) there must be enough time; (2) the focus must be on form and not on meaning; (3) the learner must know the rule. Students may monitor during written tasks (e.g. homework assignments) and preplanned speech, or to some extent during speech. Learned knowledge enables students to read and listen more so that they acquire more.

5) The affective filter hypothesis

The learner's emotional state, according to Krashen, is just like an adjustable filter which freely passes or hinders input necessary to acquisition. In other words, input must be achieved in low-anxiety contexts since acquirers with a low affective filter receive more input and interact with confidence. The filter is "affective" because there are some factors which regulate its strength. These factors are self-confidence, motivation and anxiety state. The pedagogical goal in a foreign/second language class should thus not only include comprehensible input but also create an atmosphere that fosters a low affective filter.

Krashen's theories have met criticisms from some linguists and methodologists. McLaughlin (1987: 56) argues that his models fail at every juncture by claiming that none of the hypotheses is clear in their predictions. For example, he notes that the acquisition-learning distinction is not properly defined and that the distinction between these two processes cannot be tested empirically. Although it is true that some parts of the theory need more clarification, it would be harsh to suggest that the Model is pseudo-scientific.

3.3 Summary

One observation of the acquisition theories is that none of the above-mentioned theories is complete and most of them need further and ongoing completion. Each theory, however, is important for their implications and provides invaluable information as to how a language is acquired and how language teaching should take place. Furthermore, theories guiding language learning and teaching are always evolving. Look at the views on intelligences:

Traditionally, intelligence is defined operationally as the ability to answer test items of intelligence, including exclusively linguistic competence and mathematical-logical reasoning. The inference from the test scores to some underlying ability is supported by statistical techniques that compare responses of subjects; the notion on the general faculty of intelligence is: it does not change much with age or with training or experience in that it is an inborn attribute or faculty of the individual.

Multiple intelligences theory pluralizes the traditional concept. According to Gardner (1993: 15), instead of a single dimension called intellect, on which individuals can be rank-ordered, there are vast differences among individuals in their intellectual strengths and weaknesses as well as cognitive styles; human cognitive competence is better described in terms of a set of abilities, talents, or mental skills, which he names "intelligences". For more details we will discuss in Chapter 8.

Of course, the most important implication of language acquisition theories is the fact that applied linguists, methodologists and language teachers should view the acquisition of a language as both a matter of nurture and an instance of nature. In addition, only when we distinguish between a general theory of learning and language learning can we ameliorate the conditions of L2 education.

Language teachers must apply and adapt the policies of others in the classroom creatively. If they are to adapt language models proposed by others (applied linguists) for classroom practice, it becomes more important "how" they will adopt them. How, for instance, should they utilize the findings of SLA studies conducted on syntax or natural order and use them for particular classroom settings? How should grammar points be handled? Or should there be a balance between grammar lessons and acquisition lessons just as proposed by the proponents of the Monitor Model? How should vocabulary teaching be like and how should a syllabus be designed? How will the results of language planning proposed by the government be implemented?

In the next section, some English language teaching models are presented.

4.　A brief survey of English teaching models

With the guidance of linguistic and language teaching/learning theories, various English teaching models have come into play on the stage of ELT. The following is a brief survey; more details will be dealt with in Chapter 2.

4.1　Grammar-translation method

This approach was historically used in teaching Greek and Latin and generalized to teaching modern languages. Classes are taught in the students' mother tongue, with little active use of the target language. Vocabulary is taught in the form of isolated word lists. Elaborate explanations of grammar are always provided. Grammar instruction provides the rules for putting words together; instruction often focuses on the form and inflection of words. Reading of difficult texts is started early in the course of study. Little attention is paid to the content of texts, which are treated as exercises in grammatical analysis. Often the only drills are exercises in translating disconnected sentences from the target language into the mother tongue, and vice versa. Little or no attention is given to pronunciation.

4.2   The reading approach

This approach is selected for practical and academic reasons and for specific uses of the language in graduate or scientific studies. The approach is for people who do not travel abroad, for whom reading is the one usable skill in a foreign language. The priority in studying the target language is first, reading ability and second, current and/or historical knowledge of the country where the target language is spoken. Only the grammar necessary for reading comprehension and fluency is taught. Minimal attention is paid to pronunciation or gaining conversational skills in the target language. From the beginning, a great amount of reading is done in L2, both in and out of class. The vocabulary of the early reading passages and texts is strictly controlled for difficulty. Vocabulary is expanded as quickly as possible, since the acquisition of vocabulary is considered more important than grammatical skill. Translation reappears in this approach as a respectable classroom procedure related to comprehension of the written text.

4.3   The direct approach

This approach was developed initially as a reaction to the grammar-translation approach in an attempt to integrate more use of the target language in instruction. Lessons begin with a dialogue using a modern conversational style in the target language. Material is first presented orally with actions or pictures. The mother tongue is NEVER, NEVER used. There is no translation. The preferred type of exercise is a series of questions in the target language based on the dialogue or an anecdotal narrative. Questions are answered in the target language. Grammar is taught inductively—rules are generalized from the practice and experience with the target language. Verbs are used first and systematically conjugated only much later after some oral mastery of the target language. Advanced students read literature for comprehension and pleasure. Literary texts are not analyzed grammatically. The culture associated with the target language is also taught inductively. Culture is considered an important aspect of learning the language.

4.4   The audio-lingual method

This method is based on the principles of behavior psychology. Based on the principle that language learning is habit formation, the method fosters dependence on mimicry, memorization of set phrases and over-learning. Structures are sequenced and taught one at a time. Structural patterns are taught using repetitive drills. Little or no grammatical explanations are provided; grammar is taught inductively. Skills are sequenced: Listening, speaking, reading and writing are developed in order. Vocabulary is strictly limited and learned in context. Teaching points are determined by contrastive analysis between L1 and L2. There is abundant use of language laboratories, tapes and visual aids. Great importance is given to precise native-like pronunciation. Use of the mother tongue by the teacher is permitted, but discouraged among and by the students. Successful responses are reinforced; great care is taken to prevent learner errors.

4.5   Community language learning

This methodology takes its principles from the "Counseling Learning Approach" developed by Charles Curran. It was created especially for adult learners who might fear to appear foolish; so the teacher becomes a language counselor, understanding and leading them to overcome their fears. It follows Krashen's Affective Filter Hypothesis and the Cognitive Theory where the human mind is active.

4.6   The silent way

The silent way originated in the early 1970s. The three basic tenets of the approach are that learning is facilitated if the learner discovers rather than remembers or repeats; that learning is aided by physical objects and that problem-solving is central to learning. The use of the word "silent" is also significant, as the Silent Way is based on the premise that the teacher should be as silent as possible in the classroom in order to encourage the learner to produce as much language as possible.

4.7   Functional-notional approach

Hallidays's systemic-functional linguistics exerted much impact on language teaching and learning. Notions and functions are thus attached with more and more importance. Notions are meaning elements that may be expressed through nouns, pronouns, verbs, prepositions, conjunctions, adjectives or adverbs, while functions pertain to the role language plays in its use like greeting, apologizing. The use of particular notions depends on three major factors: the functions, the elements in the situation, and the topic being discussed.

Finocchiaro (1983: 65-66) has placed the functional categories under five headings: personal (e.g. clarifying one's ideas, expressing one's thoughts), interpersonal (e.g. apologizing, extending and accepting invitations), directive (e.g. warning someone), referential (e.g. defining something, identifying items or people), and imaginative (e.g. creating rhymes, poetry, stories or plays).

4.8   Total physical response

James (1979) defines the Total Physical Response (TPR) method as one that combines information and skills through the use of the kinesthetic sensory system. This combination of skills allows the student to assimilate information and skills at a rapid rate. As a result, this success leads to a high degree of motivation. The basic tenets are:

- Understanding the spoken language before developing the skills of speaking.
- Imperatives are the main structures to transfer or communicate information.
- The student is not forced to speak, but is allowed an individual readiness period and allowed to spontaneously begin to speak when the student feels comfortable and confident in understanding and producing the utterances.

4.9   Communicative language teaching

The approach that can be broadly labeled as communicative language teaching emerged in the 1970s and 1980s as the emphasis switched from the mechanical practice of language patterns associated with the Audio-lingual method to activities that engaged the learner in more meaningful and authentic language use. Twenty years on, its influence has been so big that virtually few English teaching practices in classrooms are not claimed to be "communicative".

Above briefly mentioned are nine teaching methods/approaches, which are just part of the English teaching models, but they are of importance in the development of English language teaching. In the next chapter, we will have a more extended look at and more detailed illustration on more English teaching methods.

Questions for further discussion:

1. What are the major focuses of English subject educology?
2. How has modern technology contributed to the studies of language and language teaching theories?
3. Which factor plays a more important role in language acquisition/learning, nature or nurture? Can you list some language teaching/learning methods based on nature and nurture theories?
4. What is ZPD? What effects does it have on English learning and teaching?
5. What are the strengths and weaknesses of UG in explaining language acquisition?
6. Can you list some English teaching methods/approaches? Which one(s) do you prefer and why?

References

Austin, J. L. 1962. *How to Do Things with Words*. Oxford University Press.

Brown, H. D. 1987. *Principles of Language Learning and Teaching*. Prentice Hall, Inc.

Bruner, J. S. 1961. The Act of Discovery. *Harvard Educational Review*. 31 (Spring): 21-32

Chomsky, N. 1959. A Review of B. F. Skinner's Verbal Behavior. *Language*. Vol. 35.

Cook, V. 1991. *Second Language Learning and Language Teaching*. Arnold.

Ellis, R. 1985. *Understanding Second Language Acquisition*. Oxford University Press.

ERIC: http://eric.ed.gov/ERICWebPortal/Home.portal, retrieved March 25, 2006.

Finocchiaro, M. & Brumfit, C. 1983. *The Functional-Notional Approach*. Oxford University Press.

Fodor, J. A. 1975. *The Language of Thought*. Thomas Cromwell.

Gardner, H. 1993. *Multiple Intelligences: The Theory in Practice*. Basic Books.

James, J. A. 1979. *Learning Another Language Through Actions*. Accuprint.

Krashen, S. 1985. *The Input Hypothesis: Issues and Implications*. Longman.

Ormrod, J. 1995. *Educational Psychology: Principles and Applications*. Prentice-Hall.

McLaughlin, B. 1987. *Theories of Second-Language Learning*. Edward Arnold.

Parrot, M. 1993. *Tasks for Language Teachers*. Cambridge University Press.

Searle, J. 1969. *Speech Acts: An Essay in the Philosophy of Language*. Cambridge University Press.

Stern, H. H. 1983. *Fundamental Concepts of Language Teaching*. Oxford University Press.

Vygotsky, L. S. 1978. *Mind in Society: The Development of Higher Psychological Processes*. Harvard University Press.

陶本一. 2001. 《学科教育学》. 人民教育出版社.

CHAPTER 2
Survey of the History of English Teaching

During the past few years of the present century and the twentieth century, there seemed to be an agreement on the purpose of the English language teaching and learning, that is, to develop the learners' communicative competence.

Communicative Language Teaching claims to involve the merits of other previous methods. It is, however, necessary to know what has been done and what is being done in the field of English teaching both at home and abroad so as to serve the purpose of improving our teaching and learning, just as the saying goes: to gain new knowledge by reviewing the old.

In this chapter, we'll review the major schools and methods of foreign language teaching and learning, the development of English teaching in China and the current trends in English language teaching.

1. Main schools of English teaching in history

1.1 Grammar-translation method

It is reasonable enough to begin with Grammar-Translation Method. Language teaching had already a long history before the method became known. Grammar-Translation Method was justly termed as the Traditional Method, for it's based on teaching the old, "dead" language—Latin. The principal characteristics of the method are (Richards, 2000):

- The goal of foreign language study is to learn a language in order to read its literature or in order to benefit from the mental discipline and intellectual development that result from foreign language study. Grammar-Translation approaches the language first through detailed analysis of its grammar rules, followed by application of this knowledge to the task of translating sentences and texts into and out of the target language. It hence views language learning as consisting of little more than memorizing rules and facts in order to understand and manipulate the morphology and syntax of the foreign language.
- Reading and writing are the major focus; little or no systematic attention is paid to speaking or listening.
- Vocabulary selection is based solely on the reading texts used, and words are taught through bilingual word lists, dictionary study, and memorization.
- The sentence is the basic unit of teaching and language practice. Much of the lesson is devoted to translating sentences into and out of the target language, which is a distinctive feature of the method.
- Accuracy is emphasized. Errors are not pardoned and should be corrected at once.
- Grammar is taught deductively—that is, by presentation and study of grammar rules, which are then practiced through translation exercises (This perhaps leads to the name of the method).
- The student's native language is the medium of instruction.

At the height of the Communicative Approach to language learning in the 1980s and early 1990s, Grammar-Translation Method was labeled as outdated and old-fashioned. There were numerous reasons for this but principally it was felt that translation itself was an academic exercise rather than one which would actually help learners to use language, and an overt focus on grammar was to learn about the target language rather than to learn it. The use of mother tongue is also considered to be an interference to the learners' learning the target language.

If we examine the principal features of Grammar-Translation Method, however, we will see that not only has it not disappeared but that many of its characteristics have been central to language teaching throughout the ages and are still valid today. There are certain types of learner who respond very positively to a grammatical syllabus as it can give them both a set of clear objectives and a clear sense of achievement. Other learners need the security of the mother tongue and the opportunity to relate grammatical structures to mother tongue equivalents. Above all, this type of approach can give learners a basic foundation upon which they can then build their communicative skills. Without a sound knowledge of the grammatical basis of the language it can be argued that the learner is in possession of nothing more than a selection of communicative phrases which are perfectly adequate for basic communication but which will be found wanting when the learner is required to perform any kind of sophisticated linguistic task.

1.2 The direct method

The Grammar-Translation Method received severe criticism as time went on. Focus was on the prescriptive nature and neglecting listening and speaking of the method. With the increased opportunities of communication in the mid-nineteenth century, the reform movement on foreign language teaching became a must. The result was the appearance of several methods termed collectively as the Direct Method or the Direct Approach as some may prefer (The well-known methods of the approach are Gouin's the Series Method and the Berlitz Method). Just as what the Reform Movement advocated, the Direct Method emphasized the study of spoken language, pronunciation, the inductive teaching of grammar, and the use of the target language as the medium of instruction. The principal characteristics of the method go as follows (Richards, 2000):

- Classroom instruction was conducted exclusively in the target language.

- Only everyday vocabulary and sentences were taught.
- Oral communication skills were built up in a carefully graded progression organized around question-and-answer exchanges between teachers and students in a small, intensive class.
- Grammar was taught inductively.
- New teaching points were introduced orally.
- Concrete vocabulary was taught through demonstration, objects, and pictures; abstract vocabulary was taught by association of ideas.
- Both speech and listening comprehension were taught.
- Correct pronunciation and grammar were emphasized.

The Direct Method is "direct" in that it advocates second language learning should model first language learning and the learner's first language is not used in the class, and new vocabulary is introduced by demonstration. The Direct Method is also known as the Natural Method or Anti-grammatical Method. It vehemently opposed to teaching of formal grammar and was aware that language learning was more than the learning of rules and the acquisition of imperfect translation skills. The Direct Method enjoyed popularity in Europe for a time and was quite successful in private language schools, where paying learners had high motivation and the use of native-speaking teachers was the norm.

However, the Direct Method soon died out in the foreign language teaching field for its obvious demerits. This method believed second language should be learned in a way in which first language was acquired—by total immersion technique. But obviously second language learners have far less time and opportunity in schools, compared with small children learning their mother tongue. The Direct Method rejects the use of the printed word—but this objection is illogical since second language learner has already mastered his/her reading skills. Also Direct Methodists failed to grade and structure their materials adequately—no selection, grading or controlled presentation of vocabulary and structures, which bewildered the learners from the very beginning.

Nevertheless, many teachers did modify the Direct Method to meet practical requirements of their own schools, implemented main principles, i.e. teaching through oral practice and banning all translation into target language. Obviously compromise was needed. The Direct Method did pave the way for more communicative, oral based approach, and as such represented an important step forward in the history of language teaching.

1.3   Situational language teaching

Though the Direct Method was doomed with a short life, it paved
the way for the oral approach which led to the Situational Language
Teaching. This approach began with the work of British applied
linguists in the 1920s and 1930s. Palmer and other British linguists
developed an approach to methodology that involved systematic
principles of selection (the procedures by which lexical and
grammatical content was chosen), gradation (principles by which
the organization and sequencing of content were determined), and
presentation (techniques used for presentation and practice of items in
a course). This formed a sound systematic basis of theory and practice
for the method. The main characteristics of the method go as follows
(Richards, 2000):

- Language teaching begins with the spoken language. Material
  is taught orally before it is presented in written form.
- The target language is the language of the classroom.
- New language points are introduced and practiced
  situationally.
- Vocabulary selection procedures are followed to ensure that
  an essential general service vocabulary is covered.
- Items of grammar are graded following the principle that
  simple forms should be taught before complex ones.
- Reading and writing are introduced once a sufficient lexical
  and grammatical basis is established.

1.4   The audio-lingual method

This approach has its roots in the USA during World War II,
when there was a pressing need to train key personnel quickly
and effectively in foreign language skills. The results of the Army
Specialized Training Program are generally regarded to have been
very successful, with the caveat that the learners were in small groups
and were highly motivated, which undoubtedly contributed to the
success of the approach. The approach was theoretically underpinned
by structural linguistics, a movement in linguistics that focused on
the phonemic, morphological and syntactic systems underlying the
grammar of a given language, rather than according to traditional
categories of Latin grammar. As such, it was held that learning a
language involved mastering the building blocks of the language and
learning the rules by which these basic elements are combined from

the level of sound to the level of sentence. The audio-lingual approach was also based on the behaviorist theory of learning, which held that language, like other aspects of human activity, is a form of behavior. The main characteristics of the method go with its theories of learning as follows (Richards, 2000):

- Foreign language learning is basically a process of mechanical habit formation. Good habits are formed by giving correct responses rather than by making mistakes. Language is verbal behavior—that is, the automatic production and comprehension of utterances—and can be learned by inducing the students to do likewise.
- Language skills are learned more effectively if the items to be learned in the target language are presented in spoken form before they are seen in the written form.
- Analogy provides a better foundation for language learning than analysis. Drills enable learners to form correct analogies.
- Inductive teaching of grammar is preferred.
- The meaning that the words of a language have for the native speaker can be learned only in a linguistic and cultural context (mainly, if not solely in sentences) and not in isolation. Teaching a language thus involves teaching aspects of the cultural system of the people who speak the language.

1.5   Communicative language teaching

Communicative Language Teaching (CLT) is an approach rather than a method for it consists of set of principles about teaching including recommendations about method and syllabus where the focus is on meaningful communication, not structure and use, not usage. In this approach, students are given tasks to accomplish using language, instead of studying the language. The syllabus is based primarily on functional development (asking permission, asking directions, etc.), not structural development (past tense, conditionals, etc.). In essence, a functional syllabus replaces a structural syllabus. There is also less emphasis on error correction as fluency and communication become more important than accuracy. As well, authentic and meaningful language input becomes more important. The class becomes more student-centered as students accomplish their tasks with other students, while the teacher plays more of an observer role. Communicative language teaching is now the generally accepted norm in the field of second language teaching. CLT suggests communicative language and language acquisition, and the approach proposes way for learners to internalize a second language and to experiment in a classroom context. Therefore, the classroom context is used to create activities to teach students how to react in a real world situation, not to fake real-world situations. Its basic features are:

- The emphasis is on learning to communicate through interaction in the target language.
- The introduction of authentic texts into the learning situation (Authentic material is a must, because students cannot extrapolate to the real world from their learning on made-up material).
- Learners are provided with opportunities to focus not only on language, but also on the learning process itself.
- The learner's own personal experience, which is regarded as important contributing elements to classroom learning, is enhanced.
- The link between classroom language learning and language activation outside the classroom is to be established.

Most present-day practitioners would probably like to think that their classes are "communicative" in the widest sense of the word. Their lessons probably contain activities where learners communicate and where tasks are completed by means of interaction with other learners. To this end there will probably be considerable if not extensive use of pair, group and mingling activities, with the emphasis on completing the task successfully through communication with others rather than on the accurate use of form. During these activities the teacher's role will be to facilitate and then to monitor, usually without interruption, and then to provide feedback on the success or otherwise of the communication and, possibly, on the linguistic performance of the learners in the form of post-activity error correction. In terms of the organization of the lesson, the classic "present, practice and perform" model, where careful input of a particular structure is typically followed by controlled, less controlled and freer practice is likely to have been replaced by a more task-based approach, possibly on the lines of "test, teach, test," where the learners are given a communicative task which is monitored by the teacher and then their language use while performing the task is fine-tuned by the teacher in a lesson stage which focuses on error correction or a particular form that is causing difficulties. This is typically followed by a further task-based stage, where the initial task is repeated or a similar task is performed, ideally with a greater degree of linguistic accuracy than during the first attempt. Another feature will probably be that the traditional grammatical approach of starting the beginner's syllabus by presenting the present tense of the verb "to be" will have been replaced by a more communicative focus, with basic introductions, requests and questions enabling learners to begin communicating in English from the very first lesson.

In today's classroom we will probably see a lot of authentic listening and reading material being used and far fewer contrived texts designed to illustrate grammatical form or present items of vocabulary and with no attempt to communicate a meaningful message to the listener or reader. Perhaps the most enduring legacy of the communicative approach will be that it has allowed teachers to incorporate motivating and purposeful communicative activities and principles into their teaching while simultaneously retaining the best elements of other methods and approaches rather than rejecting them wholesale.

1.6   The natural approach

The Natural Approach was developed by Tracy Terrell and Stephen Krashen, starting in 1977. It came to have a wide influence in language teaching in the United States and around the world. It is called "Natural" for basing on the natural way of acquiring the mother tongue. The Natural Approach is based on the following principles:

- Language acquisition (an unconscious process developed through using language meaningfully) is different from language learning (consciously learning or discovering rules about a language) and language acquisition is the only way competence in a second language occurs. (The acquisition/learning hypothesis)
- Conscious learning operates only as a monitor or editor that checks or repairs the output of what has been acquired. (The monitor hypothesis)
- Grammatical structures are acquired in a predictable order and it does little good to try to learn them in another order. (The natural order hypothesis).
- People acquire language best from messages that are just slightly beyond their current competence. (The input hypothesis)

- The learner's emotional state can act as a filter that impedes or blocks input necessary to acquisition. (The affective filter hypothesis)

The Natural Approach belongs to a tradition of language teaching methods based on observation and interpretation of how learners acquire both first and second languages in non-formal settings. Such methods reject the formal (grammatical) organization of language as a prerequisite to teaching. It insists that such an approach be the only learning process which, for certain, will produce mastery of the language at a native level. The Natural Approach holds the view that the function of normal classroom teaching is just to provide comprehensible input to the students, which will naturally lead to the communicative competence. This, however, is not necessarily the case for learning a foreign language is different from learning a second language and adult learning is different from children's acquiring their mother tongue.

1.7 Total physical response

Total Physical Response is a language learning method based on the coordination of speech and action. It was developed by James J. Asher, a professor of psychology at San Jose State University, California. It is linked to the trace theory of memory, which holds that the more often or intensively a memory connection is traced, the stronger the memory will be. James J. Asher defines the Total Physical Response (TPR) method as one that combines information and skills through the use of the kinesthetic sensory system. This combination of skills allows the student to assimilate information and skills at a rapid rate. As a result, this success leads to a high degree of motivation. The basic tenets are:

- Second language learning is parallel to first language learning and should reflect the same naturalistic processes.
- Listening should develop before speaking.
- Children respond physically to spoken language, and adult learners learn better if they do that too.
- Once listening comprehension has been developed, speech develops naturally and effortlessly out of it.
- Adults should use right-brain motor activities, while the left hemisphere watches and learns.
- Delaying speech reduces stress.

- Understanding the spoken language before developing the skills of speaking.

Imperatives are the main structures to transfer or communicate information. The student is not forced to speak, but is allowed an individual readiness period and allowed to spontaneously begin to speak when the student feels comfortable and confident in understanding and producing the utterances. Some teachers hold the view that TPR only suits for the children's learning. However, it provides insight and meaningful implication for the adult's learning.

1.8   The silent way

The silent way originated in the early 1970s and was the brainchild of the late Caleb Gattegno. The last line of Benjamin Franklin's famous quote—*Tell me and I forget. Teach me and I remember. Involve me and I learn*—about teaching and learning can be said to lie at the heart of the silent way.

Following the silent way, the complete set of materials utilized as the language learning progresses include: A set of colored wooden rods, a set of wall charts containing words of a "functional" vocabulary and some additional ones, a pointer for use with the charts in visual dictation, a color coded phonic chart(s), tapes or discs, films, drawings and pictures, and a set of accompanying worksheets, a book of stories, and texts.

This method begins by using a set of colored rods and verbal commands in order to achieve the following:

To avoid the use of the vernacular, to create simple linguistic situations that remain under the complete control of the teacher, to pass on to the learners the responsibility for the utterances of the descriptions of the objects shown or the actions performed, to let the teacher concentrate on what the students say and how they are saying it, drawing their attention to the differences in pronunciation and the flow of words, to generate a serious game-like situation in which the rules are implicitly agreed upon by giving meaning to the gestures of the teacher and his mime, and to permit almost from the start a switch from the lone voice of the teacher using the foreign language to a number of voices using it. This introduces components of pitch, timbre and intensity that will constantly reduce the impact of one voice and hence reduce imitation and encourage personal production of one's own brand of the sounds.

To provide the support of perception and action to the intellectual guess of what the noises mean, thus bringing in the arsenal of the usual criteria of experience already developed and automatic in one's use of the mother tongue.

To provide a duration of spontaneous speech upon which the teacher and the students can work to obtain a similarity of melody to the one heard, thus providing melodic integrative schemata from the start.

1.9   Suggestopedia

Often considered to be the strangest of the so-called "humanistic approaches", suggestopedia was originally developed in the 1970s by the Bulgarian educator Georgi Lozanov. Extravagant claims were initially made for the approach with Lozanov himself declaring that memorization in learning through suggestopedia would be accelerated by up to 25 times over that in conventional learning methods. The approach attracted both wild enthusiasm in some quarters and open scorn in others. On balance, it is probably fair to say that suggestopedia has had its day but also that certain elements of the approach survive in today's good practice.

The approach was based on the power of suggestion in learning, the notion being that positive suggestion would make the learner more receptive and, in turn, stimulate learning. Lozanov holds that a relaxed but focused state is the optimum state for learning. In order to create this relaxed state in the learner and to promote positive suggestion, suggestopedia makes use of music, a comfortable and relaxing environment, and a relationship between the teacher and the student that is akin to the parent-child relationship. Music, in particular, is central to the approach. Unlike other methods and approaches, there is no apparent theory of language in suggestopedia and no obvious order in which items of language are presented.

The original form of suggestopedia presented by Lozanov consisted of the use of extended dialogues, often several pages in length, accompanied by vocabulary lists and observations on grammatical points. Typically these dialogues would be read aloud to the students to the accompaniment of music. The most formal of these readings, known as the "concert reading", would typically employ a memorable piece of classical music such as a Beethoven symphony. This would not be in the form of background music but would be the main focus of the reading, with the teacher's voice acting as a counterpoint to the music. Thus the "concert reading" could be seen as a kind of pleasurable event, with the learners free to focus on the music, the text or a combination of the two. The rhythm and intonation of the reading would be exaggerated in order to fit in with the rhythm of the music.

1.10 Community language learning

This methodology is not based on the usual methods by which languages are taught. Rather the approach is patterned upon counseling techniques and adapted to the peculiar anxiety and threat as well as the personal and language problems a person encounters in the learning of foreign languages. Consequently, the learner is not thought of as a student but as a client. The native instructors of the language are not considered teachers but, rather are trained in counseling skills adapted to their roles as language counselors. The language counseling begins with the client's linguistic confusion and conflict. The aim of the language counselor's skill is first to communicate empathy for the client's threatened inadequate state and to aid him linguistically. Then slowly the teacher-counselor strives to enable him to arrive at his own increasingly independent language adequacy. This process is furthered by the language counselor's ability to establish a warm, understanding, and accepting relationship, thus becoming an "other-language self" for the client.

2. Development of English teaching in China

2.1 The period of traditional English teaching

English Teaching in China possesses a long history from the church English school in the 19th century. However, the rapid development of English teaching and learning appeared much later in the 1980s for obvious reasons. The turn of foreign language teaching to Russian after the foundation of the People's Republic of China led to the stop of the development of English teaching. Though soon later English began to be taught again in China, the material of teaching focused on the political slogans and quotations of the great leaders, and the method was no more than translating these materials into and out of the target language.

English was taught for the purpose of learning a language only in the late 1970s and early 1980s, when the Communicative Approach, the Natural Approach and other experimental methods got more and more attention in foreign language teaching and learning, but Grammar-Translation Method still dominated the English teaching classroom due to the lack of opportunities of communication and the long time of "closing the door". If we read the English textbooks for the junior middle school students even in the late 1990s, we can find the book consisting of two parts: one part of pattern drills and the other part of written texts. The pattern drills (characteristics of the Audio-lingual Method) were designed for the students to learn the grammar structures and the texts for the learners or (mainly) for the teachers to translate into Chinese and explain the "major points"— mainly the grammatical rules.

2.2   The reform movement

In the late 1980s a reform movement was conducted in the English teaching in the junior middle school when "The English teaching syllabus for nine-year-system junior middle schools" was designed. The government tried to change the situation of so-called "dumb English" and set communicative competence as the purpose of English teaching. The teaching material was organized based on the structure-function system—structures for performing certain functions. Teachers were expected to change the traditional "teacher-centered" method to "student-centered" one. Test form and content also changed to some extent. The movement also had an impact on college English teaching. Activities for communication were organized both in and out of classroom. "English Corner" was organized in many middle schools, colleges, and cities. English seemed to become the "like" and pursuit of all the people of China. The reform movement was furthered by the release of "New Standard for Middle School English Teaching" by the government in 2000. "The New Standard" set quality-education as the purpose of the English course, and adopted humanism as the principle of education. Innovation on English teaching reached the height of its development. Various books and papers were written around the teaching methods, learning factors, textbook writing, and teacher education.

2.3   College English teaching

College English teaching reached its height in the late 1990s for three major reasons. The first reason is, of course, the importance and necessity of English in communication and work for the increasing opportunities of international interaction. With the rapid development of Chinese economy, more and more world-famous companies set up their branches in China. English got the first place in the college courses for students wishing to seize the chances of working in these companies and joint ventures. The second reason is the issue of the nation-wide College English Test Band 4 and Band 6 (CET4 and CET6). Many companies and working units took the certificates as the proof of language proficiency and many universities relate the certificates to the requirement for graduation. Students paid more attention to English than to their majors. The third reason is the English language examination for postgraduates. Due to the pressure of employment opportunities, more and more college students take part in the examination and English language performance forms the key factor.

No matter for what reasons, there appeared a nation-wide "English Rush". Various books for learning English occupied almost half place of the bookstores. Numerous students reading English could be found everywhere and anytime on campus. More hours for English lesson could be found in the university curriculum. Varieties of press invested money in textbook research and publishing for increasing number of consumers. Conferences for learning English were held all the year round. It's time to learn English. It's time for the "English Rush".

The "English Rush" led innovation to English teaching and learning and brought the prosperous period of English learning. The side effect, however, is also of great prominence. The "English Rush" seemed equivalent to the "English Economy Rush". The real interest, it seemed, was in the money brought by more people learning English. The name of serious English scholars could never be found in the famous leaders of learning English. In recent years many experts, including the English teachers, criticized the disadvantages of the CET4 and CET6. The burden to the students and the misleading effect of the test bore most of the criticism.

3. Current trends in English teaching

In the past few years of the 21st century, there appeared a cold reflection to English teaching and learning. People no longer try to find the short cut in English learning. Teachers and researchers come to be aware that there is no perfect textbook and perfect method in English teaching and learning. It is true that the ultimate purpose of learning English is to develop the communicative competence. However, there can be various methods of teaching and learning for the same goal. If we examine the research on the practice of English teaching both at home and abroad, we can find the following trends.

3.1   Teaching for communication

The English examination for college entrance still has great influence on English teaching and learning in middle schools and most college students are still studying English hard to pass CET. However, more and more people become aware of the importance of learning for communication.

There is no definite definition for what Communicative Language Teaching is, but there is a general distinction between a "strong" and a "weak" version. The weak version stresses the importance of providing learners with opportunities to use their English for communicative purposes and, characteristically, attempts to integrate such activities into a wider program of language teaching. The strong version, on the other hand, advances the claim that language is acquired through communication, so that it is not merely a question of activating an existing but inert knowledge of the language, but of stimulating the development of the language system itself. If the former could be described as "learning to use English", the latter entails "using English to learn it".

Whether "learning to use English" or "using English to learn it", nobody denies that the purpose of learning English is to use English. One of the tasks of language classroom is to provide opportunities for students to use English. Researchers and practitioners are now working on such communicative activities for students to really use English.

3.2   Task-based English teaching

Task-based English teaching or, rather, task-based learning for it focuses on learning rather than teaching, refers to teaching/learning a language by using language to accomplish open-ended tasks. Learners are given a problem or objective to accomplish, but are left with some freedom in approaching this problem or objective. Task-based learning offers an alternative for language teachers. In a task-based lesson the teacher doesn't pre-determine what language will be studied; the lesson is based around the completion of a central task and the language studied is determined by what happens as the students complete it. The lesson follows certain stages.

• Task

The students complete a task in pairs or groups using the language resources that they have as the teacher monitors and offers encouragement.

• Planning

Students prepare a short oral or written report to tell the class what happened during their task. They then practice what they are going to say in their groups. Meanwhile the teacher is available for the students to ask for advice to clear up any language questions they may have.

• Report

Students report back to the class orally or read the written report. The teacher chooses the order of when students will present their reports and may give the students some quick feedback on the content. At this stage the teacher may also play a recording of others doing the same task for the students to compare.

• Analysis

The teacher highlights relevant parts from the text of the recording for the students to analyze. The teacher may ask students to notice interesting features within this text. The teacher can also highlight the language that the students used during the report phase for analysis.

• Practice

Finally, the teacher selects language areas to practice based upon the needs of the students and what emerged from the task and report phases. The students then do practice activities to increase their confidence and make a note of useful language.

In the task-based language teaching, the students are free of language control. In the stages they must use all their language resources rather than just practicing one pre-selected item. A natural context is developed from the students' experiences with the language that is personalized and relevant to them. The students will have a much more varied exposure to language with task-based language teaching. They will be exposed to a whole range of lexical phrases, collocations and patterns as well as language forms. The language explored arises from the students' needs. This need dictates what will be covered in the lesson rather than a decision made by the teacher or the course book. It is a strong communicative approach where students spend a lot of time communicating.

The problem facing language teachers is how to design the tasks and how to involve the tasks in teaching the textbook. Articles have been written on the principles and characteristics of tasks and how to use tasks in teaching listening, speaking, reading and writing, and even in teaching vocabulary and grammar.

As an illustration of the trend of English language teaching in China, we conduct a detailed study on TBLT and its current situation in part four of this chapter.

3.3   Research on grammar teaching

For a time in the history of Communicative Language Teaching in China and abroad, it was misunderstood that grammar was unnecessary to teach for developing communicative competence. Krashen's Monitor Hypothesis insists that linguistic knowledge can only lead to the monitor ability rather than the communicative competence. Because of the influence of this hypothesis and the Natural Approach, grammar was ignored in English language teaching. An unexpected phenomenon appeared among the English learners—students can communicate in English, however, with numerous grammatical mistakes, or errors as some may put it.

If we take a close look at what communicative competence is, we can find grammar is a very important component of the communicative competence. Hymes considered that communicative competence included grammar, adaptability, appropriateness, and practicality. Some include the paralinguistic knowledge and socio-psychological factors in the communicative competence, but they never reject grammar. In recent years, people have been aware of the necessity and importance of grammar teaching in the foreign language context. Researchers and teachers are exploring the combination of grammar and communicative language teaching and the new way of teaching grammar. Such terms as communicative teaching of grammar, implicit teaching of grammar, etc. keep appearing in the books and journals.

3.4   Attention to learner differences

Total commitment, total involvement, and total physical, intellectual, and emotional responses are necessary to successfully send and receive messages in a second language. The learning of a second language is a complex process, involving a seemingly infinite number of variables. We have to consider who learn and teach the language—information related to learners and teachers, what—content of learning and teaching, how—the learning process, when—time or age of language learning starters, where—the learning situation, and why—reasons for and goals of learning a second language. Considering the learner factors, each learner is different from each other. Learner difference is a very important issue in foreign language teaching and learning.

All students can learn because they have multiple intelligences and ever-improving capabilities in all the domains of learning. Catering for student diversity is not intended to even out abilities and performances, but to stretch the potential of all students. Student diversity can be coped with by using different strategies such as enhancing students' motivation, adapting the central curriculum and instructional materials, modifying the styles of instruction, varying instructional grouping and adjusting assessment practices. Researchers and teachers are now exploring to what extent the learner difference influences language learning result and what the teachers should do to cope with the student diversity.

3.5   Developing learning autonomy

Learning autonomy can be said to be the ability to take charge of one's learning. On a general note, the term "autonomy" has come to be used in at least five ways:

- for *situations* in which learners study entirely on their own;
- for a set of *skills* which can be learned and applied in self-directed learning;
- for an inborn *capacity* which is suppressed by institutional education;

- for the exercise of *learners' responsibility* for their own learning;
- for the *right* of learners to determine the direction of their own learning.

The autonomous learner takes a/an (pro-) active role in the learning process, generating ideas and availing himself of learning opportunities, rather than simply reacting to various stimuli of the teacher. As we shall see, this line of reasoning operates within, and is congruent with, the theory of constructivism. The autonomous learner is a self-activated maker of meaning, an active agent in his own learning process. He is not one to whom things merely happen; he is the one who, by his own volition, causes things to happen. Learning is seen as the result of his own self-initiated interaction with the world. Within such a conception, learning is not simply a matter of rote memorization. It is a constructive process that involves actively seeking meaning from (or even imposing meaning on) events.

Autonomous learners have insights into their learning styles and strategies. They take an active approach to the learning task at hand, are willing to take risks, i.e. to communicate in the target language at all costs, and they are good guessers. They attend to form as well as to content, that is, place importance on accuracy as well as appropriateness, develop the target language into a separate reference system and are willing to revise and reject hypotheses and rules that do not apply; and have a tolerant and outgoing approach to the target language.

It is unnecessary and impossible to develop total learning autonomy for, within the learning situation in China, learners cannot be allowed to learn all by themselves. They cannot freely choose the time, situation, and the learning contents all by themselves. However, it is necessary and important for the teachers to develop the learners' ability of autonomous learning in the learning process. When students are aware that they should be responsible for their own learning, they will have higher intrinsic learning motivation. It is necessary to train the students' learning strategies (both meta-cognitive and cognitive) in order to develop the learning autonomy.

3.6   Developing automaticity in English teaching and learning

In recent years, more and more people began to pay attention to the particular strange phenomena that most Chinese students can have high scores even in very difficult tests like TOEFL and GRE but lack even the basic communicative ability. Research has been done to examine the problem and the development of automaticity in foreign language teaching and learning has been proposed.

Automatic processing is a fast, parallel, fairly effortless process which is not limited by short-term memory capacity, is not under direct subject control and performs well-developed skilled behaviors. Automatic processing typically develops when subjects deal with the stimulus consistently over many trials. Controlled processing is characterized as a slow, generally serial, effortful, capacity-limited, subject-controlled processing mode that must be used to deal with novel or inconsistent information (Schneider & Fisk, 1983). Collett (2004) considered that automaticity is the ability to effortlessly complete everyday tasks with low interference of other simultaneous activities and without conscious thought to step-by-step process. When the brain recognizes familiar tasks it processes the information and applies the correct rules to the procedure in order to reduce the demand on the working memory and allow for higher order processing of information.

In developing the learners' automaticity, the teachers should change the teaching approach. The following list is provided for consideration in teaching:

- Inductive rather than deductive teaching;
- Implicit rather than explicit teaching of the rules;
- Comprehensible and adequate input;
- Paying attention to learners' affective factors (self-esteem, anxiety, inhibition, empathy, tolerance of ambiguity, etc.);
- Learner-centered teaching;
- Task-based approach;
- Paying attention to learners' learning styles (field-dependence and field-independence, left-and-right brain functioning, reflectivity and impulsivity, visual and auditory styles);
- Paying attention to strategies training (meta-cognitive strategies, cognitive strategies, communicative strategies).

And the learners should pay attention to the following tips:

- Taking opportunities as much as possible to expose to the target language;
- Inductive rather than deductive learning;
- Focal attention on meaning while peripheral attention on forms even in the controlled stage;
- Analogic learning rather than analytical learning;
- Using communicative strategies.

3.7 Attention on CALL

Computer-assisted language learning (CALL) has been defined as the search for and study of applications on the computer in language teaching and learning and is now used routinely in a variety of instructional situations. As a result, language teachers are increasingly required to possess CALL expertise that includes both practical skills and thorough understanding of information technology (IT) theory. Teachers may need to design, implement, and evaluate CALL activities in their classrooms, they may be asked to supervise an institution-wide project or to work with other institutions to develop CALL-based exchange programs, or they may be put in charge of setting up and operating a multimedia language laboratory. It is thus becoming essential for teachers to be familiar with CALL options within the classroom, at the institutional level, and at the broader level of inter-institutional collaboration.

CALL is claimed to be effective in promoting both fluency and accuracy in the target language as well as improving motivation and learner autonomy. Therefore, in recent years, studies on CALL have been booming up and drawing more and more attention in ELT in the world.

4. A study on task-based language teaching

We have introduced many a language teaching methods above. In this section, we will have a close scrutiny on TBLT—the one English teaching approach that has attracted lots of eyeballs in the past decade in China.

4.1 Introduction

Task-based Language Teaching (TBLT) has evolved in response to a better understanding of the way languages are learnt. Traditionally, it is held that learning a language involves mastering the building blocks of the language and learning the rules by which these basic elements are combined from the level of sound to the level of sentence; it has been regarded as a process of mastering a succession of steps, each one building on the one before. Teachers present the target language in ready-to-assimilate pieces, starting with the easy parts and gradually moving towards the harder parts. Learners must master each part sequentially and incorporate it into their knowledge of the target language.

By contrast, the present view of language learning, mainly based upon research findings in linguistics, psychology, and pedagogy, is that learners do not acquire the target language in the order it is presented to them, regardless of how careful and thoughtful the teachers and textbook writers are in organizing the process. As Ellis (1994) puts it, language learning is a developmental, organic process that follows its own internal agenda. Errors are not necessarily the result of bad learning, but are part of the natural process of inter-language forms gradually moving towards target forms.

Such a view of language learning has deepened implications for language teaching, and has resulted in the development of various task-based approaches. These approaches are somehow disparate, but they share a common concept: giving learners tasks to transact, rather than items to learn, provides an environment which best promotes the natural language learning process. By engaging in meaningful activities, such as problem-solving, role-playing, discussions, etc., the learner's inter-language system is stretched and expanded. These tasks rely on a successful transfer of meaning in order to be completed, and are supposed to focus the learners' attention more closely on the comprehensibility of the language they and their partners are using, thus increasing the likelihood that inter-language forms will be pushed towards target language norms (Foster, 1999).

In the past few years, TBLT has been introduced into China and among Chinese English teachers and researchers it has apparently been enjoying growing popularity. However, many scholars (Wen 2001, for example) maintain that although this type of instruction is widely believed to be innovative, a close scrutiny on its effectiveness in China is needed.

Indeed, a disregard for differences in socio-economic conditions, educational ideologies and systems and other factors that help define teaching and learning conditions can mislead Foreign Language Teaching (FLT) practice in a country. But at the same time, we shouldn't ignore the merits of TBLT.

4.2   Basic concepts

TBLT, since its birth, has from time to time been challenged and criticized for the diversified and indefinite definitions on "task".

4.2.1 Definitions given in dictionaries

Compact Oxford English Online Dictionary[1] gives a simple definition on task: a piece of work to be done. According to Merriam-Webster Online Dictionary[2], task is a usually assigned piece of work often to be finished within a certain time or something hard or unpleasant that has to be done. Wordsmyth's[3] explanation is: a specific item of work assigned to one or something to be done that is usually very difficult or tedious.

The second and third definitions both imply work imposed by a person in authority or an employer or by circumstance. At first sight, "task" seems an unlikely candidate to form the basis of a learner-centered pedagogy which aims to motive lifelong learning, since it holds the associations of unwillingness and imposition (Littlewood, 2004).

4.2.2 Definitions given by researchers in ELT arena

Definitions on "task" put forward by ELT researchers range along a continuum according to the extent to which they insist on "communicative purpose" as an essential criterion. Littlewood (2004) selects three entry points in his review of the definition:

- Communicative purpose is not an essential criterion at all. e.g.

Breen (1987: 23): A task is a range of plans which have the overall purpose of facilitating language learning, from the simple and brief exercise type to more complex and lengthy activities such as group problem-solving or simulations and decision-making. It has a particular objective, appropriate content, a specified working procedure, and outcomes.

Williams and Burden (1997: 168): A task refers to any activity that learners engage in to further the process of learning a language.

- Moving along the continuum, some writers do not go so far to define tasks only in communicative terms but clearly think of them primarily as involving communication. e.g.

Crookes (1986): A task is a piece of work or an activity, usually with specific objective, undertaken as part of an educational course, at work, or used to elicit data for research.

---

[1] http://www.askoxford.com/concise_oed/task?view=uk, retrieved 23 Aug. 2004.

[2] http://www.m-w.com/cgi-bin/dictionary?book=Dictionary&va=task, retrieved 24 Aug. 2004.

[3] http://www.wordsmyth.net/live/home.php?script=search&matchent=task, retrieved 24 Aug. 2004

Stern (1992) associates tasks with realistic language use when he writes that communicative exercises provide opportunities for relatively realistic language use, focusing the learner's attention on a task.

- Moving further along the continuum, task is viewed as comprising only activities that involve communication.

Willis (1996): Tasks are always activities where the foreign language is used by the learner for a communicative purpose in order to achieve an outcome.

Nunan (1998a): A communication task is a piece of classroom work during which learners' attention is principally focused on meaning rather than form, that is, on what is being expressed rather than on the linguistic forms used for expressing it.

Ellis (2003) adopts the third view and uses the term "exercises" (in contrast to "tasks") for any activity in which the learners have no communicative purposes. This is similar to Estaire and Zanon's (1994) distinction: "enabling tasks" (in which the learners' attention is on linguistic aspects) and "communication tasks" (in which the learner's attention is on meaning).

Littlewood further expresses his view on the understanding of tasks by the following illustrating figures (2004).

FIGURE 2.1 The continuum from focus on forms to focus on meaning (slightly adapted)

Focus on forms ⟸			⟹ Focus on meaning	
Noncommunicative learning	Precommunicative language practice	Communicative language practice	Structured communication	Authentic communication
Focusing on the structures of language, how they are formed and what they mean, e.g. uncontextualized grammar exercises, substitution drills, pronunciation drills, awareness-raising activities	Practicing language with some attention to meaning but not communicating new messages to others, e.g. 'question and answer' practice (Who is sitting next to you?)	Practicing pre-taught language in a context where it communicates new information, e.g. information-gap activities or 'personalized' questions	Using language to communicate in situations eliciting pre-learnt language, but with some unpredictability, e.g. structured role-play	Using language to communicate in situations where the meanings are unpredictable, e.g. creative role-play, more complex problem-solving and discussion
'Exercises' ⟸	(Ellis)		⟹ 'Tasks'	
'Enabling tasks' ⟸	(Estaire and Zanon)		⟹ 'Communicative tasks'	

FIGURE 2.2 Two dimensions in task-based foreign language learning

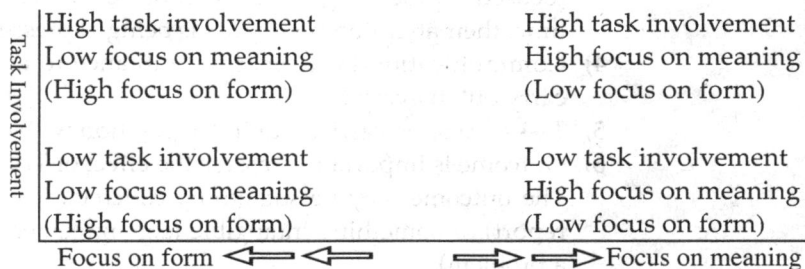

	High task involvement Low focus on meaning (High focus on form)	High task involvement High focus on meaning (Low focus on form)
Task Involvement	Low task involvement Low focus on meaning (High focus on form)	Low task involvement High focus on meaning (Low focus on form)

Focus on form ⇐ ⇐   ⇒ ⇒ Focus on meaning

According to Littlewood (2004), it is better to consider two dimensions that are crucial to understanding tasks. The first dimension is the continuum from focus on forms to focus on meaning. The second is the degree of learner-involvement that a task elicits and in TBLT teachers should aim at as high a level of task involvement (mind-engagement) as possible.

Although experts and researchers in the field of language teaching try very hard to make things clear on the definition of "task", it is clear that sometimes they make both other people and themselves bewildered. Bruton (2002), for instance, discusses tasks for eight pages, but admits that the reader does not really know what he has been discussing, since "the definition of task is an issue in itself". On the one hand, it is often a tough job to label things, especially to label things in a "perfect" or even "proper" way. On the other, it is not always easy to draw a crystal-clear line between "communicative" and "non-communicative" tasks. Meaning and form are closely interconnected. "We use different grammatical forms to signal differences of meaning. In fact, good oral grammar exercises can and should be both meaningful and communicative" (Nunan, 1989).

4.2.3 The common features of TBLT shared by researchers today

It is not easy to give a proper definition on task, neither is it easy to define TBLT. However, it is not difficult to sum up the common features of TBLT commonly-held today.

1) TBLT is objective-oriented, i.e. learners work purposefully towards an objective.
2) TBLT does not oppose "the teaching of grammar", because the objective of TBLT can be language-focused, e.g. to discover rules of grammar.

3) In TBLT classroom work, learners' attention is principally focused on meaning rather than on form, i.e. for most of the time, their attention is on what is being expressed.
4) Communication tasks bear resemblance to activities people carry out in everyday life.
5) Tasks are often carried out in cooperation with others.
6) Outcome is important to assess the effect of TBLT.
7) The outcome may be something concrete, (e.g. a timetable, a report) or something intangible (e.g. agreement or solution to a problem).

4.3   Advantages of using TBLT

In the following section, we look at the merits of TBLT in comparison with other language teaching approaches.

4.3.1 Comparison between traditional approaches and TBLT

As reviewed in the former parts, TBLT rises in response to a better understanding of the way languages are learnt.

First, it embodies a fundamental change of "focus" from "teaching perspective" to "learning perspective". In language teaching classes, teachers should consider how to provide opportunities for students to form hypotheses about the foreign language and how to test the hypotheses in practice. The learning process is overwhelmingly emphasized compared with the traditional teaching methods like grammar-translation, silent way, oral-aural method. TBLT bases on the students' needs in designing its teaching syllabus and process. Skehan (1998) points out that task difficulty should be carefully controlled that students can pay proper attention to language forms to prevent fossilization in TBLT process. Richards and Rodgers (2001) explain the aim of using TBLT: facilitate students' interaction in carrying out tasks by providing them with natural language learning environments. In the process of expressing oneself and trying to understand others, interaction naturally helps them to check and remedy his hypotheses.

Second, TBLT puts the meaningful learning process, rather than the product, in the primary place. When communicative tasks become the major component of language program, meaningful learning comes into function and meaning negotiation can enhance language learning process. According to Long (1983a), students acquire new knowledge more efficiently when the input is comprehensible to them through negotiation and interaction process in the classroom. Long proposes three ways to make language input more comprehensible: (1) simplifying input; (2) making use of context; (3) fixing and adjusting interactive structure. In TBLT, both language-production process and feedback-obtaining process are regarded as important to the development of learners' language proficiency. However, this does not mean TBLT pays no attention to product; rather, product is a measure to evaluate the efficiency of the whole process. What's more, students' emotion, personality, social ability, etc. get involved comprehensively.

Third, the learning units are no longer discrete language items preset by experts and scholars in TBLT, but mainly tasks negotiated by teachers and learners. The traditional teaching approaches regard language as sequential, separate, discrete pieces which can be piled up by learners in the process of learning. But in the 1970s the discussion over "language communication is a synthetic process" began to put the discrete view in an embarrassing situation. In TBLT, tasks serve as the mediation of learning and the presentation and learning of language forms are embedded in them. TBLT regards language as dynamic, multilayer, rather than static, linear system. At the same time, the selection of teaching materials is no longer a top-down "decree", but a selection based on the learners' needs and bottom-up negotiation between language learners and teachers.

Fourth, teacher's role has changed in TBLT. In traditional approaches, the language teacher is regarded as the controller, and sole knowledge source. In a TBLT English classroom, the teacher is a facilitator, creating the kind of atmosphere which enhances pupils' participation and impels them to learn English; the teacher is an inspirer; transmitting to his students the wish to discover new things, to find possible answers and to put them forward. The teacher is the one who helps and cooperates with his students, stimulates their curiosity, raises their interest and encourages them to practice English.

4.3.2 Comparison between other communicative approaches and TBLT

The above listed features of TBLT seem to be shared by other communicative approaches like procedural language teaching (which also emphasizes the process of learning). Then, what is special about TBLT? One point is that TBLT is not radical compared with procedural teaching. In procedural syllabi, the teaching contents and activities are totally negotiated by teachers and students without any default while TBLT bases its design and selection of tasks on the analysis of the students' needs. Another point is the attention on grammar. The traditional approaches focus overwhelmingly on language forms and the procedural approaches reject grammar teaching. When Long and Crookes (1992) put forward their task syllabus, they advocate "focus on form" rather than "focus on forms". To them, the former represents a proper attention on grammar in TBLT. They propose using language learners' grammar errors as clues, selecting proper time to arouse the learners' attention on grammar. Littlewood (2004) points out that compared with other communicative language teaching approaches, "structured communication tasks" and "authentic communication tasks" take on a more central role in a TBLT. They serve not only as major components of the methodology but also as units around which a course may be organized. These units provide a link between outside-classroom reality and inside-classroom pedagogy. At the interface with outside-classroom reality, communicative tasks enable the course to be organized around "chunks of communication" which reflect students' needs, interests, and experiences. At the interface with inside-classroom pedagogy, they provide an organizing focus for the individual components of language (structures, vocabulary, and so on) that students have to learn in order to communicate.

4.3.3 Aim of using TBLT in China

To be brief, the aim of using TBLT is to help to cause a paradigm change of ELT: a change from focus on "what is to be taught" in language classes to "how the language is learned in use".

In China, English language teaching has long been criticized for its dear investment and low efficiency, for the production of hundreds and thousands of "deaf" and "mute" learners. With the rapid development of China's economy and ever-increasing socio-cultural exchange with the international society, a new paradigm of foreign language teaching in China is becoming urgent. We need more qualified foreign language users with integrated skills, rather than language users who can merely read. In terms of English teaching method, more emphasis is put on regarding language as a means to an end rather than simply an end. As commented by Scarcella & Oxford (1992), the segregated, product-oriented form of instruction which includes syllabus design, curriculum arrangement, and student placement, is usually founded on pragmatic, administrative decisions rather than on a conceptually sound theory of language learning and teaching. Sometimes teachers and administrators think it is logistically simpler to present courses on writing divorced from speaking, or on listening severed from reading; and sometimes they believe it is impossible to concentrate effectively on more than one language skill at a time. Such classes often disintegrate into a mere examination of forms and structures. But the reality is that, it is very difficult to segregate the language skills from each other in a vigorous way while still maintaining any degree of communication. Isolation of the skills often leads to a communication deadlock.

In a word, the import of TBLT is meant to bridge ELT practice in China with the world, to make our English education move along with the times.

Questions for further discussion:

1. What are the merits and demerits of the Grammar-Translation Method?
2. Compare the Grammar-Translation Method with the Direct Method.
3. Is there an ideal teaching method? How do you choose teaching methods for your classroom?
4. How can Task Based English Teaching be effectively used in the context of China?
5. What does it mean to cater for student diversity? How can this goal be achieved in classroom teaching?
6. How can learners' automaticity be effectively developed?

References:

Breen, M. P. 1987. Learner contributions to task design. In C. N. Candlin and D. F. Murphy (Eds.), *Language Learning Tasks, Lancaster Practical Papers in English Language Education, (7)*: 23-46. Prentice Hall International (UK).

Bruton, A. 2002. From tasking purposes to purposing tasks. *ELT Journal 56*/3: 280-288.

Collett, J. 2004. *Automaticity: Skill Building*. Perry, Johnnie.

Crookes, G. 1986. Task Classification: A Cross-disciplinary Review. *Technical Report, 4.* Center for Second Language Classroom Research. Social Science Research Institute. University of Hawaii, Honolulu.

Ellis, R. 1994. *The Study of Second Language Acquisition*. Oxford University Press.

Ellis, R. 2003. *Task-based Language Teaching and Learning*. Oxford University Press.

Estaire, S. & Zanon, J. 1994. *Planning Classwork—A Task-based Approach*. Heinemann.

Foster, P. 1999. Key concepts in ELT. *ELT Journal, 53*/1. Oxford University Press.

Littlewood, W. 2004. The task-based approach: some questions and suggestions. *ELT Journal, 58*/4: 319-326.

Long, M. 1983a. *Native Speaker/Non-native Speaker Conversation in the Second Language Classroom*. Clarke and Handscombe.

Long, M. H., & Crookes, G. 1992. Three approaches to task-based syllabus design. *TESOL Quarterly, 26*(1): 27-56.

Nunan, D. 1988a. *The Learner-Centered Curriculum*. Cambridge University Press.

Nunan, D. 1989. *Designing Tasks for the Communicative Classroom*. Cambridge University Press.

Richards, G. 2000. Why use computer technology. *English Journal, 90*(2): 38-41.

Richards, J. C. & Rodgers, T. S. 2001. *Approaches and Methods in Language Teaching*. Cambridge University Press.

Scarcella, R.C. & Oxford, R. L. 1992. *The Tapestry of Language Learning*. Heinle & Heinle.

Schneider, Walter, & Arthur D. Fisk. 1983. Attention Theory and Mechanisms for Skilled Performance, in Richard A. M. (ed.) *Memory and Control of Action*. North-Holland Publishing Company.

Skehan, P. 1998. *A Cognitive Approach to Language Learning*. Oxford University Press.

Stern, H. H. 1992. *Issues and Options in Language Teaching*. Oxford University Press.

Wen, Q. F. 2001. *Applied Linguistics: Research Methods and Thesis Writing*. Foreign Language Teaching and Research Press.

Williams, M. & Burden, R. L. 1997. *Psychology for Language Teachers: A Social Constructive Approach*. Cambridge University Press.

Willis, J. 1996. *A Framework for Task-based Learning*. Longman.

CHAPTER 3
English Syllabus Evaluation and Design

The choice of a syllabus is a major decision to make in language teaching, and it should be made as consciously and with as much information as possible. Moreover, at various times during their careers, professionals in the field of language teaching find themselves involved in important tasks quite removed from actual classroom instruction, like making plans for courses and writing teaching materials.

The purposes of this chapter are:
- Helping to-be teachers and in-service teachers to appraise their experience of different types of syllabus and describe syllabuses they have used or seen in action;
- Broadening their experience of ways in which syllabuses can be specified and described;
- Introducing some key concepts in syllabus design and showing how these concepts can be used in order to appraise any type of syllabus;
- Helping them design and develop their own teaching materials.

1. Definition of syllabus

1.1 Key terms

The course a teacher teaches, or intends to teach, is very likely to be based on some kind of written syllabus. But what is a syllabus? What is the relationship between syllabus and course and curriculum?

Owing to different understandings among scholars and researchers, it is very difficult, even impossible for people to make clear demarcations between these terms. Generally speaking, in the field of language educology, a "course" is often taken to mean a real series of lessons (e.g. the writing course delivered in 2005 to sophomore English-major students in a university), while a "syllabus" can be taken to be something rather more abstract, with fewer details of the blow by blow conduct of individual lessons. Thus we might quite properly write rather different courses, with different materials, but based on the same syllabus. This happens a lot in publishing. For example, when notions and functions became popular as a basis for course design, various ELT publishers published course-books based on what became known as a "notional/functional" syllabus. And each course book was different.

However, it can also work the other way round. This is clearly illustrated in White's (1988) definition on syllabus—the specification and ordering of content of a course or courses. So, we may start with the demand for a course, for a specific group of learners over a specific length of time, and then we design a syllabus for it.

When it comes to curriculum and syllabus, things are more complicated, since some scholars use them interchangeably and tend not to distinguish them at all; thus, in a broad sense, a syllabus also involves the following four aspects:

FIGURE 3.1 Four aspects involved in a syllabus

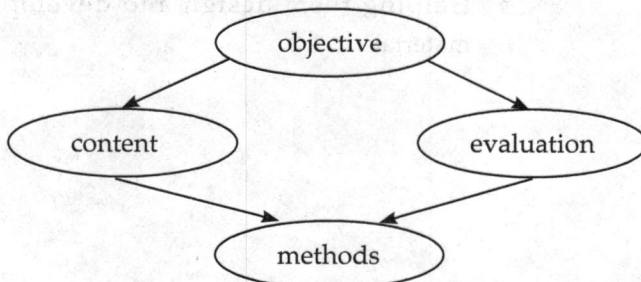

Others would like to provide them with quite different connotations. Dubin and Olshtain (1986) believe that "a curriculum contains a broad description of general goals by indicating an overall educational-cultural philosophy which applies across subjects together with a theoretical orientation to language and language learning with respect to the subject matter at hand. A curriculum is often reflective of national and political trends as well", while "a syllabus is a more detailed and operational statement of teaching and learning elements which translates the philosophy of the curriculum into a series of planned steps leading towards more narrowly defined objectives at each level".

Candlin (1984) states that curriculum is connected with language learning, learning purpose and experience, evaluation, and the role relationships of teachers and learners, while syllabus is a more concrete term, referring to the actual events in the classroom.

As for syllabus design there are some approaches that regard it in a narrow perspective. This view makes a distinction between syllabus design and methodology. The former is connected with selection and grading of content, while methodology is concerned with the selection of learning tasks and activities (Nunan, 1994: 5). While syllabus design refers to the "what" of a language program, methodology is concerned with the "how".

Stern (1984) defines syllabus as connected with content, structure, and organization, while curriculum development is viewed as connected with implementation, dissemination and evaluation. For Yalden (1984) syllabus is connected not only with learners' needs and aims, but also with the selection and grading of content, tasks and activities.

It should be pointed out that in the 1970s syllabuses were specified not only as far as grammar was concerned but also in terms of functional skills for a successful communication. According to Nunan (1994), every syllabus should pay attention to grammatical components, functional skills as well as to notions, topics, themes, activities and tasks. Needs analysis, connected with learners' expectations, some constraints and resources for implementation, has to be carried out for designing of a successful syllabus.

Of course, we don't mean to provide a clearer definition on syllabus, or draw a sharper line between the terms. Rather, we will adopt a broad vision on syllabus for our discussion. By the way, as far as the word "design" is concerned, a major point of debate in curriculum and syllabus development is concerned precisely with how much design should go into a particular course, that is, how much should be negotiated with the learners, how much predetermined by the teacher, and how much left to the chance and the mood of the participants on the day. This notion is bound up with the idea of the "focus on the learner", and more recently with ideas of control and initiative in the classroom (Skelton & Willis, 2004)[1].

1.2　Features of a syllabus

According to Ur (2000: 176), a syllabus specifies all the things that are to be taught in the course for which the syllabus has been designed: it is therefore comprehensive. The actual components of the list may be either the—"what" items (words, structure, topics), or process—the "how" items (tasks, methods) or both. The items are usually ordered, having components that are considered easier or more essential earlier, and more difficult and less important ones later. This ordering may be fairly detailed or rigid, or general and flexible.

The primary characteristic of the syllabus is that it has explicit objectives, usually declared at the beginning of the document, on the basis of which the components of the list are selected and ordered.

Another characteristic is that it is a public document, which means that the syllabus is both the formulation of pedagogical goals and an instrument of educational policy. It is available for scrutiny not only by the teachers who are expected to implement it, but also by the consumers, including the learners, their parents etc. Under this characteristic is the principle of accountability: the composers of the syllabus are answerable to their target audience for the quality of their document.

There are, other, optional features displaced by some syllabuses and not by others. For instance, some syllabuses delimit the time framework of their components (prescribing that certain items should be dealt with in the first week); some would mention some particular preferred approach or methodology to be used in classrooms.

Dubin and Olshtain (1986) hold that whatever a syllabus is called, it is a document which ideally describes:

1. What the learners are expected to know at the end of the course, or the course objectives in operational terms.

---

[1] http://www.philseflsupport.com/csd1.htm, retrieved 21 Jan. 2005.

2. What is to be taught or learned during the course, in the form of an inventory of items.
3. When it is to be taught, and at what rate of progress, relating the inventory of items to the different levels and stages as well as to the time constrains of the course.
4. How it is to be taught, suggesting procedures, techniques, and materials.
5. How it is to be evaluated, suggesting testing and evaluating mechanisms.

2. Importance of syllabus

The objectives of a syllabus describe the specific outcomes or products of the courses. As a result, objectives guide teachers; they also help learners understand where the courses are going and why. Furthermore, the inventory of items, suggested methodology, measurement, and timetable provide reference for teachers and learners in the process of teaching and learning.

The task for language teachers is to realize the syllabus as a course of action by whatever methodological means seem most appropriate for the activation of learning (Widdowson, 1990). The syllabus itself is an inert abstract object. It is a set of bears for teacher action and not a set of instructions for learner activity. What learners do is not directly determined by the syllabus but is a consequence of how the syllabus is methodologically mediated by the teacher in the pursuit of his own course of instruction.

Since a language teaching syllabus involves the integration of subject matter (what to talk about) and methodological matter (how to talk about it); choices of syllabi can range from the more or less purely linguistic, where the content of instruction is the grammatical and lexical forms of the language, to the purely semantic or informational, where the content of instruction is some skill or information and only incidentally the form of the language.

For teachers who need to work on their own for a syllabus, the fundamental point is to decide what gets taught and in what order. For this reason, the theory of language explicitly or implicitly underlying the language teaching method will play a major role in determining what syllabus should be adopted. Theory of learning also plays an important part in determining the kind of syllabus to use.

3. Different types of syllabi

Although there has been much confusion over the years as to what different types of content are possible in language teaching syllabi and as to whether the differences are in syllabus or method, several distinct types of language teaching syllabi exist, and these different types may be implemented in various teaching situations.

3.1   Eight types of syllabi

In the past decades, a great deal of attention has been paid to the particular language elements that are included in a syllabus and to the organizational system according to which they are presented. Discussions have typically considered the trade-offs, advantages, and disadvantages of the major syllabus types: the structural-grammatical syllabus, the semantic-notional syllabus, the functional syllabus and the situational syllabus (Dubin & Olshtain, 1986).

In this section, we briefly introduce eight types of syllabi. It must be pointed out that although the different types of language teaching syllabi are treated here as though each occurred "purely", in practice, they rarely occur independently of each other. Almost all actual language teaching syllabi are combinations of two or more of the types defined here. For a given course, one type of syllabus usually dominates, while other types of content may be combined with it. Furthermore, different types of syllabi are not entirely distinct from each other. For example, the distinction between skill-based and task-based syllabi may be minimal. In such cases, the distinguishing factor is often the way in which the instructional content is used in the actual teaching procedure.

3.1.1 A structural (formal) syllabus

Based on Behaviorist Psychology and Structural Linguistics, the structural, grammatical or linguistic syllabus is centered round grammatical items. The content of language teaching is a collection of the forms and structures of the language being taught. Examples include nouns, verbs, adjectives, statements, questions, subordinate clauses, tenses, articles, and so on.

For many years, language teachers, syllabus designers and testers tend to think in terms of units of language. They also tend to think of these units as being organized in some way, with similar language bits being grouped together, on the grounds that a well-marshaled inventory will be more comprehensible to the learner than an unorganized list (Palmer, 1974).

As a whole, structural syllabus designers tend to list things which can be easily systematized. According to the advocators of formal syllabi, the notion of grammatical analysis does not seem incomprehensible or absurd—even students can often identify verbs, nouns and so forth—and grammatical description gives the impression that it is accurate, and factual. Having learnt paradigms and pattern sentences, learners are in a position to use this knowledge to generate their own sentences to express their own meanings. Although under what conditions this actually happens is another matter, structural syllabus has been a very popular one in foreign language teaching. Even today we can see its presence in many English textbooks in China.

3.1.2 A notional/functional syllabus

Following a notional/functional syllabus, the content of the language teaching is a collection of the functions that are performed when language is used, or of the notions that language is used to express or both of them. This kind of syllabi focuses on identifying the meanings that learners might need to express (the notions) and the communicative acts they would wish to engage in (the functions). The notional or semantic-notional syllabus came into focus in the early 1970s and placed the semantic unit in the center of syllabus organization. Such a syllabus is organized around themes relating to broad areas of meaning such as space, time, entertainment, size, age, color, comparison, etc. The functional syllabus, which developed alongside the notional syllabus with various attempts to combine the two, focuses on the social functions of language as the central unit of organization. Thus, a functional syllabus is concerned with elements such as informing, agreeing, invitation, suggestion, apology, refusal, etc.

This semantically-based syllabus was the first major alternative (to the traditional structural syllabus) to be developed. Initially, this seems a far better way of organizing a syllabus. Learning how to book a ticket, how to check in at the airport is obviously useful; and the sets of functions can help learners get connected with real-life language use. The notional-functional syllabus seemed a very sensible idea at the beginning.

However, it is not without problems to define and specify such a syllabus. Like the grammatical syllabus, the notional/functional syllabus also risks becoming exhausted at a relatively early stage. And meanwhile it is hard to classify and divide all the notions and functions. Another problem with the notional functional syllabus is that it is often taught using a phrase-book approach, which, in itself, is not generative. If the learner knows the phrase for one situation he/she is in, he/she is all right, but for anything more complex, trouble arises. As a result, the lack of generative ability is a pitfall with a notional/functional syllabus, especially when it is used alone.

3.1.3 A lexical syllabus

A lexical syllabus is often derived from a detailed analysis of a carefully selected corpus of language that reflects the language of the target discourse community.

The analysis can offer the syllabus designer lists of the most frequently used words, their meanings and information about their typical grammatical and lexical environments, i.e. the collocations and patterns that words occur in. Although a lexical syllabus may also include grammar, expressions of notions and functions, its organizing principle is lexical, and as such it can account for a far higher proportion of text than other syllabus types. Another advantage of a lexical syllabus is that it is clear, unambiguous and accessible— everybody can recognize what a word is, and its phrases and patterns are fairly easily identifiable.

But one problem with lexical syllabus is with its exemplification: a lexical syllabus would often cover at least half a page per word. Most of the highly frequent words have at least three or four different meanings, making an inventory of tripled or quadrupled items. And one can argue that learners would rather take with them a good dictionary.

3.1.4 A situational syllabus

The situational syllabus has probably been known in language learning for many years with the tourist phrase book, the forensic English book, the secretary English book, etc. The content of situational syllabus is a collection of real or imaginary situations in which language is used. A situation usually involves several participants who are engaged in some activity in a specific setting. The language occurring in the situation involves a number of functions, combined into a plausible segment of discourse. The primary purpose of a situational language teaching syllabus is to teach the language that occurs in the situations. Examples of situations include: seeing the dentist, complaining to the hotel, booking a ticket on the phone, meeting a new student, and so on.

The pitfalls with notional/functional syllabus are identified in situational syllabus. Besides the inexhaustible situations, the lack of generative feature incurs much of its criticism.

3.1.5 A skill-based syllabus

The content of language teaching in a skill-based syllabus is a group of specific abilities that are important for language use. Compared with situational syllabi, skill-based syllabi group linguistic competencies (pronunciation, vocabulary, grammar, and discourse) together into generalized types of behavior, such as listening to spoken language for the main idea, writing well-formed paragraphs, giving effective oral presentations, and so on. The primary purpose of skill-based instruction is to learn the specific language skill. A secondary purpose is to develop more general competence in the language, learning only incidentally some information that may be available while applying the language skills.

In ELT practice, we should avoid using skill-based syllabus alone. After all, to infer meaning from context, there are linguistic operations to be made, and words to be learnt, not just skills to be performed. More or less any text could potentially be used for any skill, and no skill can be clearly severed from other skills. Another problem with skill-based syllabus is what list of skills could be understood in the same way by all potential participants. If a syllabus aims to "work out meaning from context", it is hard to know what would be regarded as success.

3.1.6 A content-based syllabus

The first goal of instruction for a content-based syllabus is to teach some content or information using the language that the students are also learning. The subject matter is primary, and language learning occurs incidentally to the content learning. The content teaching is not organized around the language teaching, but the other way round. With content-based instruction learners are helped to acquire language through the study of a series of relevant topics, each topic exploited in systematic ways and from different angles.

Content syllabuses certainly give learners a lot of exposure to the language, which is expected. However, it is not enough to produce a syllabus that is merely a list of topics. Language teachers and learners will have difficulty judging which particular items of language to focus on more closely. So far the world immersion programs have not provided enough evidence on natural acquisition happening, with no overt focus on language form to make the content more comprehensible. Another problem is that it is hard to ensure that the topics and texts chosen will give a sufficiently balanced exposure to the language that is representative of the target situation. Needs analysis can be of some help; however, it cannot solve the problem between form and meaning.

3.1.7 A process syllabus

The questions raised in content-based syllabuses apply equally to the process syllabus, which emphasizes a lot the negotiation process and rights of the learners in deciding on the learning content and methods. In many cases, learners are encouraged to choose for themselves which "pathways" to follow through "banks" of activities and materials, motivated by their own interest. But it is almost impossible to ensure that they each receive an adequately balanced exposure to the language of their target discourse community. And the assessment—to give them a fair and authentic evaluation—is another big challenge.

3.1.8 A task-based syllabus

Based on the notion of "learning to use a language in the process of carrying out tasks", the content of the task-based language teaching is a series of preplanned, complex and purposeful tasks that the students want or need to perform with the language they are learning. The tasks are usually defined as activities with a purpose other than language learning, but, as in a content-based syllabus, the performance of the tasks is approached in a way that is intended to develop second language ability. Language learning is subordinate to task performance, and language teaching occurs only as the need arises during the performance of a given task. Tasks integrate language (and other) skills in specific settings of language use.

Task-based teaching differs from situation-based teaching in that while situational teaching has the goal of teaching the specific language content that occurs in the situation (a predefined product), task-based teaching has the goal of teaching students to draw on resources to complete some piece of work (a process). The students draw on a variety of language forms, functions, and skills, often in an individual and unpredictable way, in completing the tasks. A lot of tasks that can be used for language learning are, generally, tasks that the learners actually have to perform in real life. Examples include: applying for a job, making a class almanac, producing a musical play, talking with a colleague, getting housing information over the telephone, and so on. Content-based language teaching is primarily concerned with information, while task-based language teaching is concerned with communicative and cognitive processes.

Like with other types of syllabuses, problems harass task-based syllabus. Out of them, the first is people have different understandings on "task". The second is the balance between form and meaning.

Generally speaking, the eight types of syllabi are presented along the continuum of form-function/meaning, usage-use, beginning with the one based most on structure, and ending with the one based most on language use. Language is a relationship between form and meaning, and most instruction emphasizes one or the other side of this relationship. As commented by Dubin & Olshtain (1986), course designers who carefully consider the various approaches to syllabus design may arrive at the conclusion that a number of different ones are needed and are best combined in an eclectic manner in order to bring about positive results.

Nowadays, one is unlikely to find a course book or indeed a course that uses only one of these forms of syllabi. More often than not, in the "Multi-syllabus" course books, there will be one or two major organizing factors, such as grammar and/or functions, with topics selected to illustrate the grammatical or functional items. Other features like lexis, phonology, and skills practice are often subservient to the main strands and are built in along the way. The following presents different perspectives on syllabus types.

3.2   Synthetic and analytic syllabi

Long and Crookes distinguish between *synthetic* syllabuses that "segment the target language into discrete linguistic items for presentation one at a time" (1992: 28) and *analytic* syllabuses, which "present the target language as whole chunks at a time, without linguistic interference or control" (1992: 29). The former are characterized as being based on the breaking down of language into discrete parts, presenting them deductively or inductively, in linear additive fashion and assuming that learners will synthesize the pieces for use in communication. Analytic approaches, on the other hand, are characterized as being based on the assumption that people of all ages learn languages best, inside or outside the classroom, not by treating the languages as an object of study, but by experiencing them as a medium of communication.

Synthetic syllabuses require the learner to digest the various components of language and later synthesize them for communication. Analytic syllabuses expose learners to whole chunks of language and require the learners to perceive regularities in the input and induce rules. While synthetic syllabuses assume that language can be learned in parts and therefore require the learner to synthesize and integrate these parts so as to acquire functional abilities, analytic syllabuses come from the opposite direction and assume that learners are able to perceive regularities in the language they encounter and induce their own rules.

The predominant approach in foreign language instruction over close to fifty years now was built on a synthetic syllabus, a legacy that is, of course, most visible in the continued dominance of grammar (Grammar Translation, Audio-lingual Method, the Silent Way and Total Physical Response are assumed to be guided by synthetic syllabuses), even as we attempt to make it more "communicative" or more "proficiency-oriented" or more analytic (Natural Approach and the Process Syllabus are assumed to be analytic). As Long and Crookes point out, a number of basic flaws disqualify synthetic conceptualization (1992: 30-34). Firstly, it has a static, target language, product orientation and does not consider the learner and the process of learning itself. Moreover, structural analyses are conducted on an idealized native-speaker version of the language although there is little evidence that these analytical units can serve as meaningful acquisition units for the learner. Besides, the approach assumes a model of language acquisition that is not supported by research findings, which clearly show learners going through lengthy stages of both non-target-like forms and non-target-like use of forms, and even showing temporary deterioration and u-turns in the long period of inter-language development, not the projected steady improvement.

In its place Long and Crookes suggest consideration of an analytic syllabus which takes tasks as the unit of analysis because they provide a vehicle for the presentation of appropriate target language samples to learners—input which they will inevitably reshape via application of general cognitive processing capacities— and for the delivery of comprehension and production opportunities of negotiable difficulty. And new perspectives of form-function relationships are perceived by learners as a result. The notion of tasks can then be built into syllabus design through several steps: (a) a needs analysis "in terms of the real-world *target tasks* learners are preparing to undertake—buying a train ticket, renting an apartment, reporting a chemistry experiment, taking lecture notes, and so forth"; (b) classification of the identified tasks into *task types* (e.g. serving food, serving beverages); and (c) the creation of *pedagogic tasks* which are "increasingly complex approximations to the target tasks" and are the basis of the work of teachers and students (Long & Crookes, 1992: 44).

However, the pure analytic syllabus has also met with a lot of criticism. For instance, the pitfalls with and failures of the analytic meaning-based methods (otherwise termed "non-interventionist") such as the Natural Approach, the Content Syllabus and the Process Syllabus are ascribed to the lack of a "focus on form". Many scholars (Willis 1996, for instance), then propose to build the essentials of linguistic elements into syllabus design but emphasize the importance of interaction and the accomplishment of tasks as a means of promoting language skills. "Focus on form" can be implemented by means of pedagogic tasks intended to bring formal features to learners' attention. This may even at times result in attention to individual linguistic features when problems of production or comprehension arise.

3.3   Product-oriented and process-oriented syllabi

Among educational theorists and researchers in the field of ELT, distinctions have also been made between product-oriented syllabuses, which aim at knowledge and skills that learners should gain as a result of instruction, and process-oriented syllabuses, which put an emphasis on the learning experiences themselves.

Product-oriented syllabuses can be analytically or synthetically planned. In a synthetic language teaching strategy language is taught bit by bit thus gradually making one unified whole. This strategy was connected with acquiring of grammatical structures. In an analytic syllabus the aim is the communicative structures with different degrees of difficulty. The truth is that form and function should be studied together, not in isolation. The well-known functional-notional syllabus is presented as a synthetic syllabus (Widdowson, 1979). With analytic syllabuses the stress is on situations, topics, themes, school and academic subjects. Language is used as a vehicle for communication.

Process-oriented syllabuses are in fact task-based or procedural syllabuses. They stimulate learning by involving the learner in activities of all sorts (e.g. information-gap activities, opinion-gap activities, reasoning-gap activities, etc.). These activities come as a result of processing or understanding language. Candlin's criteria have been suggested for the selection of good tasks, such as "promote attention to meaning, purpose, negotiation", "draw objectives from the communicative needs of learners", "provide opportunities for meta-communication and meta-cognition", "promote sharing of information and expertise", etc. (after Candlin 1987, in Nunan 1994: 45-46). What matters in a task-based syllabus is the degree of contextual support provided for the learner, the cognitive difficulty of the task, the amount of language input and background knowledge that are required, the psychological stress, etc. Content syllabuses are also connected with the analytic approach to syllabus design. They are usually derived from some subject area.

In the arena of Task-Based Language Teaching, the question of grading tasks has been raised again and again. This is determined by the cognitive and performance demands made upon the learner. Any type of text can be taken and exploited by devising various activities that are different in their level of difficulty.

As has been mentioned, in today's ELT circle, the notion and practice of either process-oriented syllabuses or product-oriented syllabuses, either analytic syllabuses or synthetic syllabuses have been blamed for their biases and flaws. As a result, more and more scholars are suggesting the notion of an integrated syllabus.

In summary, we can draw a list in the following:

Productive syllabus:
- traditional syllabus (before structural syllabus was used)
- structural syllabus
- lexical syllabus
- semantic syllabus: situational/notional/functional

Process syllabus:
- Task syllabus
- Procedural syllabus

3.4   An integrated syllabus

The "integrated" or "mongrel" character of the syllabus contains the following characteristics:

1. Its content (and also the methodology) is focused on the language as well as on the learner and the learning process.
2. It contains elements from various language teaching and learning approaches. A combination of structures, functions, skills, and tasks is deemed necessary in order to realize the modern, overall goal of studying a foreign language—to use it accurately and fluently for communicative purposes.
3. It builds into itself both analytic and synthetic aspects.

Each of the three language-learning methods mentioned— the structural, functional, and task-based approaches—contributes important elements to an integrated EFL syllabus.

- **The structural component**

One of the fundamental reasons for the study of grammar is that it is a familiar language learning approach with a long and successful history. Another reason is that it answers the need to impose order upon the seeming chaos of everyday language. Yet perhaps the most obvious reason is that it supports correct use of the language by paying attention to form.

Grammar instruction is an important aspect of language learning, but since its focus is on form, it does not provide students with opportunities to learn how to communicate in the new language (Ellis, 1993: 91). To provide these opportunities, other language learning approaches must be employed.

- **The functional component**

Nunan (1988a: 34) maintains, "In general, functions may be described as the communicative purpose for which we use language." Linguistic competence as the goal of language learning has been seen as too narrow, and social-linguists have argued that communicative competence, i.e. knowledge of how to use language in everyday life, is equally important. This importance was further emphasized by Halliday, whose functional approach to language learning centers on the interpersonal or communicative nature of language (Breen, 1987: 88).

In order to select and grade the functions to be taught, a needs analysis must be employed (Nunan, 1988b: 37). However, the order in which language functions such as greeting, requesting, and refusing are taught is not absolute, as there is no research indicating that some functions are mastered more easily than others.

Whereas the functional and structural components supply essential (synthetic) parts of the content of the integrated syllabus, the context or analytic aspect of the study material is furnished by the task-based element.

- **The task-based component**

Crookes (1986: 1) defines a task as "an activity, usually with a specified objective, undertaken as a part of an educational course or at work". Tasks, also known as "activities" or "exercises," may aim at fluency or accuracy of language use by focusing on meaning or on form. Some examples of task activities are: listing, matching, problem solving, writing a story, or designing a poster. Tasks may be performed by groups, pairs, or individual students (Willis, 2000: 8), and may be used to teach grammar, functions, notions, or skills. The communicative aspect of the use of tasks, even when performed individually, lies in the need to report the results to other students and/or to the teacher.

The content of a task-based syllabus is formed by exercises and activities of a practical nature. Realistic tasks, such as using timetables to plan a trip by train, are regarded as activities that stimulate learning in a natural way. The use of authentic tasks is seen as a more effective way of language learning since it provides a purpose for the use of a language other than simply studying words and phrases for their own sake. Another reason for the effectiveness of the use of tasks is that they mobilize the learners' L1 competence, i.e. the abilities and knowledge they already possess in their first language.

It is for these pedagogic reasons that teachers turn to task-based learning and attempt to construct the exercises that form the core of a mixed syllabus.

4. Guidelines to syllabus choice/design

Although various types of syllabuses are defined here in isolated contexts, it is very rare for one type of syllabus to be used exclusively in actual teaching settings. Syllabus types are usually combined in more or less integrated ways, with one type as the organizing basis around which the others are arranged and related. In this regard, when talking about syllabus choice and design, it should always be kept in mind that the issue is not which type to choose but which types, and how to relate them to each other.

Dubin & Olshtain (1986: 45-54) suggest three dimensions should be taken into consideration in choosing and designing a language syllabus: (a) language content, or the specific matter to be included; (b) process or the manner in which language content is learned; (c) product, or outcomes such as the language skills that learners are expected to master.

Alongside the content dimension, key questions to be asked are:

1. What elements, items, units, or themes of language content should be selected for inclusion in the syllabus?
2. In what order or sequence should the elements be presented in the syllabus?
3. What are the criteria for deciding on the order of elements in the syllabus?

Questions about the process dimension:

1. How should language be presented to facilitate the acquisition process?
2. What should be the roles of teachers and learners in the learning process?
3. How should the materials contribute to the process of language learning in the classroom?

Questions concerning the product/outcome dimension:

1. What knowledge is the learner expected to attain by the end of the course? What understandings based on analyses of structures and lexis will learners have as an outcome of the course?
2. What specific language skills do learners need in their immediate future, or in their professional lives? How will these skills be presented in the syllabus?
3. What techniques of evaluation or examination in the target language will be used to assess course outcomes?

In the case of teachers' general needs in their work, the following steps are put forward in preparing a practical language teaching syllabus:

1. Determine, to the extent possible, what outcomes/needs are desired for the students in the instructional program. That is, as exactly and realistically as possible, define what the students should be able to do as a result of the instruction.
2. Rank the syllabus types mentioned above in line with their likelihood of leading to the products/outcomes desired.
3. Evaluate resources in expertise available (for teaching, needs analysis, materials choice and production, etc.), in materials, and in training for teachers.

4. Rank the syllabi relative to resources available. That is, determine what syllabus types would be the easiest to implement given resources available.

5. Compare the lists made under No. 2 and No. 4. Making as few adjustments to the earlier list as possible, produce a new ranking based on the resources' constraints, taking into account the constraints contributed by teacher and student factors described earlier.

6. Making out a final ranking, taking into account all the information produced by the earlier steps.

7. Designate one or two syllabus types as dominant and one or two as secondary.

8. Review the question of combination or integration of syllabus types and determine how combinations will be achieved and in what proportion.

9. Translate decisions into actual teaching units.

Of course, in making practical decisions about syllabus design, one must take into consideration all the possible factors that might affect the practicality and teachability of a particular syllabus. By starting with an examination of each syllabus type, tailoring the choice and integration of the different types according to local needs, one may find a principled and practical solution to the problem of appropriateness and effectiveness in syllabus design.

5. Evolution of English syllabi in China

5.1   A glimpse at the college English syllabus change

College English here refers to English language courses taught to non-English majors in the universities and colleges all over China. College English Teaching in China has roughly experienced four stages since 1977, according to Lu (2001)[1]:

- The stage of resurrection (1977-1982)
- The stage of improvement (1982-1986)
- The stage of advancement (1986-1994)
- Making a step forward (1994-)

---

[1] http://www.baleap.org.uk/pimreports/2001/shu/Lu.htm, retrieved 15 Sep. 2004. As college English has been a most important and eye-catching strand in the field of ELT in China, in many cases, it is singled out for study and analysis.

Over the years, Chinese linguists and English language teachers agreed that a national English syllabus is necessary, which should serve as a guideline in all the universities and colleges. Throughout the stages, revising work has been done by the revising teams to improve the efficiency of English language teaching. Revision is more a question of examining and modifying the existing syllabus than building up a whole operation. Finding out changes in needs survey and what has already been done and what has not been done is essential in deciding goals and objective modification, content selection and sequencing. The following is an exemplifying analysis on the 1999 syllabus.

In the needs survey, the revising team did three questionnaires in 1996. The questionnaires cover:
- administrators' and teachers' expectations of college students' English proficiency for the 21st Century;
- graduates' actual use of English in their affiliations;
- employers' comments on graduates' English proficiency.

And the tests were on students' vocabulary and their English proficiency upon entering universities. Those three questionnaires and two tests have laid the basic foundation for the revision of the syllabus.

1) Goals and objectives setting

The 1999 version of the syllabus has been improved in setting the goals as, "…to develop a strong reading ability for the students and a fairly good ability for listening, speaking, writing and translating so that students are capable of EXCHANGING information in the target language…" (Revising Team, 1999).

2) Content selection and gradation

- In theory, the 1999 version of the National English Syllabus is a combination of several types of product syllabus. (Lu, 2001)
  a. It is traditional because it has a pre-designed content and it sets out what is to be taught and learned. Moreover, it is composed of a list of linguistic structures and a list of words.
  b. It is structural because it emphasizes teaching the structure and the vocabulary of the language, and it encourages students to make a comparison between their native language and the target language.
  c. It is situational because it realizes the importance that different social situations may need different features of language.
  d. It is functional because it gives priority to the needs of the

students and takes the desired "communicative capacity" as a starting point, and what is more, its organization is not determined solely by grammatical considerations but takes communicative categories into account. It is concerned with both accuracy and fluency.

- In practice, it combines the 1985 version of College English Syllabus applicable to undergraduates of science and engineering with the 1986 version of College English Syllabus applicable to undergraduates of humanities, which emphasizes the common core of the language.

- It stresses the importance of continuous study of college English by making objectives within two stages. The foundation stage is supposed to be finished in the first two years, which is to develop students' receptive skills (listening and reading) as well as productive skills (speaking, writing and translating). The advanced stage is in the last two years of universities. Students usually have specialized English, introducing them to scientific texts in the English language relating to their professions.

- Once again it gives special attention to reading, because it is a source of information and a means of consolidating and extending one's knowledge of the language. This is particularly necessary in Chinese context, where the main purpose for students to learn English is to read materials on their own special subjects.

- It pays enough attention to productive skills of speaking and writing as a result of the needs analysis. For the first time, those two skills are treated as equal with listening and translating.

- Another important decision of the syllabus is that all students have to finish college English Band 4, even if they are minorities and from remote areas.

- Requirements of reading, listening, speaking, and writing have been raised to meet the needs of the students and the society.

- Reading in specialized English has been improved to specialized English which requires not only reading, but also balance-developed language skills such as listening, speaking, writing and translating.

As far as the contents are concerned, the 1999 version of the syllabus can be considered a well-developed and rich syllabus.

3) Syllabus implementation procedures

Following Lu (2001), the procedures of the 1999 version of syllabus can be illustrated in the following figure.

Figure 3.2 Implementing procedures of a syllabus

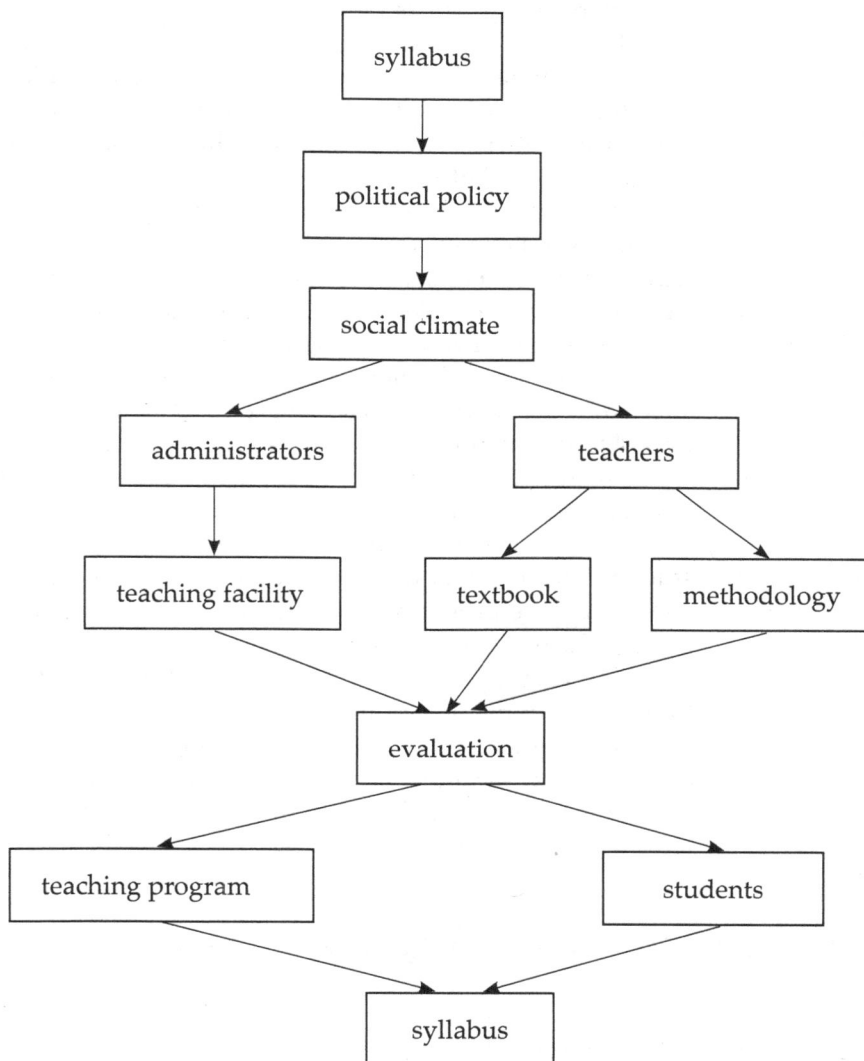

```
                        ┌─────────────┐
                        │   syllabus  │
                        └──────┬──────┘
                               ↓
                        ┌─────────────┐
                        │political policy│
                        └──────┬──────┘
                               ↓
                        ┌─────────────┐
                        │social climate│
                        └──┬───────┬──┘
                   ┌───────┘       └───────┐
                   ↓                       ↓
          ┌──────────────┐        ┌──────────────┐
          │administrators│        │   teachers   │
          └──────┬───────┘        └──┬────────┬──┘
                 ↓                   ↓         ↓
        ┌─────────────────┐  ┌──────────┐ ┌────────────┐
        │teaching facility│  │ textbook │ │ methodology│
        └────────┬────────┘  └────┬─────┘ └─────┬──────┘
                 └────────────┐   │   ┌─────────┘
                              ↓   ↓   ↓
                        ┌─────────────┐
                        │  evaluation │
                        └──┬───────┬──┘
                   ┌───────┘       └───────┐
                   ↓                       ↓
        ┌──────────────────┐      ┌──────────────┐
        │ teaching program │      │   students   │
        └────────┬─────────┘      └──────┬───────┘
                 └──────────┐   ┌─────────┘
                            ↓   ↓
                        ┌─────────────┐
                        │   syllabus  │
                        └─────────────┘
```

4) Suggestions for improvement

The 1999 syllabus is a well-developed proportional syllabus including both language structure and function, emphasizing fluency as well as accuracy. However, the following observations are forwarded for its improvement.

The syllabus intends to be a continuation of what students have learned in high school. Yet there are still many repetitions due to the strong desire of completion and perfection in systemic teaching of vocabulary and grammar, etc.

The syllabus is applicable to about 5 million students in more than 1000 Chinese universities and colleges. Though it has clarified that students should be taught in accordance with their aptitude, the options are not enough to cover such a huge gap. Consequently some requirements might be too high for some students but too low for other students. For instance, vocabulary requirement for Band 4 is low for some key university students, but too high for students from remote areas. Listening and speaking are high in a general term; even students of English majors will need more efforts to reach such goals.

The speed for intensive reading is set at 70 words per minute, which is too specific because learners' reading speed is largely affected by the contents of reading texts and by their knowledge about the subjects. One may read articles on his own subject very fast but slow down with articles of different contents. And it is impossible to limit or predict reading materials in advance.

Evaluation should consist of two aspects: to evaluate or test the students in the program; and to assess the teaching as well as the over-all course program. The syllabus seems to neglect the second aspect, which is as significant as the first.

Following the innovation to CET4 and CET6 in 2005, we are glad to see some of the defects in 1999 syllabus have been eliminated and the general situation has improved. With higher and higher demand on ELT quality in China, the Ministry of Education (MOE) is expected to take more and faster moves in implementing English teaching reform in the near future.

5.2   A general picture of English syllabus in China

5.2.1 Backdrop

- The orientation of a people or government toward language learning and teaching has always been subject to social, economic and political needs (Huang & Xu, 1999)[1]. As China strengthens its communication with and accelerates its steps to join the world family, a variety of indicators reveal the growing emphasis in China on English language study.

---

[1] Huang Yuan-yuan and Hua-li Xu.1999. Article on ESL Syllabus, retrieved 13 Feb. 2003. For details see http://www.eslmag.com/modules.php.

To cope with the trend, English syllabuses at all stages are undergoing adjustments.

- The goal of language teaching is shifting from linguistic competence to communicative competence and the mode of teaching from single skill development to integrated skills training. A comparison of two syllabuses for the secondary school, one from 1980 and one from 1985 will reveal changes in aims, objectives, methodology and vocabulary goals (Huang & Xu, 1999):

Syllabus from 1980
- Aim: Provide students with an ability to gain certain information through English
- Objective: Not clearly defined
- Methodology: Teacher-centered, grammar-translation
- Vocabulary: From 500 upward

Syllabus from 1985
- Aim: Provide students with an ability to gain information through English for their professional needs
- Objective: Proficient reading ability, certain listening ability and elementary speaking and writing ability
- Methodology: Student-centered
- Vocabulary: Functional and notional from 1,600 to 4,000

A comparison of the two syllabuses indicates that although the aims were similar, the 1985 syllabus gave an explicit objective for sub-skills. The 1985 syllabus demanded a student-centered approach (unlike the 1980 syllabus) and the vocabulary goals were increased dramatically on the basis of investigations done in 1982 and 1983 on the changing needs of students completing secondary school.

At the tertiary level, a giant step forward in the 1999 university syllabus is that the aim "to gain information through English" has been replaced by "to exchange information through English". The 1999 syllabus stipulates a national standardized test (CET Band 4) as a means of evaluating students' English level at the end of their second year in a university. Criteria are set for both receptive and productive skills to help students develop interpreting, reasoning, negotiating and expressing abilities. In reading and listening, for instance, there are skills such as grasping the gist, distinguishing facts from opinions, inferring writer's/speaker's attitude, etc. Productive skills such as presenting opinions, developing arguments, giving a short speech on familiar subjects, etc. are fundamental requirements.

5.2.2 Intercultural communicative competence in English syllabus

As early as the 1960s, when "communicative approach" just began to prevail, Ruth R. Cornfield, a distinguished American scholar of communications in education, managed to give a new answer to the first question concerning FLT (foreign language teaching): "Why do we teach and learn a foreign language?" His book, *Foreign Language Instruction: Dimensions and Horizons*, set communication to the goal of FLT (Liu, 2003)[1].

By "communicative competence", Hymes means a competence of when to speak, when not, and as to what to talk about with whom, when, where, in what manner (Stern, 1983: 111). This implies that its focus is intuitive grasp of social and cultural rules and meanings that are carried by utterances. Furthermore, it suggests that language teaching recognizes a social, interpersonal and cultural dimension and attributes to it just as much importance as to the grammatical and phonological aspect. Therefore, the goal of FLT should be to develop the learner's communicative competence: a competence to use the foreign language for communication with people of different cultural backgrounds.

In China, the current English teaching syllabi of various levels are mixtures of grammatical, notional-functional and communicative features. This shows the development of TEFL in China, for it is widely agreed that in learning a language, it is necessary to develop one's ability to use the language in addition to learning the formal rules of the language and the thought of teaching a language for communication is accepted by most, if not all, people in the TEFL circles. In the syllabi, the ultimate goal of TEFL has been set at "developing students' communicative competence", and cultural aspect of TEFL has been taken into account. For instance[2]:

In *College English Syllabus (For Non-English Majors, Revised Edition, 1999)*:

The Teaching Objective:

The teaching objective of college English is to help students develop a relatively strong reading ability and general skills of listening, speaking, writing and translating, and by so doing make students able to use English for communication and to enhance their awareness of cultural differences.

---

[1] Liu Lianzhang. http://iteslj.org/Articles/Liu-Goals.html. retrieved 9 Mar. 2003.

[2] The quotations are translated by Liu Lianzhang from the Chinese version.

Apparently, the above quotation demonstrates three facts.

- One, "communicative competence" as the goal of TEFL is no longer "half hidden" and it has got to its feet firmly in the thoughts and conceptualization of TEFL, which is intended to keep abreast of the age and to serve the development of the modern society.
- Two, cultural instruction, which is believed by many to be an integral part of TEFL, has ceased to be cold-shouldered and has been brought to people's attention.
- Three, communicative competence as the goal of TEFL has something to do with the cultural dimension of TEFL; the former may not be reached without concern for the latter.

All these add up to an encouraging and inspiring trend of TEFL—teaching and learning for real intercultural communication. To reflect the nature of TEFL more accurately, some scholars even insist that the goal of TEFL be defined as "intercultural communicative competence" rather than the somewhat ambiguous "communicative competence" or "language skills". Gladly, we have seen this developing trend in ELT in China.

Questions for further discussion:

1. What are the basic distinctions between syllabus and curriculum?
2. What are the common features of a syllabus?
3. How important is a syllabus to language teaching? How to design a teaching syllabus?
4. What are the common types of syllabi?
5. Which type of syllabus do you prefer and why?
6. What distinguishes a synthetic syllabus from an analytic syllabus?
7. What is an integrated syllabus? What advantages does an integrated syllabus have?
8. Look for an English teaching syllabus and evaluate it in line with the knowledge you acquired from this chapter.

References:

Breen, M. 1987. Contemporary Paradigms in Syllabus Design. *Language Teaching*, 20/1: 81-92 and 20/2:157-174.

Candlin, C. 1984. Syllabus design as a critical process, in C. J. Brumfit (ed.) 1984. *General English Syllabus Design*. Pergamon.

Crookes, G. 1986. Task Classification: A Cross-disciplinary Review. *Technical Report,4*. Center for Second Language Classroom Research. Social Science Research Institute. University of Hawaii, Honolulu.

Dubin, F. & Olshtain, E. 1986. *Course Design*. Cambridge University Press.

Ellis, R. 1993. The structural syllabus and second language acquisition. *TESOL Quarterly, 27*: 91-113.

Huang, Y. Y. & Xu, H. L.1999. Article on ESL Syllabus. For details see http://www.eslmag. com/modules.php. retrieved 13 Feb. 2003.

Liu, L. Z. http://iteslj.org/Articles/Liu-Goals.html. Retrieved 9 Mar. 2003.

Long, M. H., & Crookes, G. 1992. Three approaches to task-based syllabus design. *TESOL Quarterly, 26*(1): 27-56.

Lu, Z. S. 2001. http://www.baleap.org.uk/pimreports/2001/shu/Lu.htm, retrieved 15 Sep. 2004.

Nunan, D. 1988a. *The Learner-Centered Curriculum*. Cambridge University Press.

Nunan, D. 1988b. *Syllabus Design*. Oxford University Press.

Nunan, D. 1994. *Syllabus Design*. Oxford University Press.

Palmer, F. 1974. *The English Verb*. Longman.

Skelton & Willis. 2004. http://www.philseflsupport.com/csd1.htm, retrieved 21 Jan. 2005.

Stern, H. H. 1983. *Fundamental Concepts of Language Teaching*. Oxford University Press.

Stern, H. H. 1984. Introduction, review and discussion, in C. J. Brumfit (ed.) 1984. *General English Syllabus Design*. Pergamon.

Ur, P. 2000. *A Course in Language Teaching: Practice and Theory*. Foreign Language Teaching and Research Press.

White, R. 1988. *The ELT Curriculum: Design, Innovation & Management*. Blackwell.

Widdowson, H. G. 1979. *Explorations in Applied Linguistics*. Oxford University Press.

Widdowson, H. G. 1990. *Aspects of Language Teaching*. Oxford University Press.

Willis, J. 1996. *A Framework for Task-based Learning*. Longman.

Willis, J. 2000. A Holistic Approach to Task-Based Course Design. *The Language Teacher*, 24/2: 7-11.

Yalden, J. 1984. Syllabus design in general education, in C. J. Brumfit (ed.) 1984. *General English Syllabus Design*. Pergamon.

CHAPTER 4
Teaching of Different Language Skills

Effective communication is a fundamental part of all professional disciplines. As social beings, we need to master and develop effective communication skills. When it comes to learning a foreign language, this means developing skills that allow one to process what other people express and to communicate what one wants to convey in that language.

For almost six decades now research and practice in English language teaching has identified the "four skills"—listening, speaking, reading, and writing—as of paramount importance. In textbooks and curricula in widely varying contexts, ESL classes around the world tend to focus on one or two of the four skills, sometimes to the exclusion of the others (Brown, 2001: 217). In this chapter, we will look at how the four skills are taught in the field of ELT; we will also look at the teaching of grammar and vocabulary.

Human beings have fashioned the four basic skills by relating them to each other by two parameters:

- the direction of communication: receiving or producing the message
- the mode of communication: oral/aural or written

The relationships of the four skills can be represented in the following chart:

FIGURE 4.1 Relationship of the four skills

	Oral	Written
Receptive	Listening	Reading
Productive	Speaking	Writing

Of course, offshoots go hand in hand with any single mode, regardless of listening, speaking, reading or writing, in that besides these four, there are other modes of communication. Lumped together under nonverbal communication are various visually perceived messages delivered through gestures, facial expressions, proximity, and so forth. Graphic art (drawings, paintings, diagrams) is also a powerful form of communication. Moreover, with the development of modern science and technology, the lines between different skill forms are getting blurred. Online chatting, for instance, is both oral-based and written-based.

However, none of the language skills can be mastered easily with regard to second or foreign language learning, which poses a complex and labyrinthine picture to language educators. Experiences and studies have shown that written and oral communication has to be practiced extensively to be mastered while nonverbal communication means are often too elusive to teach. For learners of a foreign language, attention to the four different skills does indeed pay off as learners discover the differences among these four primary modes of performance along with their interrelationships.

1. Teaching of listening

Teaching listening skills is one of the most difficult tasks for EFL/ESL teachers. This is firstly because successful listening skills are acquired over time and with lots of practice. The process can be frustrating for students because there are no such rules to follow as in grammar teaching, and also because the effect of learning does not show up in a short time.

One serious inhibitor for students is mental block. While listening, a student may suddenly find that he or she doesn't understand what is being said. At this point, some students just tune out or seek for "alternatives" to cope with situations like a listening test. Other students convince themselves that they are not able to understand spoken English well and as a result, create problems for themselves. The following is an introduction to the landscape of listening comprehension.

1.1 Introduction to listening comprehension

Being a receptive dimension, listening is the ability to identify and understand what others are saying. This involves understanding a speaker's accent and pronunciation, his grammar and his vocabulary, and grasping his meaning. In the first language domain, most language users have all the skills and background knowledge needed to understand what they hear, so people probably aren't even aware of how complex a process it is: Listening to and understanding speech involves a number of basic processes, some depending upon linguistic competence, some depending upon previous knowledge that is not necessarily of a purely linguistic nature, and some depending upon psychological variables that affect the mobilization of these competence and knowledge in the particular task situation.

1.1.1 Listening situations

There are usually two kinds of listening situations in which we find ourselves:
- interactive
- non-interactive

Interactive listening situations concern authentic language use situations and include face-to-face conversations and phone calls, in which people are interlocutors—alternately listening and speaking, and in which any side may have a chance to ask for clarification, repetition, or slower speech from our conversation partner. Non-interactive listening situations are listening to the radio, TV, films, lectures, or sermons. In such situations people usually don't have the opportunity to ask for clarification, slower speech or repetition. Some non-interactive listening situations are less authentic in that they are specially designed and adapted for instructional purposes.

1.1.2 Listening skills

The following is a list of listening skills. The listener has to:

- discriminate among the distinctive sounds in the new language
- recognize stress and rhythm patterns, tone patterns, intonation contours
- recognize reduced forms of words
- distinguish word boundaries
- recognize typical word-order patterns
- recognize vocabulary and retain chunks of words in the short memory
- detect key words, such as those identifying topics and ideas
- recognize grammatical word classes
- recognize basic syntactic patterns
- recognize cohesive devices
- predict what people are going to talk about
- guess unknown words or phrases without panic
- use one's own knowledge of the subject to help one understand
- identify relevant points; reject irrelevant information
- retain relevant points (note-taking, summarizing)
- recognize discourse markers, e.g. *well*; *oh, another thing is*; *now, finally*; etc. and cohesive devices, e.g. *such as* and *which*, including linking words, pronouns, references, etc.

Adapted from Richards (1983, cited in Omaggio 1986: 126)

More specifically with the segmental and suprasegmental features of English pronunciation, students need to know and understand[1]: (Kuji, Kanagawa-ken, etc. 2004)

- how words link together (liaison)
- how vowels weaken (the central vowel)
- how sounds mix together (assimilation)

---

[1] Adapted from http://www.abax.co.jp/listen/, retrieved 18 Oct. 2004.

- how sounds disappear (elision)
- how syllables disappear (ellipsis)
- how helping sounds are used between vowel sounds (intrusion)
- how intonation helps with conversational turn taking (intonation)
- how stress signals new information (prominence)
- how to use knowledge of intonation and stress to guess meaning (strategies)...

From the above list, we can conclude that when teaching listening, we need to focus not only on the English language system (grammar, pronunciation and vocabulary, etc.), but also on how English is used. The problem with many a listening class, is that they simply get stuck at English language system and miss how English is used in situations of real life. In other words, listening concerns two parallel processes.

1.1.3 Bottom-up/top-down listening

◆ Bottom-up listening process[1]

According to Morley (2001), Bottom-up refers to that part of the aural comprehension process in which the understanding of the "heard" language is worked out proceeding from sounds to words to grammatical relationships in lexical meanings.

The following lists some Bottom-up skills compiled by Peterson (1991) and Brown (2001):

- discriminating between intonation contours in sentences
- discriminating between phonemes
- recognizing syllable patterns
- being aware of sentence fillers in informal speech
- recognizing words
- differentiating between content and function words by stress pattern
- finding the stressed syllable
- recognizing when syllables or words are dropped
- recognizing words when they are linked together in streams of speech

---

[1] Bottom up listening skills, or bottom up processing, refers to the decoding process, the direct decoding of language into meaningful units, from sound waves through the air, through our ears and into our brain where meaning is decoded. To do this, students need to know the code. How the sounds work and how they string together and how the codes can change in different ways when they're strung together.

- using features of stress, intonation and prominence to help identify important information
◆ Top-down listening process[1]

Top-down processing refers to the attribution of meaning, drawn from one's own world knowledge, to language input. It involves the listener's ability to bring prior information to bear on the task of understanding the "heard" language (Morley, 2001).

A list of top-down skills from Peterson (1991) and Brown (2001):

- discriminating between emotions
- getting the gist
- recognizing the topic
- using discourse structure to enhance listening strategies
- identifying the speaker
- evaluating themes
- finding the main idea
- making inferences

1.2   The process of listening comprehension

1.2.1 Three stages of listening

Listening is a decoding—making sense of the message—process. Each short stretch of meaningful material heard has to be:

- recognized as meaningful and understood on perception,
- held in the short term memory long enough to be decoded,
- related to what has gone before and/or what follows (Saricoban, 1999)[2].

Out of this process come pieces of information that can be stored in the long term memory for recall later. The whole process is showcased in the form of a model (Abbott & Wingard, 1985):

1. Perception of sounds, letter shapes, etc.
2. Initial recognition of meaning of short stretches.
3. Material held in short term memory.
4. Related to material already held in short term memory.
5. Related to material arriving in short-term memory.

---

[1] Top-down processing refers to how we use our world knowledge to attribute meaning to language input; how our knowledge of social convention helps us understand meaning.

[2] Saricoban 1999. The Internet TESL Journal, Vol. V, No. 12. Retrieved online 18 June 2002.

6. Meaning extracted from message and retained in long-term memory.

7. Gist recalled later.

Experts in the field of teaching listening skills usually divide the above listening process into three stages:

1. Pre-listening (purpose and requirement must be given at this stage),

2. During (while) listening,

3. Post-listening activities (like feedbacks in the form of speaking).

Pre-listening stage

In the pre-listening stage, teachers need to bear in mind that all students bring different backgrounds to the listening experience. Beliefs, attitudes, and biases of the listeners will affect the understanding of the message. In addition to being aware of these factors, teachers should show students how their backgrounds affect the messages they receive.

Pre-listening activities are required to establish what is already known about the topic, to build necessary background, and to set purpose(s) for listening. Students need to understand that the "Act of listening requires not just hearing but also thinking, as well as a good deal of interest and information that both speaker and listener must have in common. Speaking and listening entail ... three components: the speaker, the listener, and the meaning to be shared; speaker, listener, and meaning form a unique triangle". (King, 1984: 177)

There are several strategies that students and their teachers can use to prepare for a listening experience:

• *Activating Existing Knowledge:* Students should be encouraged to ask the question: What do I already know about this topic? From this teachers and students can determine what information they need in order to get the most from the message. Students can brainstorm, discuss, read, view films or photos, and write and share journal entries.

• *Building Prior Knowledge:* Teachers can provide the appropriate background information including information about the speaker, topic of the presentation, purpose of the presentation, and the concepts and vocabulary that are likely to be embedded in the presentation.

• *Establishing Purpose:* Teachers should encourage students to ask, "What is my purpose? Am I listening to understand/remember/evaluate/be entertained/support?"

- *Using a Listening Guide:* A guide provides an overview of the presentation, its main ideas, questions to be answered while listening, a summary of the presentation, or an outline. For example, students could use a guide such as the following during a presentation in class.
  Situation:
  Speaker's name:
  Date:
  Occasion:

During listening

1) Making use of rate gap

Students need to understand the implications of rate in the listening process. People listen and think much faster than the normal conversation rate. Students have to be encouraged to use the "rate gap" to actively process the message:

They can run a mental commentary on it; they can doubt it, talk back to it, or extend it. They can rehearse it in order to remember it; that is, they repeat interesting points back to themselves. They can formulate questions to ask the speaker ... jot down key words or key phrases ... They can wonder if what they are listening to is true, or what motives the speaker has in saying it, or whether the speaker is revealing personal feelings rather than objective assessments. (Temple & Gillet, 1989: 55)

2) While-listening activities[1]:

- Connecting: make connections with people, places, and ideas they know;
- Clarifying meaning: determine what the speaker is saying about people, places, and ideas;
- Questioning: pay attention to those words and ideas that are unclear;
- Making predictions: try to determine what will be said next;
- Making inferences: determine speaker's intention by "listening between the lines" and infer what the speaker does not actually say;
- Reflecting and evaluating: respond to what has been heard and make judgement.

---

[1] Adapted from http://ingilish.com/ma1.htm. retrieved 21 May 2004.

3) Teachers' help during listening

Teachers can use specially designed while-listening activities to train students' reasoning and thinking capability. The following is an example (Temple & Gillett, 1989: 101):

Choose a story with clear episodes and action. Plan your stops just before important events.

a. At each stop, elicit summaries of what happened so far, and predictions of "what might happen next".
b. Accept all predictions as equally probable.
c. Ask the students to explain why they made particular predictions and to use previous story information for justification.
d. Avoid "right" or "wrong"; use terms like "might happen", "possible", or "likely".
e. After reading a section, review previous predictions and let the students change their ideas.
f. Focus on predictions, not on who offered them.
g. Involve everyone by letting the students show hands or take sides with others on predictions.
h. Keep up the pace! Do not let discussions drag; get back to the story quickly.

Teachers can also encourage guided imagery aids when students are listening to presentations that have many visual images, details, or descriptive words. Students can form mental pictures to help them remember while listening.

4) Fostering critical thinking while listening

Critical thinking plays a major role in effective listening. Listening in order to analyze and evaluate requires students to evaluate a speaker's arguments and the value of the ideas, appropriateness of the evidence, and the persuasive techniques employed. Effective listeners apply the principles of sound thinking and reasoning to the messages they hear at home, in school, in the workplace, or in the media.

Planning and structuring classroom activities to model and encourage students to listen critically is important. Students should be encouraged to learn to:

a) *Analyse the message*

Critical listeners are concerned first with understanding accurately and completely what they hear (Brownell, 1996). Students should identify the speaker's topic, purpose, intended audience, and context. The most frequent critical listening context is persuasion. They should ask relevant questions and restate perceptions to make sure they have understood correctly. Taking notes will enhance their listening.

b) *Analyse the speaker:*

Critical listeners must get information about and understand the reliability of the speaker. Is the speaker credible?

c) *Analyse the speaker's evidence:*

Critical listeners must understand the nature and appropriateness of the evidence and reasoning. What evidence is used? Facts? Statistics? Examples? Reasons? Opinions?

d) *Analyse the speaker's reasoning:*

Critical listeners must understand the logic and reasoning of the speaker. Is this evidence developed in logical arguments such as deductive, inductive, causal, or analogous?

e) *Analyse the speaker's emotional appeals:*

Critical listeners must understand that persuaders often rely on emotional appeal as well as evidence and reasoning. Critical listeners, therefore, must recognize effective persuasive appeals and propaganda devices.

By understanding and practicing the principles of objective thinking, students can prepare themselves to listen effectively in most situations.

After listening

Students need to act upon what they have heard to further clarify meaning and extend their thinking. Well-planned post-listening activities are just as important as those before and during. Some examples:

- Students can ask questions to clarify their understanding and confirm their assumptions.
- Students can talk about what the speaker said, and identify parallel incidents from life and literature.
- Students can summarize a speaker's presentation orally, in writing, or as an outline.
- Students can review their notes and add information that they did not have an opportunity to record during the speech.
- Students can analyse and evaluate critically what they have heard....

To sum up, there is an association between expectation, purpose, and comprehension; therefore a **purpose** should be first of all given to learners (Saricoban, 1999). Teachers should train students to understand what is being conveyed to get them to disregard redundancy, hesitation, and ungrammaticality. The major problem is the actual way listening material is presented to the students. Teachers should give a clear **lead** in what students they are going to hear; use some kind of visual backup for them to understand; give questions and tasks in order to clarify the things in their minds; and be sure that these tasks help in learning, not confusing. Students should learn how to use the environmental **clues**: the speaker's facial expression, posture, eye direction, proximity, gesture, tone of voice.

1.2.2 Schema and listening practice

1) Schema and listening

As mentioned, there are two simultaneous and complementary ways of processing information in listening: the top-down processing and the bottom-up processing. According to the schema theory, activating students' knowledge of a topic before they listen gives them a frame of reference to make predictions about what they will hear. The process of comprehension is guided by the idea that input is overlaid by the pre-existing knowledge in an attempt to find a match. The listeners must relate textual materials to their background knowledge, so that the new input from a passage is mapped against some prior schema. Comprehension is enormously improved when the speaker's schema or organizational pattern is perceived by the listener. Therefore, students should be taught various **styles** (e.g. short story, essay, poetry, play), organizational **patterns** (e.g. logical, chronological, spatial), transitional **devices** and so on. Effective listeners can follow spoken discourse when they recognize key signal expressions such as the following:

- Exemplifying words: for example, for instance, thus, as an illustration
- Time words: first, second, third, meanwhile, next, finally, at last, fortnight
- Addition words: in addition, also, furthermore, moreover, another example
- Result words: as a result, so, accordingly, therefore, thus
- Contrast words: however, but, in contrast, on the other hand, nevertheless

2) Activities to activate students' schema
Word association (brainstorming) tasks

In this method, students respond to a key word or expression such as "Olympic games". They can write down as many related words and phrases as possible in several minutes. While they write, they should not worry about the words and sentences they write, but just pay attention to the content. The teacher can summarize and write down the main ideas on the board.

Teachers can also use the semantic webbing method. Teachers graphically connect the various concepts and key words surrounding a particular topic on the blackboard, helping students to see the possible relationship between ideas discussed. This process will enable them to connect what they are going to listen with what they have already known.

Pre-questioning

Pre-listening questions induce a selective attention strategy. In textbooks in which questions always follow a passage, we may ask the students to read the questions first. By reading the questions, students may build up their own expectations about the coming information, and also by trying to find answers to these questions, their prior knowledge on the topic can be activated. For instance:

- Who are the three actors/actresses the speaker talks about in this conversation?
- What are the relationships between them?

Of course, this method may not be very appropriate for all kinds of texts. It is best used for passages that provide factual information. If the listening passage is too long, one possible solution for the teacher is to divide the text into sections and implement the approach section by section.

List of ideas/suggestions

When the passage contains lists, even short lists of ideas/suggestions or whatever, it is often a good idea to use list making as the pre-listening activity. This way the students can use their lists during the listening stage. While making the list, the students can use the words and phrases they have already known, or they can ask their partners for help. Any checking type activity carried out while listening can then be limited to matching with known language. This can increase the likelihood of students succeeding with the task. So it is a very motivating activity, especially for the lower level students.

Pictures and graphs reading

Pictures and graphs should be observed and read carefully, especially with younger learners because they are good at reading pictures. If a teacher want to check whether students can name some of the items in the listening text, pre-listening "picture reading and discussing" is an effective way of reminding or teaching the students of lexis which they may have forgotten or don't know yet. It will also help students to focus their attention on the coming topic. This is very good for narrative or descriptive passages.

Schema-activating tasks usually have two primary goals: a) to bring to consciousness the tools and strategies that good listeners use when listening, and b) to provide the necessary context for that specific listening task. When instructors design these kinds of activities, they should remember the pre-listening process should not last longer than the actual listening activity. The learners' proficiency is also a factor to consider; the activities should not be too demanding, otherwise the students will lose their interest.

1.2.3 Students' level and listening task planning

In listening training, helping learners to distinguish sounds, teaching to isolate significant content and informational items for concentration may be provided by controlled listening exercises. One exercise is to give them certain performance objectives—to give them general informational questions that they should be able to answer after listening to the material for the first time. These questions should require only the isolation of facts clearly revealed in the material. Questions that require application or inference from the listening materials are best used at later stages or more advanced students.

More controls are necessary at less advanced learners. Sheets containing sequentially organized and significant questions on context and content—questions that call for one-word answers—serve as useful guides for the student. Such questions help him filter out and listen for significant information. The questions themselves suggest the content and provide the student with an organizational frame for selective listening.

For listening comprehension exercises, teachers should use materials cast in real-life situations. Listening exercises should be as natural as the situations from which they grow. In other words, an exercise in listening comprehension must be as close as possible to a "sample or slice of life"—neither a contrived situation nor an artificially delivered discourse. By means of this, a teacher has a great deal of work to do, and has to be a very creative person in order to teach listening communicatively.

1.3   Methods used in the teaching of listening

In the current practice of teaching listening, more and more scholars have realized that it should be taught not only as product and skill, but also as process and cognition. In this section, some listening teaching models are reviewed.

1.3.1 The "default" method

In most classrooms around China, the commonest way to teach listening is to teach it as product: have students listen to some English materials, then the teacher asks a few comprehension questions. If the students have problems understanding the contents, the teacher plays the recording again and asks the questions again. If the students still don't understand, they will be told to practice more and sooner or later they'll get used to English and will be able to understand.

Language-wise, the teacher might pick out a particular grammar point or some difficult words to explain. If a passage uses the present perfect tense quite a bit, the teacher might go over some of the differences between the simple past and the present perfect tense.

1.3.2 The integrated method

In recent years, listening teaching is more and more regarded as a process of cognition for language learners. In this sense, listening, as a receptive skill, is combined with productive skills. If students simultaneously produce something, the teaching is considered more communicative and as a result, the teaching of *integrating language skills* zooms in. The purposes of building listening into integrated language skills are:

a) To practice and extend the learners' use of a certain language structure or function, and b) To develop the learners' ability in the use of two or more of the skills within real contexts and communicative framework.

Integrated activities provide a variety in the classroom and thus maintain motivation and allow the recycling and revision of language which has already been taught separately in each skill. In modern practice of language teaching, integrated course has become a trend in language classrooms. The problem is how language teachers are able to combine different language skills effectively in the process of teaching. In the following section, we provide some examples of English language teaching to make listening classroom more effective, productive and interesting.

1.4   Examples of English listening teaching

Example I: A lesson plan[1]

Topic: Beauty Contest
Duration: 20 minutes
Level: Upper Intermediate
Materials and aids: Pictures, blackboard, tape, tape-recorder
Objectives: By the end of the lesson the students will obtain basic knowledge of beauty contest.
Pre-listening Activities: The teacher asks students what they are going to listen to, according to the paper information. A discussion atmosphere is created. At this stage pictures are used effectively.
During Listening Activities: While students are listening to the tape the teacher asks them to take some notes.
Post-listening Activities: The teacher writes some questions on the board and asks them to answer the questions. They are also stimulated to talk and participate in the activities designed.

i) PRE-LISTENING ACTIVITIES

The teacher hangs the pictures on the board and tries to make the students talk about the subjects.

T: Do you think that they are beautiful?
S: . . .
T: Can you guess the name of the first competitor?
S: . . .
T: Can you guess the height of the second competitor?
S: . . .
T: What nationality does the third girl belong to? What is your opinion?
S: . . .

ii) DURING LISTENING ACTIVITIES

The teacher asks students to listen to the tape very carefully and gives information lists to them. While listening to the tape students try to fill in the blanks with appropriate information. If no information appears for any blank on the list, students are asked to put a cross on the blank provided for the required information.

---

[1] Adapted from The Internet TESL Journal, Vol. V, No. 12, December 1999, retrieved 24 Oct. 2003.

Elizabeth Mccornick	Alexandra Bellomonti	Suzanne Kerrigan
Nationality: Weight: 53 Age: 21 Languages: Hobbies: Profession: Height:	Nationality: Italian Weight: 51 Age: Languages: Hobbies: Profession: Height:	Nationality: Weight: Age: 22 Languages: Hobbies: Profession: Height:

iii) POST-LISTENING ACTIVITY

The teacher writes on the board some questions. Students answer these questions to test whether they understood what they have listened or not.

1. Whose name is the best? Why do you think so?
2. Who is the tallest one of all?
3. What nationality does the first one belong to?
4. Who can speak two languages?
5. Whose favorite film star is Leonardo Di Caprio?

iv) ASSIGNMENT/FOLLOW-UP

Make a poster for the beauty contest in groups of three.

Example II: Diversified listening activities

1) Listening activities for songs[1]

Pre-listening activities

- Give students the title of the song and ask them to predict the lyrics.
- Give students the words of a song with an "either/or" choice for certain words in each line. Students choose which word is more likely in each case and then listen and check if they were correct.
- Dictate a list of words which appear in the song—in a random order and add a few extra words which don't appear.

While listening activities

- Students listen and delete extra words which they do not hear.
- Students listen and fill gaps (open cloze or multiple choice).

---

[1] Adapted from Katherine Bilsborough, British Council, http://www.teachingenglish. org, retrieved 3 Aug. 2004.

After listening activities
- Students listen to a song and make a note of 8 words they hear. Then they use these words as the basic vocabulary for composing another song in pairs.
- Students listen to a song, draw a picture to represent what they hear and then explain their pictures in small groups.
- Students brainstorm all of the words that they have heard and then listen again and check to see how many are correct.

2) Active listening activities[1]

Students are often asked to listen to tapes or to their teacher talking, but it can be just as useful to encourage them to listen to each other in a more active way. Learning to listen to each other more carefully can build their ability and confidence in real-life situations.

- **Dual dictation**

Ask students to get into pairs to write a dialogue. When student A is speaking, student B should write down what they are saying and vice versa. When they have finished the conversation, they should check what each other has written and put the two sides of the conversation together. Volunteers can perform their dialogues to the rest of the class, or to swap with other pairs.

This activity works best if students are given a theme or role, e.g.
- o   A conversation between friends about holidays
- o   An argument between siblings
- o   An interview with a famous person

- **Class memory quiz**

Ask one student at a time to go to the front of the class. Ask the rest of the class to ask any questions they like (as long as they are not too personal!), e.g.
- o   What is your favorite color/food/band?
- o   What did you have for lunch?
- o   Which country would you most like to visit?

Let students make a note of the answers. When all of the students (or half of the students, if you have a large group) have been interviewed, explain that you are going to hold a quiz about the class. Get the students into small teams and ask them to put their hands up if they know the answer to a question, e.g.

---

[1] Adapted from Kate Joyce, British Council. http://www.teachingenglish.org. Retrieved 5 Aug. 2004.

o Which student likes Oasis?

o What is Marie's favorite food?

o Which two students would like to be famous actors?

Award a point to the first team to answer correctly. This game can be a lot of fun, and encourages students to listen to each other.

3) Dictation I[1]

Dictation is a common form of practicing listening abilities of students. It can take different forms.

- **Think about meaning**

Quantifying sentences

Teacher dictates sentences. Students have to add a quantifier to the "key" words used. For example,

SENTENCE DICTATED ....QUANTIFIERS ADDED

He gets home *late* in the evening .... at 10 pm

They live in a *large* flat ....almost 100 square meters

It saves *time* ....by many hours

She gets up fairly *early* at the weekend .... at 7 a.m.

He *often* leaves town .... every week

- **Fill the gap**

Dictate, leaving blanks by saying "mmm". The students have to fill the gaps.

For example, students complete the sentence with an appropriate pronoun (with "she or he").

1. _____ is a good goal keeper.

2. _____was 80 and lived alone, but _____ lives happily knitting all day long.

Alternatively, the teacher can dictate a story and ask students to fill in the blanks with verbs, etc.

- **Associations**

Set the groups in pairs, student A and student B. Dictate 2 words that are similar, student A writes word 1 and student B word 2. They add more words related to the words dictated. For example:

STUDENT A .... STUDENT B................. ADDED WORDS

wood .... bark ....trees, chair

would............................. may............................. modal, might

bee .... buzz.............................honey, sting

---

[1] Adapted from Liliana Borbolla, Mexico at http://www.teachingenglish.org. Retrieved 14 Oct. 2003.

4) Dictation II[1]

A. *Shadow dictation*

Choose a writer and a listener. Teacher reads a paragraph (normal speed). While one writes the other just listens. Then have both to re-construct the story. Teacher reads the story again so they can compare their versions.

B. *Passing the buck*

Teacher dictates one sentence. The students exchange their sentences. Then everyone underlines the mistakes they find in the sentence. Teacher dictates the second one. Students exchange their paper again. Now they underline the mistakes on the second sentence and correct the ones in the previous one. Whole class review all the sentences dictated.

C. *Word fields*

Teacher dictates. One student writes, the other monitors. (pair work)

Then the teacher asks them to circle all the words related to a certain topic. For example,

In the following story, find the words related to sports.

She sat in the **corner**. She took a sip of her coffee and spat it out because it was **foul**. Her **goal** that evening had been to finish her essay, but there had been constant interruptions. For a start, her boyfriend had dropped in. She had heard him **whistling** as he came up the path and jumped up like a **shot** to let him in. But they had had a row that had just made him very **defensive**. As he thought about it she tried to **block** his memory from her mind.

5) Sounds, spelling and pronunciation training

i) *Silent letter*

a. Write the words and underline the silent letter.

Christmas   platform   knee   sandwich   wrong

b. Write the number of letters and the silent letter(s).

honest ....6...h

daughter.......................8... g h

cupboard......................8...p

ii) *Listening for stressed syllables*

Teacher dictates the words and students write in the appropriate column according to the word stress.

---

[1] Adapted from Liliana Borbolla at http://www.teachingenglish.org. Retrieved 5 Sep. 2003.

FIRST SYLLABLE	SECOND SYLLABLE
coffee	canteen
forty	cassette
record	record

6) Interactive listening and speaking

Interactive listening is a very important part in listening training. For different learners, different activities can be designed.

Lower levels[1]

1) Choose any dialogue, for example a dialogue involving someone checking into a hotel.

2) Tell students that they are going to hear part of a conversation in a hotel or whatever other situation you have chosen.

3) Ask them to predict what they think they will hear.

4) Tell students that they will only hear one side of the conversation. Tell them that you are the receptionist etc. and that you will be speaking to them. They have to write down what you say.

5) Dictate each line of the receptionist's side of the conversation.

6) After dictating all of the receptionist's part, then elicit it from the students or alternatively ask them to write it on the board. Check the language.

7) Students then formulate their responses to the receptionist's side of the dialogue. Check these with the whole class and write them on the board.

8) Act out the conversation with the whole class. Leave the dialogue on the board. You are one side of the dialogue, the students the other side.

9) At a later date, for example at the beginning or end of a subsequent lesson, re-enact the conversation to see how well students are able to respond.

Higher levels

At higher levels the teacher can do the same as outlined above but using a variety of text types. Alternatively the following can be done:

1) Tell students that they are to listen to utterances from a variety of situations.

2) Give them the different situations in a random order. Then dictate each utterance. Students have to match the utterance

[1] Adapted from Rolf Donald. http://www.teachingenglish.org. Retrieved 13 Sep. 2004.

with the situation.

3) Check with the whole class. Then dictate the utterances again. This time students have to write down the whole utterance. Check the utterances with the class.

4) Students then formulate possible responses to the utterances.

5) Check these with the class.

6) Students then take it in turn, in pairs/groups, to say and respond to the different utterances.

7) A further stage is to ask students to build up a 30-second interaction using one or more of the different utterances.

As students realize that they are getting more proficient at responding appropriately in a variety of situations, then their self-confidence will increase also.

7) Predicting language for context

This simple activity encourages students to predict language for situations before they listen[1].

- Choose a lexical group, such as feelings, locations/places, types of people, jobs. For example:
  - o Locations/places: a bank, a petrol station, a school, a hospital...
  - o Jobs: a doctor, a shop assistant, a bus conductor, an office worker...
  - o Feelings: happy, excited, sad, disappointed, bored, fascinated...
- Place the students in small groups. Put each word on a separate piece of paper and put them in a pile for each group, face down.
- A student takes a slip of paper and says something that would be spoken in the context given by the piece of paper. The other students have to guess the context.
  - o For example, a student picks the word "doctor" and says, "I'll give you these, and you need to take them twice a day, before meals." The other students shout out the word "doctor". The fastest wins a point. The next student draws a card...

The teacher could use more than one context at a time, but be sure the students know which lexical sets are in use.

---

[1] Adapted from Gareth R. at http://www.teachingenglish.org. Retrieved 13 Sep. 2004.

The above lists some examples of listening activities. Of course, in teaching listening the teacher's active and creative role should be greatly encouraged.

2. Teaching of speaking

2.1 General introduction to speaking skill

Speaking is the productive skill in the oral mode. Teachers often tend to assume that conversation in the language classroom involves nothing more than putting into practice the grammar and vocabulary skills taught elsewhere in the course. But actually, like listening skill, speaking is much more complicated than it seems and involves more than just pronouncing and reading aloud words.

2.1.1 Speaking situations and "conversation"

- *Speaking situations*

Generally speaking, there are three kinds of speaking situations in which we often find ourselves:

- Interactive
- Partially interactive
- Non-interactive

Interactive speaking situations include face-to-face conversations, telephone calls, and on-line talking usually with audio-visual aids, in which interlocutors are alternately listening and speaking, and in which they have a chance to ask for clarification, repetition, or slower speech from our conversation partner. Some speaking situations are partially interactive, such as when giving a speech to a live audience, where the convention is that the audience does not interrupt the speech. The speaker nevertheless can see the audience and judge from the expressions on their faces and body language whether or not he or she is being understood. Some few speaking situations may be totally non-interactive, such as when recording a speech for a radio or TV broadcast.

- *Conversation*

Conversation can be what normally occurs in everyday life. It is a spoken interaction between two or more people. The conversation involves such actions as the exchange of information, the creation and maintenance of social relationships, the negotiation of status and social roles as well as deciding on joint actions.

In technical terms of discourse analysis, the basic unit of a conversation is an **exchange**. An exchange consists of two **moves** (an initiating move and a response). Example 1):

A: Would you like a cup of tea? (initiation)

B: No, thank you. (response)

We can give a function to each move. In the case above we have *offering* (A) and *declining* (B). To do so we need to take account of factors such as who the speakers are and where and when the conversation occurs. And, a conversation in real life situation can be much more complicated. Example 2):

A: Excuse me?

B: Me?

A: How do I get to the school library from here?

B: Where is my umbrella?

The potential for an exchange to be diversified is always there in real life. During a conversation, usually:

- one part speaks at a time;
- the speakers change their turns;
- the length of any contribution varies;
- there are techniques allowing the other party or parties to speak.

Therefore, students need to develop the sense when someone is about to finish. Besides, to hold the floor, students need to know expressions like *Wait,* or *Another point* as well as fillers such as *Er, Mmm, Well*, etc. As regards to topics, cultural awareness must be built in students: different cultures talk about different things in their everyday lives. That is why both teachers and students need to develop a sense of taboo subjects if they are to avoid offence.

2.1.2 Macro- and micro-skills

One of the most significant differences between speaking and writing forms of information is that listeners often have one chance to hear your talk and can't "re-read" when they get confused. Being clear is particularly important if the audience can't ask questions during the talk. There are some macro and micro skills involved to communicate your points effectively.

Macro-skills
- Planning for thoughts/ideas/topics to be expressed
- Evaluating the target listeners/audience and situation of speaking
- Monitoring the speaking process
- Adjusting speech if necessary
- Understanding the related background/culture/world knowledge
- Reflecting on the tactics and strategies used in the process of speaking
- Appraising the listener's purpose, intention, strategy in communication

Micro-skills
Some of the micro-skills involved in speaking:[1]
- Pronouncing the distinctive sounds of a language clearly enough so that people can distinguish them. This includes making tonal distinctions.
- Using stress and rhythmic patterns, and intonation patterns of the language clearly enough so that people can understand what is said.
- Using the correct forms of words, including the tense, case, or gender.
- Putting words together in correct word order.
- Using vocabulary appropriately.
- Using the register or language variety that is appropriate to the situation and the relationship to the conversation partner.
- Making the main ideas stand out from supporting ideas or information.
- Making the discourse hang together so that people can follow what you are saying.

2.2 Oral English errors and oral proficiency test

Oral test is interrelated to the error analysis in speaking. More profound theories concerning testing come in Chapter 8, though.

---

[1] Adapted from http://www.nclrc.org/essentials/speaking/assessread.htm. Retrieved 13 Oct. 2004.

2.2.1 General background

A lot of research has been done on error analysis in second language educology. Corder (1967, 1971), Richards (1974), Dulay & Krashen (1982), Widdowson (1978), Henderickson (1978), Ellis (1994) are among those who have contributed to the theories and practice of L2 error analysis, which is a complex issue itself.

One contributor to its complexity is that the root of errors can be traced to a rather wide range of factors. Taylor (1986, cited from Ellis 1994: 57) puts forward four broad error sources: psycho-linguistic, socio-linguistic, cognitive and discourse structure. As to error analysis, Ellis states, "It concerns the nature of second language knowledge system and difficulties learners have in using it in production" (1994: 57). The following is Ellis' view on the psycholinguistic sources of error (Ellis, 1994: 58):

Error ⎡— competence: transfer, intra-lingual, unique problems

⎣— performance: processing problems, communicative strategies

In oral English, all kinds of errors may occur, especially to foreign language learners, resulting in various problems like whether students' oral errors should be corrected, to what extent, and how their errors should be corrected.

Another typical problem is what criteria should be based on in the evaluation of the oral performance. Influenced by different attitudes towards students' oral errors in L2 acquisition, oral English test, an important means to monitor and pinpoint the students' errors in communication, has been put under various and colorful references.

2.2.2 Studies on English errors of second language learners

Selinker (1972) identifies five processes believed to be kernel to second language learning and acquisition, each of which can force non-native items, rules, and subsystems to appear and possibly remain indefinitely in the inter-language systems of language learners. The five processes are: language transfer, transfer-of-training, strategies of second language learning, strategies of second language communication, and overgeneralization of target language rules.

Ellis (2000: 43) believes that there are rules or, at least, regularities in the way which native speakers hold conversations. In the United States, for example, a compliment usually calls for a response and failure to provide one can be considered a socio-linguistic error. Furthermore, in American English compliment responses are usually quite elaborate, involving some attempt on the part to play down the compliment by making some unfavorable comment. Ellis illustrates by giving the following example:

A: I like your sweater.

B: It's so old. My sister bought it for me in Italy some time ago.

According to Ellis, B stands for the typical American way to respond to a compliment; L2 learners however, behave differently. A Chinese learner of English's response can often be "It's not good at all." Sometimes they fail to respond to a compliment at all. This shows that the acquisition of discourse rules, like the acquisition of grammatical rules, also reflects the types of errors in L2 acquisition.

Schmidt (1983: 168) comments that a good or a poor language learner depends very much on one's definition of language and of the content of SLA. If language is seen as a means of initiating, maintaining, and regulating relationships and carrying on the business of living, one who neglects the fixed rules and does not very often emphasize the accuracy of communication can be regarded as an effective language learner. If one views language as a system of elements and rules, with syntax playing a major and determining role, then the judgment can be different.

Regardless of the individual differences of studies on second language errors and the sources, one point can be safely reached: Errors in second language acquisition include not only linguistic errors, but more, such as communicative strategies. And we are warranted to say that the errors made on the linguistic levels of pronunciation, words and syntax are more superficial, which can be regarded by native speakers as "speaking badly", compared with errors made on the level of pragmatics and social-linguistics, which can often be regarded as "behaving badly", i.e. making a pragmatic error is far more serious than a linguistic one because grammatical errors may reveal a speaker to be a less proficient language user, while pragmatic failures reflect badly on him or her as a person. Consequently, pragmatic error is often the major cause of cross-cultural miscommunication for L2 learners. And, in oral test, all these factors should be taken into consideration.

2.2.3 A spoken English test (SET) grade table for Chinese college students

FIGURE 4.2 A spoken English test grade table

Name of the attendee:

Language competence

I. Pronunciation						
inaccurate	1	2	3	4	5	accurate
II. Grammar (syntax, tense, morphology)						
incorrect	1	2	3	4	5	correct
III. Vocabulary						
scarce	1	2	3	4	5	abundant
IV. Text (cohesion, coherence)						
poorly-organized	1	2	3	4	5	well-organized
V. Pragmatic (language functions)						
inappropriate	1	2	3	4	5	appropriate
VI. Socio-linguistic (register, dialect)						
foreign	1	2	3	4	5	native

Strategic competence

VII. Paralinguistic features						
monotonous	1	2	3	4	5	various
VIII. Turn-taking and negotiation						
inflexible	1	2	3	4	5	flexible
IX. Circum-locution						
inflexible	1	2	3	4	5	flexible
X. Body language						
unnatural	1	2	3	4	5	natural

Total:

Reference:

Class A	above 45	Fully able to communicate in English
Class B	40 - 44	Able to communicate in English with few difficulties
Class C	35 - 40	Able to communicate in simple English
Class D	30 - 34	Able to communicate in limited English with great difficulties
Class E	below 30	Unable to communicate in English

Signature of the Judge(s):

Language competence mainly evaluates two aspects of the attendee's oral English level: organizing ability and pragmatic ability. The former includes pronunciation and prosodic features (whether the learner can pronounce correctly and whether the intonation, pitch, rhythm are good), grammar (whether the grammatical features are correctly put in the utterances), capacity of vocabulary (whether the learner has grasped a certain amount of English vocabulary to make sure the expressions are colorful, meaningful and abundant), text (whether the learner can organize the chunks of language in a coherent and unified whole). The latter is on the pragmatic aspect of language use, i.e. whether the learner can understand the illocutionary meaning and give appropriate responses and whether the utterances are suitable to various simulated social settings. Strategic competence reflects the student's ability in using paralinguistic features like "er", "uh", "um", and other voice effects; the student's ability in holding and switching turns in conversation; the student's ability in paraphrasing and seeking for clearer information; the student's ability in using body language, i.e. whether the student uses eye contact, gestures, facial expression, nods, etc. to help him or her to better communicate with others.

2.2.4 A sample checklist of oral presentation

Of course, sometimes the oral performance can take the form of presentation. The following is a sample checklist that might be used when evaluating oral presentations.

FIGURE 4.4 A checklist table of oral presentations

Presenter (print):
Title of Presentation (print):
Time allowed:
Evaluator(s):

Organization and Content (45%):	Poor		Average	Excellent	
Appropriate Introduction	1	2	3	4	5
Clear Thesis	1	2	3	4	5
Presentation Organization	1	2	3	4	5
Adequate Support for Ideas (Weighted 2x)	2	4	6	8	10
Definite Conclusion	1	2	3	4	5
Visual Aids (Appropriateness & Effectiveness)	1	2	3	4	5
Q & A Session-Knowledge of Topic	1	2	3	4	5
Use of Allotted Time	1	2	3	4	5

(to be continued)

Presence (20%):	Poor		Average	Excellent	
Physical Appearance, Neatness, and Grooming	1	2	3	4	5
Posture, Gestures, and Movement	1	2	3	4	5
Eye Contact	1	2	3	4	5
Interaction with Audience	1	2	3	4	5
Delivery and Grammar (35%):					
Enthusiasm and Vocal Variation (freedom from monotone)	1	2	3	4	5
Preparation and Knowledge of Materials	1	2	3	4	5
Effectiveness of Delivery Method	1	2	3	4	5
Vocabulary and Use of Appropriate Words	1	2	3	4	5
Freedom from Distracting "Uh" & "Like", etc.	1	2	3	4	5
Pronunciation, Enunciation, Audibility, and Clarity	1	2	3	4	5
Grammar	1	2	3	4	5

Grade:

Comments:

2.2.5 Error correction

It is natural for some learners to experience difficulty in pronouncing certain sounds and groups of sounds in another language. Some Chinese and Japanese speakers of English, for example, have trouble with /l/ and /r/. Some learners have trouble with the beginning sounds in the words "three" and "thanks". Giving too much attention to the correction of pronunciation in the early stages of language learning can make learners worried and reluctant to speak because of fear of making errors (Brown & Nation, 1997)[1].

It is worth thinking about why errors occur, because this can help teachers decide what to do about them.

For each cause listed, suggestions for the teacher are given in brackets (Brown & Nation, 1997).

1) The learner makes an error because the learner has not had sufficient chance to observe the correct form or to develop sufficient knowledge of the language system. (Don't correct the learner but give

---

[1] Robert Sanborn Brown & Paul Nation. 1997. Teaching Speaking: Suggestions for the Classroom. http://www.jalt-publications.org/tlt/files/97/jan/speaking.html. Retrieved 23 Aug. 2005.

more models and opportunities to observe.)

2) The learner makes an error because the learner has not observed the form correctly. (Give a little correction by showing the learner the difference between the correct form and the learner's error.)

3) The learner makes an error because of nervousness. (Don't correct. Use less threatening activities—or, if appropriate, joke with the student to lighten the mood.)

4) The learner makes an error because the activity is difficult, that is, there are many things the learner has to think about during the activity. This is sometimes called cognitive overload. (Don't correct. Make the activity easier or give several chances to repeat the activity.)

5) The learner makes an error because the activity is confusing. Use of tongue twisters, for instance, for pronunciation can be confusing. (Don't correct. Improve the activity.)

6) The learner makes an error because the learner is using patterns from the first language instead of the patterns from the second language. (Give some correction. If there has been plenty of opportunity to develop knowledge of the second language, then some time should be spent on correction to help the learner break out of making errors that are unlikely to change. Errors resistant to change are sometimes called *fossilized errors* and imaginative correction is often needed to break the fossilization. If there has not been a lot of opportunity to develop knowledge of the second language, correct by telling the learner what to look for when observing people using the second language. This is called *consciousness raising*. It does not actually teach the correct form but makes the learner more aware of what to look for to learn it.)

7) The learner makes an error because the learner has been copying incorrect models. (Correct the learner and provide better models.)

This range of causes shows that the teacher should not rush into error correction, but should consider whether the error is worth the interruption and, if it is, the teacher should consider possible causes and then think of appropriate ways of dealing with the error.

2.2.6 On pronunciation correction

In China, pronunciation is a paramount issue to many English learners.

The teaching and correction of pronunciation to learners past the age of puberty is often a difficult task. The audiolingual method argues that native-like pronunciation is one of the most important aspects of language proficiency. However, as Ueno reports, "The research on this issue [whether specific instruction can improve students' pronunciation] is inconclusive. In a recent survey... almost half of the recent experiments on this subject show no improvement in students' production of target-language sounds" (Ueno, 1994: 1). There is some hope that specific pronunciation instruction may be effective in improving students' perception or overall comprehension of the target language. Moreover, to use a sports metaphor, a beginning tennis player must "develop and automatize basic muscle skills necessary to perform the new physical tasks. Similarly, a language learner must practice the new motor skills involved in producing the sounds of the target language" (Ueno, 1994: 2).

The following are simple suggestions for correcting pronunciation (Brown & Nation, 1997).

1) Say "What?" and see if the learner is capable of self-correction.

2) Give the correct form for the learner to copy. If the learner cannot copy it after two or three attempts, then some explanation and guidance may be needed.

3) Explain how to make the correct form and, if necessary, what is wrong with the incorrect expressions. For example, to make the "th" sound as in "then", say "Put your tongue between your teeth and make a long sound." or "Put your tongue like this."

2.3   How to teach speaking

L1 studies have shown that beyond the context of any classroom, almost all children exposed to a language in normal circumstances will learn it unconsciously. There are certain features in the process:

Firstly, they are usually exposed to language which they more or less understand even if, sometimes, they lack the ability to produce the same language spontaneously themselves. Second, they are motivated to learn the language in order to be able to communicate, which is mainly an oral business. And finally they have opportunities to use the language they are learning, thus checking their own progress and abilities.

Although these features of natural language acquisition can be difficult to replicate in the classroom, there are elements that are no doubt worth imitating. Obviously, within the classroom environment students don't get the same kind of exposure as those who are "picking up" the language. As English educators, we should try to work on **motivation, language exposure, maximized talking time** and offer **chances to use** the language. The following are some important aspects to be considered in teaching oral English.

2.3.1 Goals setting and procedures of teaching speaking

The ultimate goal of teaching speaking skills is communicative efficiency. Learners should not only be able to make themselves understood, but use their current proficiency to the fullest. They should try to avoid confusion in the message due to faulty pronunciation, grammar, or vocabulary, and to observe the social and cultural rules that apply in each communication situation. To help students develop communicative efficiency in speaking, instructors can use a balanced activities approach that combines language input, structured output, and communicative output.

Language input comes in the form of teacher talk, listening activities, reading passages, and the language heard and read outside of class. It gives learners the material they need to begin producing language themselves. Language input may be content oriented or form oriented.

- Content-oriented input focuses on information, whether it is a simple weather report or an extended lecture on an academic topic. Content-oriented input may also include descriptions of learning strategies and examples of their use.
- Form-oriented input focuses on ways of using the language: guidance from the teacher or other sources on vocabulary, pronunciation, and grammar (linguistic competence); appropriate things to say in specific contexts (discourse competence); expectations for rate of speech, pause length, turn-taking, and other social aspects of language use (socio-linguistic competence); and explicit instruction in phrases to use to ask for clarification and repair miscommunication (strategic competence).

In the presentation part of a lesson, an instructor should combine content-oriented and form-oriented input. The amount of input that is actually provided in the target language depends on students' listening proficiency and also on the situation.

Structured output focuses on correct form. In structured output, students may have options for responses, but all of the options require them to use the specific form or structure that the teacher has just introduced, sometimes in combination with previously learned items.

In *communicative output*, the learners' main purpose is to complete a task, such as obtaining information, developing a travel plan, or creating a video. To complete the task, they may use the language that the instructor has just presented, but they also may draw on any other vocabulary, grammar, and communication strategies that they know. In communicative output activities, the criterion of success is whether the learner gets the message across.

In everyday communication, spoken exchanges take place because there is some sort of information gap between the participants. Communicative output activities involve a similar real information gap. In order to complete the task, students must reduce or eliminate the information gap. In these activities, language is a tool, not an end in itself. In a balanced activities approach, the teacher uses a variety of activities from these different categories of input and output. Learners at all proficiency levels, including beginners, benefit from this variety; it is more motivating, and it is also more likely to result in effective language learning.

2.3.2 Three key issues in speaking classes

According to Brown & Nation (1997)[1], there are three key items in speaking classes: (1) form-focused instruction; (2) meaning-focused instruction; and (3) opportunities to improve fluency.

1) Form-focused speaking
- Repetition drills and substitution drills

When learners first begin to speak in another language, their speaking will need to be based on some form-focused learning. An effective way to begin is to base speaking on some language chunks/formulized expressions—useful, simple memorized phrases and sentences. These may be greetings, simple personal descriptions, and simple questions and answers. They can be practiced in *Repetition drills*. The teacher says a phrase or sentence several times and then asks the learners to repeat. Some learners can be called on to repeat individually, and then the class may repeat together. Because it is helpful to give learners quite a lot of repetition practice in beginning level courses, the teacher needs to find ways of varying repetition activities to keep the learners interested.

a. The teacher varies the speed. The teacher says the sentence slowly and the learners repeat. Then the teacher says the phrase a little

[1] Robert S. Brown & Paul Nation. 1997. Teaching Speaking: Suggestions for the Classroom. http://www.jalt-publications.org/tlt/files/97/jan/speaking.html. Retrieved 21 Feb. 2004.

faster until the phrase is being said at normal speaking speed.

b. The teacher varies the way of choosing who is to repeat the sentence. The teacher utters the sentence repeatedly and asks different individuals to repeat it. This variation can also include choosing individuals or choosing the whole class to repeat the sentence.

c. The teacher can vary the content of the sentence. That is, the teacher can substitute a word for one of the words in a sentence. So instead of only saying "How do you like the city traffic?" the learners might also be called on to repeat "How do you like this English song?"

In this stage of controlled practice, it is important to make sure students pronounce each word correctly and clearly. It is important for teachers to sample and correct.

- The role of drills

The use of drills should be seen as merely one kind of form-focused activity that needs to be balanced with other types of form-focused activities, as well as with meaning-focused and fluency development activities.

Drills play a useful part in a language course in helping learners to be formally accurate in their speech and in helping them to quickly learn a useful collection of phrases and sentences that allow them to start using the language as soon as possible. As their proficiency and experience in the language develop, most of these sentences and phrases may be reanalyzed and incorporated into the learners' system of knowledge of the language. Language use based on memorization can be the starting point for more creative use of the language.

2) Meaning-focused speaking

In addition to form-focused speaking, language learners should also be exposed to and given opportunities to practice and use meaning-focused communication, in which they must both produce and listen to meaningful oral communication.

Brown & Nation (1997) suggest the following:

a. The meaning-focused speaking activity follows some form-focused instruction. That is, the teacher presents some new vocabulary or grammatical features, gives the learners some practice, and then uses a meaning-focused activity to help the learners use and remember these items.

b. Before the learners speak on a topic or take part in an activity, they work in pairs or groups of three or four to prepare. This gives the learners the chance to learn new items from each other.

c. The learners are given topics to talk about. They prepare at home, using dictionaries, reference texts, reading sources, and so forth. Here is an example called *Newspaper talks*. Each learner has to choose a short and interesting article from an English language newspaper to present to the class. The learner must not read the article aloud to the class but must describe the main points of the article. The class should then ask the presenter questions.

d. Many speaking activities involve some kind of written or picture input in the form of a worksheet. In a "Who Gets the Heart" activity, for example, a group of three or four students must decide from a list of several possible candidates who is to receive the only available heart for transplantation. None of the patients will survive without the new heart. They are a Nobel Prize winner in medical research (a 58-year-old male with no family), a homemaker (a 34-year-old female), an Olympic athlete (a 22-year-old female, married with no children), an Academy award winning film director (female, 38-year-old, two children), and a 45-year-old homeless male. The students must rank in order which of these people is most deserving of the heart. Then, each student presents his/her case to the group. Based on these presentations, and the ensuing discussion, the group must choose one candidate for the transplant. Then, each group must present its conclusion to the class as a whole.

3) Development of speaking fluency

Fluency in speaking is the aim of many language learners. Signs of fluency include a reasonably fast speed of speaking and only a relatively small number of pauses and "ums" and "ers". These signs indicate that the speaker does not have to spend a lot of time searching for the language items needed to express the message.

Timed story telling is a useful technique for developing fluency. First the learners choose a topic or are given a topic with which they are very familiar. This kind of recounting is very effective because the chronological order of the events will make it easier to recall and repeat. The learners can work in pairs or small groups. Learner A tells a story to Learner B or more group members and has a time limit (four minutes, for instance) to do this. The audience just listens and does not interrupt or question Learner A. When the time turns up, the teacher says, "Change audience"; Learner A then moves to a new Learner B or group of listeners. Then the teacher says "Start" and Learner A tells exactly the same story to the new partner(s) but this time has only three minutes to tell it. When the three minutes are up, the teacher again stops it. With a new partner, Learner A now has two minutes to tell the story.

Of course, there are other methods and techniques to develop speaking fluency, which teachers can learn from each other or create on their own.

2.3.3 Strategies for developing speaking skills

Many language teachers and learners tend to think that the ability to speak a language is the product of language learning. However, speaking is also a crucial part of the language learning process. Effective instructors teach students speaking strategies—using minimal responses, recognizing scripts, and using language to talk about language—that they can use to help themselves expand their knowledge of the language and their confidence in using it. These instructors help students learn to speak so that the students can use speaking to learn.

1) Using minimal responses

Language learners who lack confidence in their ability to participate successfully in oral interaction often listen in silence while others do the talking. One way to encourage such learners to begin to participate is to help them build up a stock of minimal responses that they can use in different types of exchanges. Such responses can be especially useful for beginners.

Minimal responses are predictable, often idiomatic phrases that conversation participants use to indicate understanding, agreement, doubt, and other responses to what another speaker is saying. Having a stock of such responses enables a learner to focus on what the other participant is saying, without having to simultaneously plan a response.

2) Recognizing scripts

Some communication situations are associated with a predictable set of spoken exchanges—a script. Greetings, apologies, compliments, invitations, and other functions that are influenced by social and cultural norms often follow patterns or scripts. So do the transactional exchanges involved in activities such as obtaining information and making a purchase. In these scripts, the relationship between a speaker's turn and the one that follows it can often be anticipated.

Instructors can help students develop speaking ability by making them aware of the scripts for different situations so that they can predict what they will hear and what they will need to say in response. Through interactive activities, instructors can give students practice in managing and varying the language that different scripts contain.

3) Using language to talk about language

Language learners are often too embarrassed or shy to say anything when they do not understand another speaker or when they realize that a conversation partner has not understood them. Instructors can help students overcome this reticence by assuring them that misunderstanding and the need for clarification can occur in any type of interaction, whatever the participants' language skill levels are. Instructors can also give students strategies and phrases to use for clarification and comprehension check.

By encouraging students to use clarification phrases in class when misunderstanding occurs, and by responding positively when they do, instructors can create an authentic practice environment within the classroom itself. As they develop control of various clarification strategies, students will gain confidence in their ability to manage the various communication situations that they may encounter outside the classroom.

2.3.4 Principles for designing speaking activities

In designing speaking activities, various patterns are followed by foreign language teachers. However, most experts agree on the following principles:

1) Maximum foreign talk (students' talk time in the foreign language)
2) Even participation (equal opportunities for students of different levels)
3) High motivation (the topic; the types of tasks; a clear objective)
4) Right language level (avoid giving up or reverting to native language)

2.4 Developing speaking activities

1) Traditional speaking activities and real communication activities

Traditional classroom speaking practice often takes the form of drills in which one person asks a question and another gives an answer. The question and the answer are structured and predictable, and often there is only one correct, predetermined answer. The purpose of asking and answering the question is to demonstrate the ability to ask and answer the question.

In contrast, the purpose of real communication is to accomplish a task, such as conveying a telephone message, obtaining information, or expressing an opinion. In real communication, participants must manage uncertainty about what the other person will say. Authentic communication involves an information gap; each participant has information that the other does not have. In addition, to achieve their purpose, participants may have to clarify their meaning or ask for confirmation of their own understanding.

To create classroom speaking activities that will develop communicative competence, instructors need to incorporate a purpose and an information gap and allow for multiple forms of expression. However, quantity alone will not necessarily produce competent speakers. Instructors need to combine structured output activities, which allow for error correction and increased accuracy, with communicative output activities that give students opportunities to practice language use more freely.

2) Structured output activities

Two common kinds of structured output activities are *information gap* and *jigsaw* activities. In both, students complete a task by obtaining missing information, a feature the activities have in common with real communication. However, information gap and jigsaw activities also set up practice on specific items of language. In this respect they are more like drills than like real communication.

Information gap activities

- Filling the gaps in a schedule or timetable: Partner A holds an airline timetable with some of the arrival and departure time missing. Partner B has the same timetable but with different blank spaces. The two partners are not permitted to see each other's timetables and must fill in the blanks by asking each other appropriate questions. The features of language that are practiced would include questions beginning with "when" or "at what time". Answers would be limited mostly to time expressions like "at 8:15" or "at ten in the evening".

- Completing the picture: The two partners have similar pictures, each with different missing details, and they cooperate to find all the missing details. In another variation, no items are missing, but similar items differ in appearance. For example, in one picture, a man walking along the street may be wearing an overcoat, while in the other the man is wearing a jacket. The features of grammar and vocabulary that are practiced are determined by the content of the pictures and the items that are missing or different. Differences in the activities depicted lead to practice of different verbs. Differences in number, size, and shape lead to adjective practice. Differing locations would probably be described with prepositional phrases.

Jigsaw Activities[1]

Jigsaw activities are more elaborate information gap activities that can be done with several partners. In a jigsaw activity, each partner has one or a few pieces of the "puzzle", and the partners must cooperate to fit all the pieces into a whole picture. The puzzle piece may take one of several forms. It may be one panel from a comic strip or one photo from a set that tells a story. It may be one sentence from a written narrative. It may be a tape recording of a conversation, in which case no two partners hear exactly the same conversation.

- In one fairly simple jigsaw activity, students work in groups of four. Each student in the group receives one panel from a comic strip. Partners may not show each other their panels. These pictures have a clear narrative line and the partners are not likely to disagree about the appropriate sequencing. The task can be made more demanding, however, by using pictures that lead themselves to alternative sequences, so that the partners have to negotiate among themselves to agree on a satisfactory sequence.
- More elaborate jigsaws may proceed in two stages. Students first work in groups (for instance, 4 groups) to receive information. Each group receives a different part of the total information for the task. Students then reorganize into groups of four with one student from A, B, C, and D respectively, and use the information they received to complete the task. Such an organization could be used, for example, when the input is given in the form of a tape recording. Groups A, B, C, and D each hear a different recording of a short news bulletin. The four recordings all contain the same general information, but each has one or more details that the others do not. In the second stage, students reconstruct the complete story by comparing the four versions.

---

[1] See http://www.nclrc.org, retrieved 3 Nov. 2004.

Structured output activities can form an effective bridge between instructor modeling and communicative output because they are partly authentic and partly artificial. Like authentic communication, they feature information gaps that must be bridged for successful completion of the task. However, where authentic communication allows speakers to use all of the language they know, structured output activities lead students to practice specific features of language and to practice only in brief sentences, not in extended discourse. Also, structured output situations are contrived and more like games than real communication, and the participants' social roles are irrelevant to the performance of the activity. This structure controls the number of variables that students must deal with when they are first exposed to new material. As they become comfortable, they can move on to true communicative output activities.

3) Communicative output activities

Communicative output activities allow students to practice using all of the language they know in situations that resemble real settings. The most common types of communicative output activity are *role plays* and *discussions*.

Role plays

In a role play, students are assigned roles and put into situations that they may eventually encounter outside the classroom. Because role plays imitate life, the range of language functions that may be used expands considerably. Also, the role relationships among the students as they play their parts call for them to practice and develop their socio-linguistic competence. They have to use language that is appropriate to the situation and to the characters. Students usually find role playing enjoyable, but students who lack self-confidence or have lower proficiency levels may find it intimidating at first. To succeed with role plays:

- Prepare carefully: Introduce the activity by describing the situation and making sure that all of the students understand it.
- Set a goal or outcome: Be sure the students understand what the product of the role play should be, whether a plan, a schedule, a group opinion, or some other product.
- Use role cards: Give each student a card that describes the person or role to be played. For lower-level students, the cards can include words or expressions that the person might use.
- Brainstorm: Before you start the role play, have students

brainstorm as a class to predict what vocabulary, grammar, and expressions they might use.

- Keep groups small: Less-confident students will feel more able to participate if they do not have to compete with many voices.
- Give students time to prepare: Let them work individually to outline their ideas and the language they will need to express them.
- Be present as a resource, not a monitor: Do not correct their pronunciation or grammar unless they specifically ask you about it.
- Allow students to work at their own levels: Each student has individual language skills, an individual approach to working in groups, and a specific role to play in the activity. Do not expect all students to contribute equally to the discussion, or to use every grammar point you have taught.
- Do topical follow-up: Have students report to the class on the outcome of their role plays.
- Do linguistic follow-up: After the role play is over, give feedback on grammar or pronunciation problems you have heard. This can wait until another class period when you plan to review pronunciation or grammar anyway.

Discussions

Discussions, like role plays, succeed when the instructor prepares students first, and then gets out of the way:

- Prepare the students: Give them input (topical information and language forms) so that they will have something to say and the language with which to say it.
- Offer choices: Let students suggest the topic for discussion or choose from several options.
- Set a goal or outcome: This can be a group product, such as a letter to the editor, or individual reports on the views of others in the group.
- Use small groups instead of whole-class discussion: Large groups can make participation difficult.
- Keep it short: Give students a defined period of time for discussion. Allow them to stop sooner if they run out of things to say.
- Allow students to participate in their own way: Not every student will feel comfortable talking about every topic. Do not expect all of them to contribute equally to the conversation.

- Do topical follow-up: Have students report to the class on the results of their discussion.
- Do linguistic follow-up: After the discussion is over, give feedback on grammar or pronunciation problems you have heard. This can wait until another class period when you plan to review pronunciation or grammar anyway.

4) Fluency promotion activities

The following examples adapted from Brown & Nation (1997)[1] are oriented to promoting students' fluency in speaking:

In the *Headlines* activity, students create newspaper "headlines" that will serve as the basis for the speaking activity. The learners all think of an interesting or exciting thing that has happened to them. Then each learner writes a newspaper headline referring to that specific event. The teacher should give some examples to help the learners, such as "NBA Embraces Yi". Half of the learners hold their headlines up for the rest of the class to see. Those not holding up a headline go to hear a story behind the headline that interests them. Each story can be told to no more than two people at a time. When the story is done, the listeners should circulate to a second headline that interests them. The tellers will thus have to repeat their story several times. After there has been plenty of opportunities to tell the stories, the other half of the class hold up their headlines and, in similar fashion, tell their stories.

5) Activity continuum: Towards communicative competence

According to Littlewood (1981), there is a continuum of classroom activities:

- Controlled performing
- Memorized dialogues
- Contextualized drills
- Cued dialogues
- Discourse chains
- Role play
- Improvisation
- Creativity

In training students' communicative competence, Littlewood suggests moving gradually from the controlled activities to fully creative, communicative activities with real life purpose.

---

[1] See http://www.jalt-publications.org/tlt/files/97/jan/speaking.html. Retrieved 21 Feb. 2004.

3. Teaching of reading

3.1 Introduction to reading

According to the AFT[1] (American Federation of Teachers), reading is the fundamental skill upon which all formal education depends. Research now shows that a child who doesn't learn the reading basics early is unlikely to learn them at all. Any child who doesn't learn to read early and well will not easily master other skills and knowledge, and is unlikely to ever flourish in school or in life.

Reading is the receptive skill in the written mode. It can develop independently of listening and speaking skills, but often develops along with them, especially in societies with a highly-developed literary tradition. Reading can help build vocabulary that helps listening comprehension at the later stages, particularly. The following is a look at skills, goals and techniques of teaching reading.

3.1.1 Micro-skills & macro-skills involved

1) *Micro-skills*

- Deciphering the script. In an alphabetic system, this means establishing a relationship between sounds and symbols. In a pictograph system, it means associating the meaning of the words with written symbols.
- Recognizing vocabulary
- Picking out key words, such as those identifying topics and main ideas
- Figuring out the meaning of the words, including unfamiliar vocabulary, from the (written) context
- Recognizing grammatical word classes (parts of speech): noun, adjective, etc.
- Detecting sentence constituents, such as subject, verb, object, etc.
- Recognizing basic syntactic patterns
- Using both knowledge of the world and lexical and grammatical cohesive devices to make the foregoing inferences, predict outcomes, and inferring links and connections among the parts of the text

---

[1] For more details see http://www.aft.org/topics/reading/index.htm, retrieved 12 May 2006.

- Getting the main point or the most important information
- Distinguishing the main idea from supporting details

2) *Macro-skills*

Some macro-skills involved in reading:

- Planning on the purposes to read
- Planning for what sorts of books/materials to read
- Previewing and predicting of the main idea
- Evaluating the reading speed and comprehension of reading
- Monitoring the general reading process
- Adjusting speech or material if necessary
- Obtaining the related background/culture/world knowledge
- Reflecting on the tactics and strategies used in the process of reading
- Appraising the difficulty, style, and other features of the reading materials
- Exchange with others reading strategies to promote one's reading skills

3) *An illustration of reading skills*

◆ **Word attack skills**: letting the reader figure out new words (Halvorson, 1992).

The skills come from the following:

- Seeing language as made up of units of sound and units of meaning
- Seeing print as letters symbolizing sounds, words, and discourse units of language such as sentences, paragraphs, and quotations
- Seeing relationships of ideas and the ability to infer, evaluate, and conclude

◆ **Comprehension skills**: helping readers predict the next word, phrase, or sentence quickly enough to speed recognition. (*SIL International* 1999)[1]

Comprehension is based on:

- readers' prior knowledge
- information presented in the text, and
- the use of context to assist recognition of words and meaning

◆ **Fluency skills**: helping readers see larger segments, phrases, and groups of words as wholes (Gudschinsky, 1973).

---

[1] See http://www.sil.org/lingualinks, retrieved 24 Jan. 2005.

Here are some examples of fluency skills:
- Immediately recognizing letters and frequent clusters of letters
- Learning frequent words by sight
- Seeing phrases as wholes
- ◆ **Critical reading skills**: helping readers see the relationship of ideas and use these in reading with meaning and fluency (Halvorson, 1992).

Critical reading skills are the ability to analyze, evaluate, and synthesize what one reads.
- recognizing questions and expecting answers
- recognizing cause and effect
- recognizing steps in a process
- recognizing comparisons
- recognizing generalization and itemization

3.1.2 Goal of teaching reading

Language instructors generally want to "produce" students who, even if not having complete control of the grammar or an extensive lexicon, can "take care of" themselves in communication situations. In the case of reading, this means producing students who can use reading strategies to maximize their comprehension of text, identify relevant and non-relevant information, and tolerate less than word-by-word comprehension.

To accomplish the goal, instructors should focus on the process of reading rather than on its product[1]:
- Develop students' awareness of the reading process and reading strategies by asking students to think and talk about how they read in their native language.
- Allow students to practice the full repertoire of reading strategies by using authentic reading tasks and encourage students to read to learn.
- Show students the strategies that will work best for the reading purpose and the type of text. Explain how and why students should use the strategies.
- Have students practice reading strategies in class and ask them to practice outside of class in their reading assignments, encouraging students to be conscious of what they're doing

---

[1] Adapted from http://www.nclrc.org/essentials/reading/assessread.htm, retrieved 25 Apr. 2005.

while they complete reading assignments.

- Encourage students to evaluate their comprehension and self-report their use of strategies.
- Explicitly mention how a particular strategy can be used in a different type of reading task or with another skill.

3.1.3 Principles of teaching reading

In teaching reading, the following principles should be followed by teachers in designing and carrying out activities and tasks:

1) The process of reading is active.
2) Reader engagement is essential.
3) Reading has a purpose.
4) Content and language and structure are important.
5) Key skills are involved to train students to be better readers.

3.2   Reading stages and strategies training

3.2.1 Three stages of reading

Instruction in reading strategies is an integral part of the use of reading activities. Instructors can help their students become effective readers by teaching them how to use strategies before, during, and after reading.

Before reading: Plan for the reading task

- Set a purpose or decide in advance what to read for
- Decide if more linguistic or background knowledge is needed
- Determine whether to enter the text from the top down (attend to the overall meaning) or from the bottom up model (focus on the words and phrases)

During and shortly after reading: Monitor comprehension

- Verify predictions and check for inaccurate guesses
- Decide what is and is not important to understand
- Reread to check comprehension
- Ask for help

After reading: Evaluate comprehension and strategy use

- Evaluate comprehension in a particular task or area
- Evaluate overall progress in reading and in particular types of reading tasks
- Decide if the strategies used were appropriate for the purpose and for the task

- Modify strategies if necessary

3.2.2 Authentic materials

For students to develop communicative competence in reading, reading activities must resemble (or be) real-life reading tasks that involve meaningful communication. They must therefore be authentic in three ways.

1) *The reading material must be authentic*: It must be the kind of material that students will need and want to be able to read when traveling, or using the language in other contexts outside the classroom.

Hint: When selecting texts for student assignments, remember that the difficulty of a reading text is less a function of the language, and more a function of the conceptual difficulty and the task(s) that students are expected to complete. Simplifying a text by changing the language often removes natural redundancy and makes the organization somewhat difficult for students to predict. This actually makes a text more difficult to read than if the original were used.

Rather than simplifying a text by changing its language, make it more approachable by eliciting students' existing knowledge in pre-reading discussion, reviewing new vocabulary before reading, and asking students to perform tasks that are within their competence, such as skimming to get the main idea or scanning for specific information, before they begin intensive reading.

2) *The reading purpose must be authentic:* Students must be reading for reasons that make sense and have relevance to them. "Because the teacher assigned it" is not an authentic reason for reading a text.

Hint: To identify relevant reading purposes, ask students how they plan to use the language they are learning and what topics they are interested in reading and learning about. Give them opportunities to choose their reading assignments, and encourage them to use the library, the Internet, and foreign language newsstands and bookstores to find other things they would like to read.

3) *The reading approach must be authentic:* Students should read the text in a way that matches the reading purpose, the type of text, and the way people normally read. This means that reading aloud will take place only in situations where it would take place outside the classroom, such as reading for pleasure. The majority of students' reading should be done silently[1].

---

[1] See http://www.nclrc.org/essentials/reading, retrieved 26 Nov. 2005.

Notice: Students do not learn to read by reading aloud. A person who reads aloud and comprehends the meaning of the text is coordinating word recognition with comprehension and speaking and pronunciation ability in highly complex ways. Students whose language skills are limited are not able to process at this level, and end up having to drop one or more of the elements. Usually the dropped element is comprehension, and reading aloud becomes word calling: simply pronouncing a series of words without regard for the meaning they carry individually and together. Word calling is not productive for the student who is doing it, and it is boring for other students to listen to.

- There are two ways to use reading aloud productively in the language classroom. Read aloud to students as they follow along silently. Teachers have the ability to use inflection and tone to help them hear what the text is saying. Following along as teachers read will help students move from word-by-word reading to reading in phrases and thought units, as they do in their first language.

- Use the "read and look up" technique. With this technique, a student reads a phrase or sentence silently as many times as necessary, then looks up (away from the text) and tells you what the phrase or sentence says. This encourages students to read for ideas, rather than for word recognition.

3.2.3 Strategies for developing reading skills

1) Core reading strategies

Effective language instructors show students how they can adjust their reading behavior to deal with a variety of situations, types of input, and reading purposes. They help students develop a set of reading strategies and match appropriate strategies to each reading situation.

Strategies that can help students read more quickly and effectively include[1]:

- *Previewing:* previewing titles, section headings, and photo captions to get a sense of the structure and content of a reading selection

- *Predicting:* using knowledge of the subject matter to make predictions about content and vocabulary and check comprehension; using knowledge of the text type and purpose

---

[1] http://www.nclrc.org/essentials/reading, retrieved 26 Nov. 2005.

to make predictions about discourse structure; using knowledge about the author to make predictions about writing style, vocabulary, and content

- *Skimming and scanning:* using a quick survey of the text to get the main idea, identify text structure, confirm or question predictions
- *Guessing from context:* using prior knowledge of the subject and the ideas in the text as clues to the meanings of unknown words, instead of stopping to look them up
- *Paraphrasing:* stopping at the end of a section to check comprehension by restating the information and ideas in the text

Instructors can build learners' awareness of strategy—help students learn when and how to use reading strategies in several ways.

- By modeling the strategies aloud, talking through the processes of previewing, predicting, skimming and scanning, and paraphrasing. This shows students how the strategies work and how much they can know about a text before they begin to read word by word.
- By allowing time in class for group and individual previewing and predicting activities as preparation for in-class or out-of-class reading. Allocating class time to these activities indicates their importance and value.
- By using cloze (fill in the blank) exercises to review vocabulary items. This helps students learn to guess meaning from context.
- By encouraging students to talk about what strategies they think will help them approach a reading assignment, and then talking after reading about what strategies they actually used. This helps students develop flexibility in their choice of strategies.

When language learners use reading strategies, they find that they can control the reading experience, and they gain confidence in their ability to read the language.

2) Strategic reading for cognition

Reading is a cognitive process. It is an essential part of language instruction at every level because it supports learning in multiple ways.

- *Reading to learn the language*: Reading material is language input. By giving students a variety of materials to read, instructors provide multiple opportunities for students to absorb vocabulary, grammar, sentence structure, and discourse structure as they occur in authentic contexts. Students thus gain a more complete picture of the ways in which the elements of the language work together to convey meaning.

- *Reading for content information*: Students' purpose for reading in their native language is often to obtain information about a subject they are studying, and this purpose can be useful in the language learning classroom as well. Reading for content information in the language classroom gives students both authentic reading material and an authentic purpose for reading.

- *Reading for cultural knowledge and awareness*: Reading everyday materials that are designed for native speakers can give students insight into the lifestyles and worldviews of the people whose language they are studying. When students have access to newspapers, magazines, and web sites, they are exposed to culture in all its variety, and monolithic cultural stereotypes begin to break down.

When reading to learn, students need to follow four basic steps:

a. Figure out the purpose for reading. Activate background knowledge of the topic in order to predict or anticipate content and identify appropriate reading strategies.

b. Attend to the parts of the text that are relevant to the identified purpose and ignore the rest. This selectivity enables students to focus on specific items in the input and reduces the amount of information they have to hold in short-term memory.

c. Select strategies that are appropriate to the reading task and use them flexibly and interactively. Students' comprehension improves and their confidence increases when they use top-down and bottom-up skills simultaneously to construct meaning.

d. Check comprehension while reading and when the reading task is completed. Monitoring comprehension helps students detect inconsistencies and comprehension failures, helping them learn to use alternate strategies.

3) A grid of reading strategies[1]

The following is a reading strategy grid. English teachers can refer to the grid for strategies they want to use in their reading classrooms.

---

[1] Adapted from http://www.greece.k12.ny.us/instruction/ela/6-12/Reading/Reading%20Strategies/reading%20strategies%20index.htm. Retrieved 21 Dec. 2006.

FIGURE 4.5 Reading strategy grid

Before	During	After	Reading Strategy	Description
	√	√	Annolighting a Text	This active reading strategy links concept of highlighting key words and phrases in a text and annotating those highlights with marginal notes.
	√	√	Annotating a Text	Annotating a text is an effective strategy to promote active and critical reading skills; this strategy provides some useful acronyms that students can use to remember different elements of writer's craft when reading and annotating a text.
√			Anticipation Guide	Anticipation guides are typically used as a pre-reading strategy and help to engage students in thought and discussion about ideas and concepts that they will encounter in the text.
√			Checking out the Framework	This strategy provides students with suggestions for previewing texts of different genre in order to read strategically based on their purposes for reading the text.
	√	√	Collaborative Annotation	This strategy engages students in a process of co-constructing their interpretations of a text through a collaborative annotation activity.
√	√	√	Conversations Across Time	This reading strategy helps students to develop deeper insights by making connections between and across texts from different time periods in response to a common topic, theme, or essential question.
	√	√	Dense Questioning	The dense questioning strategy can be used to help students pose increasingly dense questions as they make text-to-text, text-to-self, text-to-world connections.
√	√	√	Frame of Reference	The frame of reference strategy teaches students how to create a mental context for reading a passage; this is accomplished by helping students to consider what they know about a topic and how they know what they know.
	√	√	Inferential Reading	The inferential reading strategy provides a list of the various types of inferences that readers make while reading even seemingly straightforward text; recognizing that there are different types of inferences helps students to analyze text more consciously and strategically.

(to be continued)

Before	During	After	Reading Stategy	Description
√	√	√	Interactive Notebook	This highly adaptable strategy encourages students to use a two-column note-taking strategy. In the right column, they take notes to synthesize essential ideas and information from a text, presentation, film, etc.; in the left-hand column, they interact with the content in any way they choose (personal connections, illustrations, etc.).
	√	√	Key Concept Synthesis	The key concept synthesis strategy helps students to identify the most important ideas in a text, put those ideas into their own words, and then make connections between among these important ideas.
	√	√	Listening to Voice	This strategy helps students to analyze and interpret writer's voice through the annotation of a passage, with particular emphasis on dictions, tone, syntax, unity, coherence, and audience.
	√	√	Metaphor Analysis	This adaptable strategy teaches students how to analyze a complex metaphor and substantiate interpretive claims using textual evidence.
	√	√	Parallel Note-taking	The parallel note-taking strategy teaches students to recognize different organizational patterns for informational texts and then develop a note-taking strategy that parallels the organization of the text.
√	√	√	QAR: Question-Answer Relationships	The QAR strategy helps students to identify the four **Q**uestion-**A**nswer **R**elationships that they are likely to encounter as they read texts and attempt to answer questions about what they have read. These include "right there" questions, "think and search" questions, "author and you" questions.
√	√	√	Questions Only	The questions only strategy teaches students how to pose questions about the texts they are reading and encourages them to read actively as they work to answer the questions they have posed.
		√	RAFT	This is a flexible post-reading strategy that helps students to analyze and reflect upon their reading through persona writing. Based on suggestions provided by the teacher or generated by the class, students choose a **R**ole, an **A**udience, a **F**ormat, and a **T**opic on which to write in response to their reading.

(to be continued)

Before	During	After	Reading Strategy	Description
√	√	√	Reciprocal Teaching	The reciprocal teaching strategy enables students to activate four different comprehension strategies—predicting, questioning, clarifying, summarizing—which they apply collaboratively to help each other understand a text they are reading.
	√	√	Socio-grams	A socio-gram is a visual representation of the relationships among characters in a literary text. Students can make use of pictures, symbols, shapes, colors, and line styles to illustrate these relationships, to understand the traits of each character, and to analyze the emerging primary and secondary conflicts.
√	√	√	Think Aloud	Skillful readers unconsciously use a range of strategies to make meaning from text. The think aloud strategy involves modeling these strategies by "thinking aloud" while reading and responding to a text. By making explicit for students what is implicit for more expert readers, it becomes possible for students to develop and apply these strategies themselves.
	√		Transactional Reading Journal	The name of this reading strategy is inspired by the work of Louise Rosenblatt (1978), who explained reading as a transactional process that occurs between the text and the reader. The Transactional Reading Journal builds on this concept (via Jude Ellis) and provides a flexible framework for engaging students in a process of active and personally meaningful interaction with a text.
√	√	√	Writer's Craft Seminar	This reading strategy teaches students how to analyze text through close reading in order to formulate a interpretive thesis that is supported through assertions and textual evidence. Students present their interpretations to the class through a seminar format.
√	√	√	KWL	This reading strategy teaches students reading in different stages: asking students what they know about the topic; what they want to know; and what they have learned.

Of course, there are many more reading strategy patterns not covered in the above grid. In Section 3.2.6, for instance, we will have a close look at the use of SQ3R method.

3.2.4 Schema and reading

As discussed in the section of teaching listening skills, all human beings possess categorical rules or scripts that they use to interpret the world. New information is processed according to how it fits into these rules, called schema. These schemata can be used not only to interpret but also to predict situation occurring in our environment. In other words, schema theory seeks to explain how we are able to cope with our constantly changing daily environment. Obviously, we do not see each circumstance as unique and unfamiliar. We are quickly able to recognize familiar elements and patterns (*schema*) in the activities unfolding around us. This enables us to behave correctly in situations as diverse as a history class, a fast food restaurant, or crossing a busy street in a large city in a foreign country.

This remarkable ability to make sense out of our ever-changing surroundings clearly depends on memory. We are somehow able to extract just those elements from our huge store of experiences, facts, smells, tastes—everything we call memory—to allow us to make at least an educated guess as to what is occurring around us. And this memory comes to us not in random bits and pieces, but in an organized form, allowing us to almost immediately distinguish a marriage ceremony from a courtroom trial, or a bus station from a school.

Schemata are important not just in interpreting information, but also in decoding how that information is presented. Schemata can be reflected in text structures (Driscoll, 1997; Halliday & Hasan, 1989). Readers use their schematic representations of text (narrative, compare/contrast, cause/effect, etc.) to help them interpret the information in the text. Moreover, the structure of formal argumentative essays is culturally determined (Kaplan, 1966). Therefore, second language writers and readers must be aware of not only having sufficient command of their second language but also of the textual structures in their second language.

In classroom reading, we essentially deal with two broad categories of schema: text schema and content schema.

Text schema

Writings such as newspaper articles are remarkably consistent and experienced readers have well developed expectations for the style of writing to be found in each section of the newspaper. The styles of news writing, feature writing and opinion writing are easily described and readers can develop effective strategies for dealing with these styles.

Content schema

Newspaper content is equally consistent. Only a limited number of topics (important elections, bad storms, championship boxing matches, etc.) are generally considered newsworthy and each has distinctive characteristics. They have their own typical settings, sequences and characters with discernable roles. And they are often described using a limited set of high-frequency words and phrases. Similarly, different styles of essays (exposition, argumentation, description and narration) can be presented.

Thus schema theory, with its focus on underlying patterns and consistencies, offers teachers clear "shortcuts" for familiarizing students with the style and content of the readings. But this should not be done in isolation. Teachers should encourage students to read extensively because that is the only way they can truly develop the background and expectations necessary to genuine comprehension.

3.2.5 Speed reading

Speed reading aims at increasing one's reading speed: understanding text more quickly. It is an essential skill in any environment where you have to master large volumes of information quickly.

The most important trick about speed reading is to know what information you want from a document before you start reading it: if you only want an outline of the issue that the document discusses, then you can skim the document very quickly and extract only the essential facts. If you need to understand the real detail of the document, then you need to read it slowly enough to fully understand it.

Speed reading aims to improve reading skills by:

- increasing the number of words read in each block
- reducing the length of time spent reading each block
- reducing the number of times your eyes skip back to a previous sentence

These are explained below:

- *Increasing the number of words in each block:* This needs a conscious effort. Try to expand the number of words you read at a time. Practice will help you to read faster. You may also find that you can increase the number of words read by holding the text a little further from your eyes. The more words you can read in each block, the faster you will read.
- *Reducing Fixation Time:* The minimum length of time needed to read each block is probably only a quarter of a second. By

pushing yourself to reduce the time you consume you will get better at picking up information quickly.

- *Reducing Skip-Back:* To reduce the number of times that your eyes skip back to a previous sentence, run a pointer along the line as you read. This could be a finger, or a pen or pencil. Your eyes will follow the tip of your pointer, smoothing the flow of your reading. The speed at which you read using this method will largely depend on the speed at which you move the pointer.

3.2.6 SQ3R reading method

SQ3R is a useful technique for fully absorbing written information. It helps the reader to create a good mental framework of a subject, into which he/she can fit facts correctly. It also helps to set study goals.

The acronym SQ3R stands for the five sequential techniques:

- *Survey:*
  Survey the document: scan the contents, introduction, chapter introductions and chapter summaries to pick up a shallow overview of the text.
- *Question:*
  Make a note of any questions on the subject coming to mind. Perhaps scan the document again to see if any stand out. These questions can be considered almost as study goals.
- *Read:*
  Now read the document. Read through useful sections in detail, taking care to understand all the points that are relevant.
- *Recall:*
  Once you have read appropriate sections of the document, run through it in your mind several times. Isolate the core facts or the essential processes behind the subject, and then see how other information fits around them.
- *Review:*
  Once you have run through the exercise of recalling the information, you can move on to the stage of reviewing it. This review can be done by rereading the document, by expanding your notes, or by discussing the material with your friends.

As an illustration of its use, the following grid is adapted from Robinson (1970):

FIGURE 4.6 Application of SQ3R reading method

Survey! Question! Read! Recite! Review!	
Before you read, Survey the chapter:	• the title, headings, and subheadings • captions under pictures, charts, graphs or maps • review questions or teacher-made study guides • introductory and concluding paragraphs • summary
Question while you are surveying:	• Turn the title, headings, and/or subheadings into questions; • Read questions at the end of the chapters or after each subheading; • Ask yourself, "What did my instructor say about this chapter or subject when it was assigned?" • Ask yourself, "What do I already know about this subject?" **Note:** If it is helpful to you, write out these questions for consideration.
When you begin to Read:	• Look for answers to the questions you first raised • Answer questions at the beginning or end of chapters or study guides • Reread captions under pictures, graphs, etc. • Note all the underlined, italicized, bold printed words or phrases • Study graphic aids • Reduce your speed for difficult passages • Stop and reread parts which are not clear • Read only a section at a time and recite after each section
Recite after you've read a section:	• Orally ask yourself questions about what you have just read or summarize, in your own words, what you read • Take notes from the text but write the information in your own words • Underline or highlight important points you've just read • Use the method of recitation which best suits your particular learning style but remember; the more senses you use the more likely you are to remember what you read, i.e., TRIPLE STRENGTH LEARNING: Seeing, saying, hearing QUADRUPLE STRENGTH LEARNING: Seeing , saying , hearing, writing!

(to be continued)

Review:
an ongoing process.
	Day One
	• After you have read and recited the entire chapter,
	  write questions in the margins for those points you have highlighted or underlined.
	• If you took notes while reciting,
	  write questions for the notes you have taken in the left hand margins of your notebook.
	Day Two
	• Page through the text and/or your notebook to re-acquaint yourself with the important points.
	• Cover the right hand column of your text/note-book and orally ask yourself the questions in the left hand margins.
	• Orally recite or write the answers from memory.
	• Make "flash cards" for those questions which give you difficulty.
	• Develop mnemonic devices for material which need to be memorized.
	Days Three, Four and Five
	• Alternate between your flash cards and notes and test yourself (orally or in writing) on the questions you formulated.
	• Make additional flash cards if necessary.
	Weekend
	Using the text and notebook, make a Table of Contents—list all the topics and sub-topics you need to know from the chapter.
	From the Table of Contents, make a Study Sheet/Spatial Map.
	Recite the information orally and in your own words as you put the Study Sheet/Map together.
	Now that you have consolidated all the information you need for that chapter, periodically review the Sheet/Map so that at test time you will not have to cram.

3.3   Developing reading activities

3.3.1 Task preparation

Developing reading activities involves more than identifying a text that is "at the right level," writing a set of comprehension questions for students to answer after reading, handing out the assignment and sending students away to do it. A fully-developed reading activity supports students as readers through pre-reading, while-reading, and post-reading activities.

1) Construct the reading activity around a purpose

Make sure students understand the purpose for reading: to get the main idea, obtain specific information, understand most or all of the message, enjoy a story, or decide whether or not to read more. Recognizing the purpose for reading will help students select appropriate reading strategies.

2) Define the activity's instructional goal and the appropriate response

In addition to the main purpose for reading, an activity can also have one or more instructional purposes, such as practicing or reviewing specific grammatical constructions, introducing new vocabulary, or familiarizing students with the typical structure of a certain type of text.

3) Check the level of difficulty of the text

The factors listed below can help you judge the relative ease or difficulty of a reading text for a particular purpose and a particular group of students.

- How is the information organized? Texts in which the events are presented in natural chronological order, which have an informative title, and which present the information following an obvious organization (main ideas first, details and examples second) are easier to follow.
- How familiar are the students with the topic? Remember that misapplication of background knowledge due to cultural differences can create major comprehension difficulties.
- Does the text offer visual support to aid in reading comprehension? Visual aids such as photographs, maps, and diagrams help students preview the content of the text, guess the meanings of unknown words, and check comprehension while reading.

Remember that the level of difficulty of a text is not the same as the level of difficulty of a reading task. Students who lack the vocabulary to identify all of the items on a menu can still determine whether the restaurant serves steak and whether they can afford to order one.

3.3.2 Student preparation

1) Use pre-reading activities to prepare students for reading

The activities used during pre-reading may serve as preparation in several ways:

- Assess students' background knowledge of the topic and linguistic content of the text
- Give students the background knowledge necessary for comprehension of the text, or activate the existing knowledge that the students possess

- Clarify any cultural information which may be necessary to comprehend the passage
- Make students aware of the type of text they will be reading and the purpose(s) for reading
- Provide opportunities for group or collaborative work and for class discussion activities
  Sample pre-reading activities:
- Using the title, subtitles, and divisions within the text to predict content and organization or sequence of information
- Looking at pictures, maps, diagrams, or graphs and their captions
- Talking about the author's background, writing style, and usual topics
- Skimming to find the theme or main idea and eliciting related prior knowledge
- Reviewing vocabulary or grammatical structures
- Reading over the comprehension questions to focus attention on finding that information while reading
- Constructing semantic webs (a graphic arrangement of concepts or words showing how they are related)
- Doing guided practice with guessing meaning from context or checking comprehension while reading

Pre-reading activities are most important at lower levels of language proficiency and at earlier stages of reading instruction. As students become more proficient at using reading strategies, teachers will be able to reduce the amount of guided pre-reading and allow students to do these activities themselves.

2) Match while-reading activities to the purpose for reading

In while-reading activities, students check their comprehension as they read. The purpose for reading determines the appropriate type and level of comprehension.

- When reading for specific information, students need to ask themselves, "Have I obtained the information I was looking for?"
- When reading for pleasure, students need to ask themselves, "Do I understand the story line/sequence of ideas well enough to enjoy reading this?"
- When reading for thorough understanding (intensive reading), students need to ask themselves, "Do I understand each main idea and how the author supports it? Does what I'm

reading agree with my predictions, and, if not, how does it differ?"

To check comprehension in this situation, students may

- Stop at the end of each section to review and check their predictions, restate the main idea and summarize the section
- Use the comprehension questions as guides to the text, stopping to answer them as they read

3.3.3 Making use of textbook reading activities

Many language textbooks emphasize product (answers to comprehension questions) over process (using reading skills and strategies to understand the text), providing little or no contextual information about the reading selections or their authors, and few if any pre-reading activities. Some newer textbooks may provide pre-reading activities and reading strategy guidance, but their one-size-fits-all approach may or may not be appropriate for different students.

Language teachers can use existing, or add their own, pre-reading activities and reading strategy practice as appropriate for their students. Don't make students do exercises simply because they are in the book; this destroys motivation.

Another problem with textbook reading selections is that they have been adapted to a predetermined reading level through adjustment of vocabulary, grammar, and sentence length. This makes them more immediately approachable, but it also means that they are less authentic and do not encourage students to apply the reading strategies they will need to use outside of class. When this is the case, use the textbook reading selection as a starting point to introduce a writer or topic, and then give students choices of more challenging authentic texts to read as a follow-up.

3.4   Reflections on teaching reading

3.4.1 On material

Traditionally, the purpose of learning to read in a language has been to have access to the literature written in that language. In language instruction, reading materials have been chosen from literary texts that represent "higher" forms of culture (Byrnes, 1998).

This approach assumes that students learn to read a language by studying its vocabulary, grammar, and sentence structure, not by actually reading it. In this approach, lower level learners read only sentences and paragraphs generated by textbook writers and instructors. The reading of authentic materials is limited to the works of great authors and reserved for upper level students who have developed the language skills needed to read them.

The communicative approach to language teaching has given instructors a different understanding of the role of reading in the language classroom and the types of texts that can be used in instruction. When the goal of instruction is communicative competence, everyday materials such as train schedules, newspaper articles, and travel and tourism web sites become appropriate classroom materials, because reading them is one way communicative competence is developed. Instruction in reading and reading practice thus become essential parts of language teaching at every level.

3.4.2 On reading purpose and reading comprehension

Reading is an activity with a purpose. A person may read in order to gain information or verify existing knowledge, or in order to critique a writer's ideas or writing style. A person may also read for enjoyment, or to enhance knowledge of the language being read. The purpose(s) for reading guide(s) the reader's selection of texts.

The purpose for reading also determines the appropriate approach to reading comprehension. A person who needs to know whether he/she can afford to eat at a particular restaurant needs to comprehend the pricing information provided on the menu, but does not need to recognize the name of every appetizer listed. A person reading poetry for enjoyment needs to recognize the words the poet uses and the ways they are put together, but does not need to identify main idea and supporting details. However, a person using a scientific article to support an opinion needs to know the vocabulary that is used, understand the facts and cause-effect sequences that are presented, and recognize ideas that are presented as hypotheses and givens.

Reading research shows that good readers

- read extensively;
- integrate information in the text with existing knowledge;
- have a flexible reading style, depending on what they are reading;
- are motivated;
- rely on different skills interacting: perceptual processing, phonemic processing, recall;
- read for a purpose.

3.4.3 On regarding reading as a process

Reading is an interactive process that goes on between the reader and the text, resulting in comprehension. The text presents letters, words, sentences, and paragraphs that encode meaning. The reader uses knowledge, skills, and strategies to determine what that meaning is.

Reader knowledge, skills, and strategies include

- Linguistic competence: the ability to recognize the elements of the writing system; knowledge of vocabulary; knowledge of how words are structured into sentences
- Discourse competence: knowledge of discourse markers and how they connect parts of the text to one another
- Socio-linguistic competence: knowledge about different types of texts and their usual structure and content
- Strategic competence: the ability to use top-down strategies, as well as knowledge of the language

The purpose(s) for reading and the type of text determine the specific knowledge, skills, and strategies that readers need to apply in the reading process to achieve comprehension. Reading comprehension is thus much more than decoding; it is also a process of cognition.

4. Teaching of writing

4.1   Introduction to writing

Writing is the productive skill in the written mode. It often seems to be the hardest of different skills, even for native speakers of a language, in that it involves not just a graphic representation of speech, but the development and presentation of thoughts in a structured way. Brown (2001) quotes Lenneberg (1967) and says that human beings universally learn to walk and talk but swimming and writing are culturally specific, learned behaviors. To some extent, this analogy is true. We learn to swim only if there is a body of water available and usually if someone teaches us. We learn to write if we are members of a literate society, and usually only if someone teaches us. Let's first get to know some basics about writing.

4.1.1 Macro- and micro-skills of writing

Macro-skills
- Planning for thoughts/ideas/topics to be conveyed onto paper
- Evaluating the target reader(s) and situation of writing
- Monitoring the writing process
- Adjusting blueprint/outline if necessary
- Absorbing the related background/culture/world knowledge
- Reflecting on the tactics and strategies used in the process of writing
- Appraising the effect of the writing product on the readers

Micro-skills
- Using the orthography correctly, including the script, spelling and punctuation conventions
- Using correct forms of words
- Putting words together in correct word order
- Using vocabulary correctly
- Using the style appropriate to the genre and audience
- Making the main sentence constituents, such as subject, verb, and object, clear to the reader
- Making the main ideas distinct from supporting ideas or information
- Making the text coherent so that other people can follow the development of the ideas
- Judging how much background knowledge the audience has on the subject

4.1.2 Major issues involved in writing

1) Types of Writing

The following is a list of writing assignments. The topics range through various discourse aims including the expressive, the exploratory, the informative, the scientific, the literary, and the persuasive (Adapted from Kinneavy, 1971):

a. Expressive
- Mission statements and vision statements
- Proposals
- Constitutions
- Legislative bills

b. Exploratory
- Definitions
- Diagnoses

- White papers
- Marketing analyses
- Opinion surveys
- Feasibility studies
- Annotated bibliographies
- "Literature" reviews
- Problem solutions

c. Informative
- News articles
- Magazine feature articles
- Reports, letters, itinerary
- Encyclopedia articles

d. Scientific
- Formal arguments from principle, e.g. applying or implementing a theory
- Arguments generalizing from particulars, e.g. testing a hypothesis

e. Literary
- Historical fiction, biography, autobiography, essay
- Ballads, poetry
- Plays, TV, or film scripts on course related issues

f. Persuasive
- Advertising campaigns
- Political speeches
- Editorials
- Social, political, or artistic criticism

2) Topics and format in different genres (Manning)[1]

For most classroom writing, teachers and students dwell on the following genres.

a. Narrative: WHO did WHAT, WHEN and WHERE they did it.

b. Persuasive/Argumentative: WHICH product to buy or WHICH politician to believe.

c. Technical/Expositive: HOW things work or HOW things happen the way they do.

d. Academic: WHETHER a particular theory or hypothesis is true.

Besides these, we also often need to deal with application writings both in class and in society. These include letters, greeting cards, memos, messages, application forms, CV, advertisements,

---

[1] Manning A. Writing Across Genres: Developing Competence in Stages. http://linguistics.byu.edu/classes/ling230am/writing_chapters/Types_of_Writing.html, retrieved 14 Mar. 2006.

invitation cards, etc. Different writing genres also differ in terms of how often we typically encounter them, how easy it is to read each kind of writing, and how soon or how easily people learn each genre. For writing teachers, it is vital to avail students of the detailed rules and conventions—or in another word—build schemata knowledge in students.

3) Characteristics of written language

Brown lists seven-point characteristics of written language (2001: 325-326):

a. **Permanence:** Once something is written down and delivered in its final form to its intended readers, the writer abdicates power to emend, to clarify and to withdraw.

b. **Production time:** For quite a few written works, they involve a variety of stretches of time.

c. **Distance:** This distance factor—"cognitive empathy" as called by Brown denotes that writers need to be able to predict the audience's general knowledge, cultural and literary schemata.

d. **Orthography:** Everything from simple greetings to extremely complex ideas is captured through the manipulation of a few dozen letters and other written symbols.

e. **Complexity:** Writers must learn how to remove redundancy, how to combine sentences, how to make references to other elements in text, etc.

f. **Vocabulary:** Writing places a heavier demand on vocabulary use than does speaking.

g. **Formality:** The conventions of each form must be followed in writing.

4) Types of writing prompts

Prompts are written to elicit writing for specific purposes. For instance, expository prompts may ask students to explain why or how, narrative prompts may direct students to recount or tell, and persuasive prompts may require students to convince or persuade. Prompts to writing assessment should be carefully selected to ensure that the subject matter is interesting and appropriate for the students. In addition, the prompts should be reviewed for any bias relating to gender, religion, race, or ethnic background.

Prompts have two basic components: the writing situation and directions for writing. The writing situation orients students to the subject on which they are to write. The directions-for-writing component sets the parameter for writing and, in the case of persuasive prompts, identifies the audience to whom the writing is directed.

Example of a Persuasive Prompt:

Writing Situation:

The principal of your school has been asked to discuss with a parent group the effects watching TV has on students' grades.

Directions for Writing:

Think about the effect watching TV has on your grades and your friends' grades.

Now write to convince your principal to accept your point of view on the effect watching TV has on grades.

4.1.3 Writing to learn vs. writing to communicate

Writing is one of the most powerful skills developed during the educational experience. Writing contains different purposes, which are very often entangled with one another. Learners are probably familiar with the "writing to communicate"[1] type of assignment: a personal/business letter that will be read by friends or business partners only, a four to five page term paper that will be read only by the instructor and counted as some percentage of the final grade.

Researching, organizing, and drafting papers are active processes that help one better understand the material and complement the experiences of classroom lectures and discussions. This type of discovery writing, therefore, may be called "writing to learn". The basic concept is to first gather facts and ideas together and then begin a period of critical analysis. The end result of this analysis will be a draft paper with the major issues organized into some logical and understandable form.

It is later during the iterative revision process of reading, editing, and proofreading that the focus is switched to the "writing to communicate" mode. The goal of writing to communicate is to involve a reader in his or her own process of discovery: the goal shifts from gathering and organizing facts to presenting facts and inferences in the most efficient manner.

Writing to learn and writing to communicate are both integral parts of the writing process. It is very hard to achieve excellence in the latter without putting forth major time and effort in the former.

---

[1] http://www.etsu.edu/scitech/langskil/reports. html#Lab Rpts-Tech, retrieved 26 Aug. 2005.

Experience with students has shown that when sufficient effort and time is invested in both types of writing, the quality of work will always be higher. The more you thoughtfully practice writing, the sharper your skills will become. This investment will yield rich rewards.

4.2   Key writing models

This section describes the major models of composition important to students—the product (or current-traditional) model, the process model, the social-theoretic (or social construction) model, and the academic paper writing.

4.2.1 Introduction

The product model developed during the 17th and 18th centuries. Most of the factors or conventions that govern writing in this model—such as audience, aims, and form—are related to two types of writing: journalism and literary criticism. Style is a major concern, and for this reason the pedagogy associated with the product model tends to focus on error correction and telling rather than showing. As a result, it involves little true writing instruction.

The process model emerged in the early 1970s as teachers and researchers began evaluating the factors that distinguish good writers from poor ones. As the name suggests, the emphasis is on writing as a process rather than on product. This model therefore aims to improve writing by helping students master a range of behaviors associated with effective composition. It restructures the current traditional classroom into a writing workshop where students collaborate on drafts of assignments in small groups. When ideally applied, the process model emphasizes group activities geared toward discovering things to say about a topic (*invention*), drafting, pausing, sharing work in progress, revising, and editing. As students work on drafts of assignments, teachers circulate among the groups, offering advice and suggestions through formative rather than summative evaluation.

The social-theoretic model developed when teachers saw that process was limited in some important ways. For example, the process model focuses on writers and their psychological states. Although it addresses audience needs, it offers little insight into the relationship between writers and audience. Especially absent is any recognition of how audience determines numerous significant features of text. In other words, the process model generally invests writers with control over their work that does not exist in real situations. As a result, in the light of related subjects such as discourse analysis and sociolinguistics, social-theoretic considerations are used to complement other models.

Academic paper writing is one of the most important writing tasks for tertiary level students. It is important to note that various academic units have their own standards for content and style for academic writing; it is the *students'* responsibility to ensure that they follow the appropriate rules. However, some analysis of the basic features of academic writing pays off.

4.2.2 Product-oriented vs. process-oriented writing

1) Product-oriented writing
Following the product oriented pattern, the teacher first gives the students a topic together with some related requirements. Then, the students will work under deadline pressure in class or at home. After they hand in their products, the teacher will correct and grade them. In most cases, teacher's feedback is limited to grammatical, structural or other mechanical errors, with little concern for the content or organization of the texts. In a word, product approach places emphasis on the end product, showing no concern for the process in writing. As a result, three areas of problems arise from this traditional approach:

- From the psychological perspective, students are prone to feel pressure in writing. Particularly, the first thing they encounter is what to say on the topic. For lacking teacher's guidance, they suffer a lot in making a start. On the other hand, because time is so limited, they tend to be hasty in getting started without much thinking. It's difficult for them to go on smoothly for their way of thinking is not clear enough. Thus, a sense of stress will pervade in them, just as Holemes (2000) states, "The need to produce a coherent, well-written text can be a great source of stress to the writer if the intervening stages in the process of creating this text are overlooked."[1]

- From the linguistic perspective, students taught in this way will not learn to use their own language so that they are not able to

---

[1] Niclola Holemes. 2000. "The use of a process-oriented approach to facilitate the planning and production stages of writing for adult students of English as a foreign or second language". http://www.developingteachers.com/articles_tchtraining/processw1_nicola.htm, retrieved 23 Apr. 2005.

express their intended meaning clearly and freely. The teaching of product writing will result in that "writing was viewed primarily as a tool for the practice and reinforcement of specific grammatical and lexical patterns; accuracy being all important whereas content and self expression given little if any priority." (Simpson, 2000)[1] It is true that a basic valuable point of writing is helping students to consolidate what they have learned, such as grammatical structures, vocabulary use and so on. However, with the improvement of writing, on the part of intermediate and advanced learners, they are not contented with the limited linguistic knowledge transmitted from teachers, but are eager to write language of their own freely and naturally.

- From the communicative perspective, there is no communicative element involved in this approach of writing. The main purpose of students' writing is to display an error-free and coherent text. The only reader kept in their mind may be their teacher, who will read and grade it primarily on the basis of language usage whereas the communicative function of language is almost completely ignored. No wonder students are inclined to feel at a loss when facing some application writing, such as letters, term papers, and so on.

2) Process-oriented writing

Writing based on process approach focuses on the process of composing rather than the final written product. In White's model, writing is viewed as a recursive process, as indicated by the following figure (White and Valerie, 1991: 4):

FIGURE 4.7 White's writing model

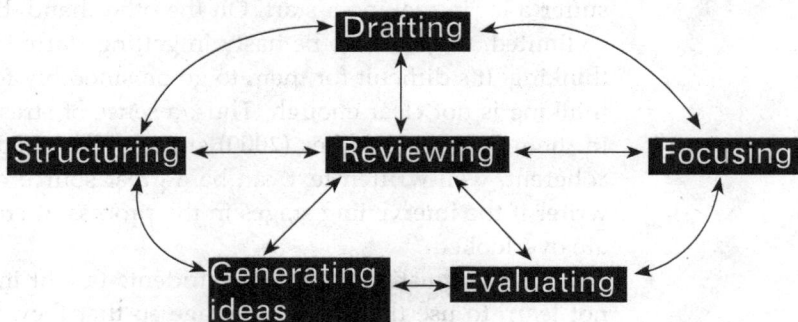

---

[1] Adam Simpson. 2000. "A Process Approach to Writing by Adam Simpson". http://www.developingteachers.com/articles_tchtraining/pw1_adam.htm, retrieved 23 Apr. 2005.

As can be seen from the figure, this model includes six procedures: generating, structuring, drafting, focusing, evaluating and reviewing, which are moving back and forth from one procedure to another. To be more specific, first of all, students must actively engage themselves in classroom activities being adopted to stimulate their ideas. By so doing, the problem "what can I say on the topic" is largely solved. Then, they focus on an established viewpoint purposefully, organize their ideas and construct them into a logical and coherent piece of work. After putting down their ideas onto the page, they get the first drafts. Subsequently, they re-examine their drafts and let others read (just like a reader of a published article) with fresh eyes. During this process, students may get feedback from others. Along with feedback, they produce more drafts until they receive satisfactory comments. Finally, with their products being handed in, the teacher will make a more sincere and effective evaluation, from which they can get more insights for the next writing task. The merits of this writing are as followings:

• Process approach is in line with humanistic education.

According to Legutke & Thomas (1991), humanistic education emphasizes that meaningful learning has to be self-initiated, even if stimulus comes from outside, the sense of discovery, the motivation have to come from the inside driven by the basic human desire for self-realization.

Process approach accords with the foregoing argument in the following ways:

a. This approach makes students' learning more meaningful and motivated. Content and meaning are given high priority. Students write purposefully rather than write for writing's sake. The learners will respond to real audience with enthusiasm, and embrace the task as it has a genuine purpose. As is summarized by White & Valerie, "... the overall aim (of process approach) is to create meaningful, purposeful writing tasks that develop the writer's skills over several drafts" (1991).

b. This approach will intrinsically stimulate students' thinking and exploring ability so that they can find out what to write on a given topic. The initial stage of idea generation plays an important role in the whole process, not merely at the beginning. This procedure is highlighted by White, "...idea-generating is particularly important as an initiating process...even in later stages, however, idea-generating continues to take place, so that the techniques used to stimulate ideas at an initial stage may still prove useful" (White & Valerie, 1991: 10). As a matter of fact, students can be seen as creators of language and ideas. "A student who is given the time for the process to work, along with appropriate feedback from readers such as the teacher or other students will discover new ideas, new sentences, and new words as he plans."(Raimes, 1983: 10)

c.　This approach may effectively moderate the students' tension.

In the pre-writing stage, compared with product approach, more time and information are provided in this approach for students through meaningful activities so that they can start without much trouble.

- Process approach adopts a communicative approach in the teaching of writing.

Communicative approach holds the basic assumption that "...the essential purpose of language is communication" (Canale & Swain, 1979: 23). Several guiding principles for communicative approach are proposed by them:

a.　A communicative approach must be based on response to the learner's communication needs;

b.　The second language learner must have the opportunity to take part in meaningful, communicative interaction;

c.　The primary objective must provide the learners with the experience needed to meet their communicative need in the second language.

3) Summary: seeking a balance

There must be a balance between process approach and product approach since too many times of revision are time-consuming and laborious. Above all, the final product is what we ultimately want. Just as Brown (2001: 322) points out, "The new emphasis on process writing must be seen in the perspective of a balance between process and product. Process is not the end; it is the means to an end."

However, as mentioned above, even the combination of product approach and process approach is not sufficient to reflect the trend of teaching writing. The social-theoretical perspective adds new blood: considering not only the writing purpose, but also the readers/ audience before and during the writing process. This new vision makes writing not only interactive between the students themselves and with their teachers, but also between the writers and the readers. A paper is written to be read, so the writer should never forget his or her audience. Above all, the student should identify an audience and develop the paper to reflect the needs and interests of that audience. Such needs include: the level at which the material will be covered, the scope of the coverage, an appropriate writing style, a logical flow of ideas, consistency of form, and a basis in documented fact.

4.3   Trends of writing teaching in classroom

4.3.1 More focus on writing process

The process approach treats all writing as a creative act which requires time and positive feedback to be done well (Stanley, 1999). Since process approach is now an influential force in teaching writing, the following is a detailed observation of it.

1) The changing roles of teacher and student

The teacher moves away from being a marker to a reader, responding to the content of student writing more than the form. Students are encouraged to think about the audience: Who is the writing for? What does this reader need to know? Students also need to realize that what they put down on paper can be changed: Things can be deleted, added, restructured, reorganized, etc.

2) Stages in a process writing approach

- Pre-writing

  The teacher needs to stimulate students' creativity, to get them thinking how to approach a writing topic. The most important thing is the flow of ideas, and the teacher can contribute with advice on how to improve their initial ideas.

- Focusing on ideas

  During this stage, students write without much attention to the accuracy of their work or the organization. The most important feature is meaning. Here, the teacher (or other students) should concentrate on the content of the writing. Is it coherent? Is there anything missing?

- Evaluating, structuring and editing

  At this stage, the writing is adapted to a readership. Students should focus more on form and on producing a finished piece of work. The teacher can help with error correction and give organizational advice.

3) Classroom activities

Here are some ideas for classroom activities related to the stages above:

- *Pre-writing*
  - o Brainstorming: Students are divided into groups to produce ideas about the topic.
  - o Planning: Students make a plan of the writing before they start. These plans can be compared and discussed in groups before writing takes place.
  - o Generating ideas: Discovery tasks such as cubing (students write quickly about the subject in six different ways—they are: 1. describe it; 2. compare it; 3. associate it; 4. analyze it; 5. apply it; 6. argue for or against it.)
  - o Questioning: In groups, students generate questions about the topic. This helps students focus upon audience as they consider what the reader needs to know. The answers to these questions will form the basis to the composition.
  - o Discussion and debate: The teacher helps students with topics, helping them develop ideas in a positive and encouraging way.
- *Focusing on ideas*
  - o Fast writing: The students write quickly on a topic for five to ten minutes without worrying about language or punctuation. Write as quickly as possible and if they cannot think of a word they leave a space or write it in their own language. The important thing is to keep writing. Later this text will be revised.
  - o Group composition: Working together in groups, sharing ideas. This collaborative writing is especially valuable as it involves other skills (speaking in particular).
  - o Varying form: This practice is closely related to genre-based approach: how different text types decide the choice of expressions, grammar, etc. The task can be designed as, for example, how would the text be different if it were written as a letter, or a newspaper article, etc.
- *Evaluating, structuring and editing*
  - o Ordering: Students take the notes written in one of the pre-writing activities above and organize them. What would come first? Why? Here it is good to tell them to start with information known to the reader before moving onto what the reader does not know.
  - o Self-editing: A good writer must learn how to evaluate their own language—to improve through checking their own text, looking

for errors, structure.

o   Peer Editing and proof-reading: Here, the texts are interchanged and the evaluation is done by other students. In the real world, it is common for writers to ask friends and colleagues to check texts for spelling, etc.

4) The importance of feedback

It takes a lot of time and effort to write, and so it is only fair that student writing is responded to suitably. Positive comments can help build students' confidence and create good feeling for the next writing class. It also helps if the reader is more than just the teacher. Class magazines, swapping letters with other classes, etc. can provide an easy solution to providing a real audience.

5) Potential problems

Writing is a complex process and can lead to learner frustration. As with speaking, it is necessary to provide a supportive environment for the students and be patient. Students may react negatively to reworking the same material, but as long as the activities are varied and the objectives clear, then they will usually accept doing so. In the long term, students will start to recognize the value of a process writing approach as their written work improves.

4.3.2 Use peer editing effectively in process writing

Since collaborative writing has become a highlight in the field of English writing, this part is devoted to the importance of peer editing in process writing. Examples and samples are then used to show the application of peer-editing in writing classes of English.

1) Importance of peer editing

Peer editing is a way for students to help each other in the process of writing. It usually follows the first draft of the composition. The most important thing about peer editing is sharing—sharing with others what one has written. This step can be a fascinating experience for students, who step out of themselves to see what they have created through the eyes of the readers. And in turn, they can use the information to improve what they have written.

Beyond creating a powerful environment for collaboration, and encouraging students to think critically about concepts, peer editing also provides a framework for content development and arouses great interest in learning. Each student brings to class unique background knowledge and perspective, as well as a set of preferences for materials of their peers. It's a two-way street. The students can gradually learn to be better writers and also good readers.

2) Methods of peer editing in practice

- Guiding questions

One way to practice peer editing is dividing the students into pairs or small groups and let them edit or proofread one another's composition (usually the first draft). It is better if the teacher gives the pair or the group the same topic for their writing. Questions can be followed after they read through the partners/members' work, guiding them to make critical and constructive comments. Of course, the questions can and should be adapted according to the level of the students. E.g.:

Discuss the idea-generating techniques that you each used to write this composition.

a. What do you think is the theme of the composition? Is it clear?
b. What convincing details does the writer use?
c. Where can the writer add supporting details or ideas to make the composition better?
d. What areas of the composition are not clear?
e. What do you like most about the writing?

- Question table

This method is much of the same as the first method in terms of the contents. But this varied form can add some color to the classroom practice by changing the bare words into charts and for younger students and some pictures and different colors can serve as decoration to make the process more interesting and attractive.

FIGURE 4.8 A question table of peer editing[1]

Peer Editing
This exercise asks you to give detailed feedback to a classmate about his or her essay. Read the essay carefully before you start the exercise, and make sure you have it handy so you can refer to it while answering the questions. Try to be as specific as you can in your comments, using examples from the essay where appropriate.

(to be continued)

---

[1] This example is adapted from http://www. eslmag. com.

1.	What do you like best about the essay?
2.	Do the opening lines grab your attention? Why or why not?
3.	What is the point of the essay? Does the writer develop this point effectively throughout the entire essay?
4.	Are there any places at which you get lost?
5.	Which paragraphs are well developed? Which paragraphs need to be revised? In what ways?
6.	Does the conclusion summarize or point forward? Can you suggest improvements?

- **Think-Aloud and Reader-Response method**

This method is adapted from Janet Giltrow's *Academic Writing* (1995).

In this method, students work in pairs. One (X) reads the other (Y)'s paper aloud while Y sits alongside taking notes. Y does not interject but simply records what the reader reports. Readers only come up with personal reactions and observations during the reading process; writers are the ones to flag problem areas for diagnosis. Only readers should speak. Good sections should also be commented upon.

Here is a possible scenario between Sally (reader) and Keith (writer):

(Sally starts reading and then has trouble with word choice or sentence structure.)

Sally, "I find this phrase is difficult. It made me confused so I had to re-read."

(Keith writes: This section is unclear. Maybe I should reword or explain it better?)

Sally, "I'm not sure of the connection between these sentences. Why are you telling me the second part about the sex education? Do you mean to say the first sentence is the cause of this one?"

(Keith writes: Revision needed. Transition should be clearer.)

Sally, "Okay, from this paragraph, I get the idea that you concentrate on how the female workers were included in the bargaining units and the two important points you want me to carry are..."

(Keith writes: This part works well! She gets what I'm saying!)

And so on.

More often than not, this process will simply confirm problems one already anticipated; other times, it will foreground areas overlooked in one's own revising. The positive commentary of what the reader understands is also a great motivator that what one's saying is coming through.

Of course, there are many other ways to organize peer editing in classroom. As a teacher, various methods or forms can be tried to arouse the students' interest in doing the work and to make the best out of the process.

3) Concerns over peer editing and some suggestions

Some teachers (accustomed to the traditional way of teaching) of ESL in China complain that if peer editing is introduced into the classroom, students will be out of control. These teachers should be reminded of using classroom as a place for free, democratic, and creative thinking. To make the process a fascinating adventure, teachers must give students time and freedom to discover, explore and remedy on their own.

With regard to concerns over the students' technical skills in peer editing, some tips for the work should be provided timely to the students:

a. Be respectful. Give the sort of helpful comments that you would like to receive.

b. Comment with simple and clear questions, such as "What do you mean by this?"

c. Be specific about strengths and weaknesses. "Your transition is weak." is less clear than "How do you connect your first and second paragraphs?" "I don't like this paragraph" is not as helpful as "This introductory paragraph doesn't show me what the main idea of this essay is."

d. You'd better write a list of comments or suggestions according to the natural order of the essay development.

e. Always remember that grammar is not everything. The main focus of a peer editing session is to see that the writer sophistication will make a paper successful.

f. Approach each other as sailors in the same boat. You're here to help each other.

Some teachers worry about the students' language level in fulfilling the task of editing. Actually, teachers can adapt the contents and activities of peer editing according to the students' level. The lower level the students, the easier task they are expected to have. The task requirements and activities can be quite flexible. In order to show this point clear, the next section is an example of college English writing class.

4) A sample of peer editing

The following is a writing prompt and response taken from a seventh grade ESL student in the United States. This material is chosen to a writing section in a college English class.

Writing Prompt: Think about an important event that changed your life style. What happened before the important event? How did you feel before the important event? How did you change because of the important event?

Student Response:

A trip to Ocean Park[1]

One time I went to Hong Kong for a trip. My uncle brought my family and his family to Ocean Park. It was a beautiful amusement park with a lot of entertainment. The best game for me was the roller coaster because it was very excited when I get on the roller coaster I felt very scared and nervous. I was afraid I might fall down! When the roller coaster started moving it was slow. Then it shifted and moved really fast. When the roller coaster went up and turned upside down I felt almost falling. But of course it didn't because I put on the seat belt. It was very dramatic that I never forget. When I get out of the roller coaster I felt very excited. It almost liked losing my spirit. I get lots of fun, indeed. I think riding on the roller coaster is not so scared after all. When I got off the roller coaster I wanted to play again, but a lot of people were standing in line so I didn't want to line up. I went to another place to play. When it is dark my dad and my uncle said "It's time to go home." I asked my dad "Can we came back to play again next time?" My dad answered "Sure we can." My feeling changed from nervous to excited and happy feeling. It's really wonderful!

Requirements of the teacher: we will use Gaudiani's (1981) method to peer edit the student's work. Gaudiani asks classes to read a student's composition in five "passes" to check meaning, style, organization, and overall effectiveness of the writing. The passes could be used over several drafts or one draft of a student's work. The following is an adaptation of Gaudiani's method for each pass:

---

[1] From Chun, K. 2001, Authentic Literacy Assessment of Culturally and Linguistically Diverse Students. www.gse.berkeley.edu, retrieved 23 July 2005.

I. Comprehension of meaning. Students listen as one of them (who is supposed to have written the above passage; if he/she does write one like this, it would be much better) reads it aloud. Class members ask for clarification of any words or expressions that they do not understand during this pass. The class can discuss and work on the parts where the meanings are not clear.

II. Analysis of prose style. After the composition has been revised for meaning, the class reads the piece once again silently, after which they comment on the style (sentence length, repetition of words, lack of precision in vocabulary or expression, etc.). When problems are discovered, the teacher asks for solution from class members.

III. Analysis of organization. Students read the composition a third time, looking now for such things as the use of topic sentences, sufficient evidence to support the topic sentence, logical connections between sentences and paragraphs, and concluding sentences.

IV. Correction of grammar. The teacher reads each sentence of the composition and asks the author and the others in the class to provide any needed grammatical correction.

V. Overview/synthesis. Finally, the class offers general comments on the effectiveness of the composition as a whole in communicating a message.

The process will not be a perfect one, but it shows how the process writing can be organized in a systematic way.

In order to make peer editing really count in process writing, ESL teachers must try to make peer editing an interlocked part of the whole writing process and meanwhile try to keep a balance between the writing process and the final product. Of course, the emphasis is aimed at training the student's writing ability, which means the method must be used flexibly to cultivate the students' potential in writing in English.

4.3.3 Conferencing: An interactive way in process writing

Brender (1998)[1] states that writing is a very personal skill, with each individual having his or her own specific problems. Writing teachers have long acknowledged these problems and have provided feedback to their students. However, many ESL/EFL students find

---

[1] Discussions in this section are quoted and adapted from Alan Brender (1998); for more details, refer to http://www.jalt-publications.org/tlt/files/98/jul/brender.html, retrieved 27 May 2004.

written comments problematic. If a person utilizes a discourse pattern from another language when writing in English, that person's writing is often labeled wordy, lacking coherence, unfocused, or unclear. For instance, Asian students are said to circle around a subject, showing it from a variety of tangential views but will not look directly at it. Consequently, teachers often urge students to "keep to the point", or to provide more details.

Because written comments may prove very difficult for ESL students to comprehend and to act upon, Zamel (1985) recommends that teachers and students carry on a face-to-face dialogue so that "dynamic interchange and negotiation" can take place. Xu (1989) contends that in one-on-one conferences, perceptive teachers can reduce students' anxiety, trace the cause of the problems, and apply strategies for enhancing language acquisition.

1) Types of conferencing

Traditional conferencing involves a short meeting (10-15 minutes) between the student and the teacher. Other forms of conferencing include: collaborative conferencing, small group conferencing, journaling, emailing, and journaling cum emailing.

In **collaborative counseling**, the teacher works individually with students in developing their papers. Marshall (1986) developed her classes around her conferencing sessions, in which she addressed meaning in the composition first, and then form. In the initial conference, students discussed their ideas for papers. In the next conference, students brought their first drafts and discussed them with the teacher. Marshall planned class lessons based on the needs students showed in the conferences. She found this method to be more efficient for the teacher and more effective for the student.

In **small group conferencing**, the teacher meets students in groups of three to ten, often divided according to writing weaknesses. Small group conferencing takes less time and offers students more feedback than regular classes. Group dynamics sometimes help students speak up and discuss their writing problems.

In **journaling**, teachers carry on a dialogue with students by responding to their journal entries. Some writing teachers ask their students to focus their journal writing on development of essay topics and on writing problems. Journaling allows the teacher and student to enter a dialogue. Moreover, students can have significant control over what they wish to discuss. For teachers, this method does not demand as much of their time as conferencing does.

Many teachers have been using **email** to communicate with their students. Cassidy (1996), in a description of a series of email assignments and other writing activities for ESL students, contends that these computer-generated exercises have improved her students' writing. Wang (1996) has combined **e-mailing with journaling** to induce what she contends is effective interaction between student and teacher.

2) Caveats with conferencing

In many ways, one-on-one conferencing is a most advantageous method for ESL students. The teacher or tutor should, however, be aware of the special needs of these students. One serious problem that often occurs in conferencing is that teachers and tutors talk down to their students. Other areas in which students are at a disadvantage in one-on-one discussions include types of questions asked, the length of pauses after questions, turn-taking, and the proportion of time each participant speaks per turn, methods of negotiating meaning, and methods of wielding power. Teachers and tutors need to listen to students more attentively and become more adept at a certain kind of listening in order to establish a non-judgmental setting where there is no penalty for trying out new ideas.

4.4 A checklist for written reports

Concerning writing, it is important to check the final product. The following is an example checklist that might be used when evaluating student papers. The student should consider such basic criteria when preparing written communications[1].

---

[1] Adapted from http://www.etsu.edu/scitech/langskil/reports.htm#LabRpts-Tech, retrieved 20 Aug. 2004.

FIGURE 4.9 A Checklist for Written Reports

Author:

Title:

Reviewer:

Organization (30%):	Poor		Avg.	Excellent	
The introduction gains the reader's attention and leads smoothly to the thesis.	1	2	3	4	5
The introduction includes a satisfactory purpose or thesis statement.	1	2	3	4	5
The body is structured and organized appropriately (weighted 2X).	2	4	6	8	10
There are adequate transitions between paragraphs and from topic to topic.	1	2	3	4	5
There is a definite conclusion and/or action statement.	1	2	3	4	5
Content and Sources (35%):					
The subject is appropriate, significant, and is presented in an interesting way (weighted 2X).	2	4	6	8	10
There is sufficient supporting material to adequately develop and clarify the subject (2X).	2	4	6	8	10
Each sub-topic or paragraph is adequately developed.	1	2	3	4	5
Material from sources is smoothly integrated with original commentary.	1	2	3	4	5
Sources are appropriately documented.	1	2	3	4	5
Grammar and Layout (35%):					
The work is free from errors in spelling (2X).	2	4	6	8	10
The work is free from errors in grammar (2X).	2	4	6	8	10
The work is free from errors in punctuation.	1	2	3	4	5
The paper is neat and orderly with correct margins, typefaces, figures, tables, etc. (2X)	2	4	6	8	10

Total score out of a possible 100 points:

Comments:

5. Teaching of grammar and vocabulary

So far in this chapter, the teaching of four language skills has been discussed. In ELT, we need also to consider the teaching of grammar and vocabulary. In this part, the issue of teaching grammar is tackled first, followed by the teaching of vocabulary.

Grammar teaching, for long, has been a core of foreign language teaching. For centuries, in fact, the dominating activity of language classroom was the study of grammar and words. However, the twentieth century, especially the 1950s onward, has changed all that dramatically. During the late 1960s and the early 1970s in the US, for instance, education went through a period where the teaching of grammar was thought to be stifling to creativity. Nowadays, language teachers are often confused by a swarm of mixed messages about the place of grammar and vocabulary in the communicative language classroom. Can we teach grammar in our classroom teaching? Or should it just be absorbed without direct teachings? How should we teach vocabulary?

The above questions are raised by Brown in his book—*Teaching by Principles: An Interactive Approach to Language Pedagogy*. In the following, we will have a detailed look at these questions.

5.1　Introduction to the teaching of grammar

Grammar is commonly defined as a system of rules governing the conventional arrangement and relationship of words in a sentence. Specifically, it is a branch of linguistics dealing with the form and structure of words (morphology) and their interrelation in sentences (syntax). The study of grammar reveals how language works.

5.1.1 Various schools of grammar [1]

1) Prescriptive grammar

The prescriptive grammar is also called *normative*, because it defines the role of the various parts of speech and purports to tell what is the norm, or rule, of "correct" usage. Prescriptive grammars state how words and sentences are to be put together in a language so that the speaker will be perceived as having good grammar. When people are said to have good grammar or bad grammar, the inference is that they obey or ignore the rules of accepted usage associated with the language they speak.

2) Historical contrastive grammar

Language-specific, prescriptive grammar is only one way to look at word and sentence formation in language. Other grammarians are primarily interested in the changes in word and sentence construction in a language over the years, for example, how Old English, Middle

---

[1] Adapted from http://www.homeschoolingplus.com/the-importance-of-grammar.aspx, retrieved 13 May, 2005.

English, and Modern English differ from one another. This approach is known as *historical grammar*. Some grammarians seek to establish the differences or similarities in words and word order in various languages. Thus, specialists in comparative grammar study use sound and meaning correspondence among languages to determine their relationship to one another. By looking at similar forms in related languages, grammarians can discover how different languages may have influenced one another.

3) Systemic functional grammar

Grammarians represented by Halliday look at grammar from a very different angle: how words, choice of words and their arrangement are used in social contexts to get messages across; to fulfill various functions. According to Halliday, language has three basic functions—ideational function, interpersonal function and textual function. In social life, the real utterances people choose to use not only depend on the speakers' mastery of the constructional knowledge of a language, but also on the purpose of using the utterance, the power relationship and distance between the speakers, and the situations of communication. Systemic functional grammar has been developed by Halliday's followers and been used extensively in fields like discourse analysis and genre study.

4) Descriptive Grammar

Some grammarians are more concerned with determining how the meaningful arrangement of the basic word-building units (morphemes) and sentence-building units (constituents) can best be described. This approach is called *descriptive grammar*. Descriptive grammars contain actual speech forms recorded from native speakers of a particular language and represented by means of written symbols. Descriptive grammars indicate what languages—often those never before written down or otherwise recorded—are like structurally.

5) The transformational-generative grammar

The above types of grammar constitute a part of linguistics that is distinct from phonology (the linguistic study of sound) and semantics (the linguistic study of meaning or content). Grammar to the prescriptivist, historian, comparativist, functionalist, and descriptivist is then the organizational part of language—how speech is put together, how words and sentences are formed, and how messages are communicated.

Transformational-generative grammarians, spearheaded by Chomsky, approach grammar quite differently as a theory of language. By TG grammar, these scholars mean the knowledge human beings have that allows them to acquire any language. Such a grammar is a kind of universal grammar, an analysis of the principles underlying all the various human grammars.

5.1.2 Grammar study through the ages

The study of grammar was first made by the ancient Greeks. With the study of grammar, Greeks developed "rhetoric" which helped them engage in logical philosophical speculation and discussion about languages.

The study of grammar was passed down quickly from the Greeks to the Romans, who translated the Greek names for the parts of speech into their own Latin; many of these Latin terms such as "nominative", "accusative" and "dative" are still used in modern grammar lessons. But the Greeks and Romans were unable to figure out how languages were related to one another. This linguistic predicament wasn't tackled until the early 20th century when Renaissance grammarians began to describe languages on their own terms—a study that was called "comparative grammar". Although grammar teaching experienced ups and downs in the past century, today, grammarians worldwide carry on the task and make further, deeper and wider studies on grammar and its related fields and subjects.

5.1.3 Grammar teaching: challenging the myths

Grammar is often misunderstood in the field of language teaching. The misconception roots from the view that grammar is a collection of arbitrary rules about static structures in the language (Larsen-Freeman, 1997). Further questionable claims are that the structures do not have to be taught, learners will acquire them on their own, or if the structures are taught, the lessons that ensue will be boring. Consequently, communicative and proficiency-based teaching approaches sometimes unduly limit grammar instruction. Of the many claims about grammar that deserve to be called myths, Larsen-Freeman challenges ten (Larsen-Freeman, 1997).

1) Grammar is acquired naturally; it need not to be taught.

It is true that some learners acquire second language grammar naturally without instruction. This is especially true of young immigrants to English speaking countries. However, this is not true for all learners. Among the same immigrant groups are learners who may achieve a degree of proficiency, but whose English is far from accurate. A more important question may be whether it is possible with instruction to help learners who cannot achieve accuracy in English on their own.

It is also true that learning particular grammatical distinctions requires a great deal of time even for the most skilled learners. Chomsky (1969) showed that native English speakers were still in the process of acquiring certain grammatical structures in English well into adolescence. Thus, another important question is whether it is possible to accelerate students' natural learning of grammar through instruction. Research findings can be brought to bear on this question from a variety of sources (see Larsen-Freeman & Long, 1991). Pienemann (1984) demonstrated that subjects who received grammar instruction progressed to the next stage after a two-week period, a passage normally taking several months in untutored development.

With regard to whether instruction can help learners acquire grammar they would not have learned on their own, some research points to the value of form-focused instruction to improve learners' accuracy over what normally transpires when there is no focus on form (Larsen-Freeman, 1995).

2) Grammar is a collection of meaningless forms.

This myth may have arisen because many people associate the term grammar with verb paradigms and rules about linguistic form. However, grammar is not unidimensional and not meaningless; it embodies the three dimensions of morphosyntax (form), semantics (meaning), and pragmatics (use). These dimensions are interdependent; a change in one results in change in another. Despite their interdependence, however, they each offer a unique perspective on grammar.

Consider the passive voice in English. It clearly has form. It is composed minimally of a form of the "be" verb and the past participle. Sometimes it has the preposition "by" before the agent in the predicate: (a) "The store was robbed by the same gang that robbed a bank last week." That the passive can occur only when the main verb is transitive is also part of its formal description.

The passive has a grammatical meaning. It is a focus construction, which confers a different status on the receiver or recipient of an action than it would receive in the active voice. For example, the store in sentence (a) is differently focused than it would be in the active sentence: (b) "The same gang robbed the store."

When or why do we use the passive? When the receiver of the action is the theme or topic, when we do not know who the agent is, when we wish to deliberately conceal the identity of the agent, when the agent is obvious and easily derivable from the context, when the agent is redundant, and so on.

To use the English passive voice accurately, meaningfully, and appropriately, students must master all three dimensions. This is true of any grammatical structure.

3) Grammar consists of arbitrary rules.

While there is some synchronic arbitrariness to grammar, not all of what is deemed arbitrary is so. If one adopts a broad enough perspective, it is possible to see why things are the way they are. Consider the following sentences: (c) "There is the book missing." (d) "There is a book missing."

Grammar books will say that sentence (c) is ungrammatical because sentences with existential "there" almost always take an indefinite noun phrase in the predicate. Why? The reason is not arbitrary. "There" is used to introduce new information, and the preferred position for new information is toward the end of a sentence. A noun phrase that contains new information is marked by the use of the indefinite article, "a" or "an", if it is a singular common noun, as in sentence.

4) Grammar is boring.

This myth is derived from the impression that grammar can only be taught through repetition and other rote drills. Teaching grammar does not mean asking students to repeat models in a mindless way, and it does not mean memorizing rules. Such activities can be boring and do not necessarily teach grammar. Of course, this does not mean there is no place for drills, but drills should be used in a meaningful and purposeful way. For example, to practice past-tense yes/no sentences in English, the teacher may ask the students to close their eyes while he/she changes five things about him/herself. He/She takes off one shoe, takes off his/her watch, puts on his/her glasses, puts on his/her sweater, and takes off his/her ring. Students are then asked to pose questions to figure out the changes he/she has made. Students may ask, "Did you take off a shoe?" or "Did you put on a sweater?" This kind of activity can be fun and, more importantly, engages students in a way that requires them to think and not just provide mechanical responses. Teaching grammar in a way that engages students may require creativity, but the teaching need not and should not be boring.

5) Students have different learning styles. Not all students can learn grammar.

Research shows that some people have a more analytical learning style than others. According to Hatch (1974), some learners approach the language learning task as "rule formers". Such learners are accurate but halting users of the target language. Others are what Hatch calls "data gatherers", fluent but inaccurate producers of the target language. This observation by itself does not address whether or not all students can learn grammar. While it may be true that learners approach language learning differently, there has been no research to show that some students are incapable of learning grammar. Students have different strengths and weaknesses. It is clear that all students can learn grammar as is evident from their mastery of their first language. As grammar is no different from anything else, it is likely that students will learn at different rates.

6) Grammar structures are learned one at a time.

This myth is demonstrably untrue. Teachers may teach one grammar structure at a time, and students may focus on one at a time, but students do not master one at a time before going on to learn another. There is a constant interaction between new inter-language forms and old. Students may give the appearance of having learned the present tense, for example, but when the present progressive is introduced, often their mastery vanishes and their performance declines. This backsliding continues until the grammar they have internalized is restructured to reflect the distinct uses of the two tenses. We know that the learning curve for grammatical structures is not a smoothly ascending linear one, but rather is characterized by peaks and valleys, backslidings and restructurings.

7) Grammar has to do only with sentence-level and subsentence-level phenomena.

Grammar does operate at the sentence level and governs the syntax or word orders that are permissible in the language. It also works at the subsentence level to govern such things as number and person agreement between subject and verb in a sentence. However, grammar rules also apply at the suprasentential or discourse level.

For example, not every choice between the use of the past and the present perfect tense can be explained at the sentence level. Often, the speaker's choice to use one or the other can only be understood by examining the discourse context. Similarly, use of the definite article with a particular noun phrase after the noun phrase has been introduced in a text is a discourse-governed phenomenon. It would be a mistake to teach students grammar only at the sentence and subsentence levels. Much of the apparent arbitrariness of grammar disappears when it is viewed from a discourse-level perspective.

8) Grammar and vocabulary are areas of knowledge. Reading, writing, speaking, and listening are the four skills.

While grammar can be thought of as static knowledge, it can also be considered a process. Language teachers would not be content if their students could recite all the rules of grammar but not be able to apply them. The goal is for students to be able to use grammar in an unselfconscious fashion to achieve their communicative ends. As with any skill, achieving this goal takes practice.

Ellis (1993) postulates that structural syllabi work better to facilitate intake than to teach learners to produce grammatical items correctly. He suggests that grammar teaching should focus on consciousness raising rather than on the practice of accurate production.

9) Grammars provide the rules/explanations for all the structures in a language.

Explaining why things are the way they are is an ongoing quest. Because languages evolve, linguists' descriptions can never be complete for all time; they have to accommodate the changing nature of language. For example, most grammar books make clear the fact that progressive aspect is not used with stative verbs; therefore, the following would be ungrammatical: (e) "I am wanting a new car." For some English speakers, the sentence is not ungrammatical, and even those who find it so would be more inclined to accept progressive aspect when it co-occurs with perfective aspect, as in : (f) "I have been wanting a new car" (for some time now).

The point is, languages change, and any textbook rule should be seen as subject to change and non-categorical. Just as grammar learning is a process—witness the persistent instability of inter-languages—so is grammar itself.

10) "I don't know enough to teach grammar."

Teachers often say this when they have opted to teach one of the other language skills, or when they choose to teach a low-proficiency class. While it is true that teachers can only teach what they know, teachers who articulate the above often know more than they think they do.

If the goals of language instruction include teaching students to use grammar accurately, meaningfully, and appropriately, then a compelling case can be made for teaching grammar. Instead of viewing grammar as a static system of arbitrary rules, it should be seen as a rational, dynamic system that is comprised of structures characterized by the three dimensions of form, meaning, and use.

5.1.4 To teach or not to teach grammar—no longer the question?

With Larsen-Freeman's challenges of the myths, it seems that to teach or not to teach grammar should no longer be the question. Without grammar, words hang together without any real meaning or sense. In order to be able to speak a language to some degree of proficiency and to be able to say what we really want to say, we need to have some grammatical knowledge. By teaching grammar we not only give our students the means to express themselves, but we also fulfill their expectations of what learning a foreign language involves.

However, the fact is even under the rush of "communicative language teaching"—communication first, meaning first, when mentioning grammar, many English teachers are still holding fast the notion of *prescriptive* grammar, thus producing a feeling of repelling. No wonder because grammar used to be taught as a discrete set of rigid rules to be memorized, practiced, and followed. During the height of the whole language movement, when teaching grammar in isolation became taboo, many teachers were left frustrated and baffled by the lack of grammar instruction in the classroom (Janice Christ)[1].

With the development of English educology and the emergence of more balanced teaching approaches (like task-based language teaching), more and more English teachers have begun to join the profession embracing ideas of *descriptive* grammar. These teachers believed that grammar instruction should be matched to the purpose of the user. Teachers found descriptive grammar theories to be more

---

[1] Janice Christy. http://www.glencoe.com/sec/teachingtoday/subject/to_teach.phtml, retrieved 14 Mar. 2004.

flexible, reflecting actual usage and self-expression over "correct" structures. Some people credit the descriptive approach with a general loosening of rules regarding grammatical structures.

If viewing the language teaching practice as a clock pendulum, behind the swing back to more attention on grammar teaching hides another reason. With the widespread institution of standards and high-stakes tests, students are expected to recognize and use correct grammar. Educators can no longer afford to assume that students acquire an accurate understanding of formal language structures through reading, writing, and speaking. Moreover, they also cannot assume that prescriptive or descriptive approaches, in isolation, are singularly effective. Rather, English teachers must embrace the notion that grammar instruction, like any other content area, should reflect current pedagogical approaches. Grammar instruction should be tailor-made to meet the needs of students, and should weave both prescriptive and descriptive practices into relevant, meaningful instruction.

5.2   Fundamentals of grammar teaching

5.2.1 Goals and techniques for teaching grammar

The ultimate goal of grammar instruction is to enable students to carry out their communication purposes. This goal has three implications[1]:

- Students need overt instruction that connects grammar points with larger communication contexts.
- Students do not need to master every aspect of each grammar point, only those that are relevant to the immediate communication task.
- Error correction is not always the instructor's first responsibility.

Overt Grammar Instruction

Older and adult students appreciate and benefit from direct instruction that allows them to apply critical thinking skills to language learning. Instructors can take advantage of this by providing explanations that give students a descriptive understanding of each point of grammar.

---

[1] Adapted from http://www.nclrc.org/essentials/grammar.htm, retrieved 24 Aug. 2004.

- Teach the grammar point in the target language or the students' first language or both. The goal is to facilitate understanding.
- Limit the time of grammar explanations, especially for younger and lower level students whose ability to sustain attention can be limited.
- Present grammar points in written and oral ways to address the needs of students with different learning styles.

An important part of grammar instruction is providing examples. Teachers need to plan their examples carefully around two basic principles:

- Be sure the examples are accurate and appropriate. They must present the language appropriately, be culturally appropriate for the setting in which they are used, and be to the point of the lesson.
- Use the examples as teaching tools. Focus examples on a particular theme or topic so that students have more contact with specific information and vocabulary.

Relevance of Grammar Instruction

In the communicative competence model, the purpose of learning grammar is to learn the language of which the grammar is a part. Instructors therefore teach grammar forms and structures in relation to meaning and use for the specific communication tasks that students need to complete.

The following is the communicative competence model for teaching the English past tense[1]:

- Distribute two short narratives about recent experiences or events, each one to half of the class.
- Teach the regular -*ed* form, using verbs that occur in the texts as examples. Teach the pronunciation and doubling rules if those forms occur in the texts.
- Teach the irregular verbs that occur in the texts.
- Students read the narratives and ask questions about points they don't understand.
- Students work in pairs in which one member has read Story A and the other Story B. Students interview one another; using the information from the interview, they then write up or orally repeat the story they have not read.

---

[1] Adapted from http://www.nclrc.org/, retrieved 26 July 2005.

Error Correction

At all proficiency levels, learners produce language that is not exactly the language used by native speakers. Some of the differences are grammatical, while others involve vocabulary selection and mistakes in the selection of language appropriate for different contexts.

In responding to student communication, teachers need to be careful not to focus on error correction to the extent of the detriment of communication and confidence building. Teachers should be skillful in letting students know when they are making errors so that they can work on improving. Teachers also need to build students' confidence in their ability to use the language by focusing on the content of their communication rather than the grammatical form.

Teachers can use error correction to support language acquisition, and avoid using it in ways that undermine students' desire to communicate in the language, by taking cues from context.

- When students are doing structured output activities that focus on development of new language skills, use error correction to guide them.

Example:

Student *(in class)*: I buy a new MP4 yesterday.

Teacher: You *bought* a new MP4 yesterday. Remember, the past tense of buy is "bought".

- When students are engaged in communicative activities, correct errors only if they interfere with comprehensibility. Respond using correct forms, but without stressing them.

Example:

Student *(greeting teacher)*: I buy a new camera yesterday!

Teacher: You bought a new camera? That's exciting! What kind?

5.2.2 Strategies for learning grammar

Language teachers and learners are often frustrated by the disconnection between knowing the rules of grammar and being able to apply those rules automatically in listening, speaking, reading, and writing. This disconnection reflects a separation between declarative knowledge and procedural knowledge.

- Declarative knowledge is knowledge about something. Declarative knowledge enables a student to describe a rule of grammar and apply it in pattern practice drills.
- Procedural knowledge is knowledge of how to do something. Procedural knowledge enables a student to apply a rule of grammar in communication.

Procedural knowledge does not translate automatically into declarative knowledge; many native speakers can use their language clearly and correctly without being able to state the rules of its grammar. Likewise, declarative knowledge does not translate automatically into procedural knowledge; students may be able to state a grammar rule, but consistently fail to apply the rule when speaking or writing.

To address the declarative knowledge/procedural knowledge dichotomy, teachers and students can apply several strategies.

1) Link knowledge needs with learning goals

Identify the relationship of declarative knowledge and procedural knowledge to learner goals for learning the language. Students can have tilted choices according to specific considerations like their career expectations.

2) Apply higher order thinking skills

Recognize that development of declarative knowledge can accelerate development of procedural knowledge. Teaching students how the language works and giving them opportunities to compare it with other languages they know allows them to draw on critical thinking and analytical skills. These processes can support the development of the innate understanding that characterizes procedural knowledge.

3) Provide plentiful, appropriate language input

Understand that students develop both procedural and declarative knowledge on the basis of the input they receive. This input includes both finely tuned input that requires students to pay attention to the relationships among form, meaning, and use for a specific grammar rule, and roughly tuned input that allows students to encounter the grammar rule in a variety of contexts.

4) Use schema knowledge to predict

Different communication situations or discourse types are characterized with different clusters of linguistic features common to those types. Verb tense and aspect, sentence length and structure, and larger discourse patterns all may contribute to the distinctive profile of a given communication type. For example, a history textbook and a newspaper article in English both use past tense verbs almost exclusively. However, the newspaper article will use short sentences and a discourse pattern that alternates between subjects or perspectives. The history textbook will use complex sentences and will follow a timeline in its discourse structure. Awareness of these features allows students to anticipate the forms and structures they will encounter in a given communication task.

5) Limit expectations for drills or rote learning

- Mechanical drills can help students memorize irregular forms and challenging structures. However, students do not develop the ability to use grammar correctly in oral and written interactions by doing mechanical drills, because these drills separate form from meaning and use.

- In contrast, communicative drills encourage students to connect form, meaning, and use because multiple correct responses are possible. In communicative drills, students respond to a prompt using the grammar point under consideration, but providing their own content. For example, to practice questions and answers in the past tense in a communicative way[1]:

Teacher: Did you go to the English corner last night?

Student 1: No, I didn't. I went to the movies. (to Student 2): Did you finish *Tom and Jerry*?

Student 2: Yes, I read it, but I didn't understand some part of it. (to Student 3): Did you understand *Tom and Jerry*?

Student 3: I read a few pages. I went to the movie last night.

5.2.3 Developing classroom grammar activities

When designing grammar activities for classroom, instructors need to make sure that grammar is taught in context, in discourse, and in communication to maintain students' interest.

For curricula that introduce grammatical forms in a specified sequence, instructors need to develop activities that relate form to meaning and use.

- Describe the grammar point, including form, meaning, and use, and give examples (structured input)
- Ask students to practice the grammar point in communicative drills
- Have students do a communicative task that provides opportunities to use the grammar point

---

[1] Adapted from http://www.nclrc.org, retrieved 26 July 2005.

For curricula that follow a sequence of topics, instructors need to develop activities that relate the topical discourse (use) to meaning and form.

- Provide oral or written input (audiotape, reading selection) that addresses the topic (structured input)
- Review the point of grammar, using examples from the material (structured input)
- Ask students to practice the grammar point in communicative drills that focus on the topic (structured output)
- Have students do a communicative task on the topic (communicative output)

When instructors have the opportunity to develop part or all of the course curriculum, they can develop a series of contexts based on the real world tasks that students will need to perform using the language, and then teach grammar and vocabulary in relation to those contexts.

For instance, students who plan to travel will need to understand public address announcements in airports and train stations. Instructors can use audio-taped simulations to provide input; teach the grammatical forms that typically occur in such announcements; and then have students practice by asking and answering questions about what was announced.

5.2.4 Making use of textbook grammar activities

Textbooks are what most language teachers follow in teaching grammar. Textbooks usually provide one or more of the following three types of grammar exercises.

- Mechanical drills: Each prompt has only one correct response, and students can complete the exercise without attending to meaning.
- Meaningful drills: Each prompt has only one correct response, and students must attend to meaning to complete the exercise.
- Communicative drills: The prompt or question is life-oriented, and open-ended and students can have their own answers in line with their understanding.

To use textbook grammar exercises effectively, instructors need to recognize which type they are, devote the appropriate amount of time to them, and supplement them as needed.

Recognizing Types

Before the teaching term begins, inventory the textbook to see which type(s) of drills it provides. Decide which you will use in class, which you will assign as homework, and which you will skip.

Assigning Time

When deciding which textbook drills to use and how much time to allot to them, keep their relative value in mind.

- Mechanical drills are the least useful because they bear little resemblance to real communication. They do not require students to learn anything; they only require parroting of a pattern or rule.
- Meaningful drills can help students develop understanding of the workings of rules of grammar because they require students to make form-meaning correlations. Their resemblance to real communication is limited by the fact that they have only one correct answer.
- Communicative drills require students to be aware of the relationships among form, meaning, and use. In communicative drills, students test and develop their ability to use language to convey ideas and information.

Supplementing

In case that the textbook provides few or no meaningful and communicative drills, instructors may want to create some to substitute for mechanical drills.

5.3 Planning a grammar lesson

The example of grammar lesson planning is adapted from Tanya Cotter (2005)[1] from the British Council. Tanya presents a grammar teaching model in the form of PPP (Presentation, Practice, Production). With the emphasis on a communicative approach and a wealth of stimulating resources, teaching grammar does not necessarily mean endless conjugation of verbs or grammar translation; Tanya shows us this in the PPP model.

First, let's take a look at the deductive approach and inductive approach.

- A deductive approach is when the rule is presented and the language is produced based on the rule. (The teacher gives the rule.)
- An inductive approach is when the rule is inferred through some form of guided discovery. (The teacher gives the students a means to discover the rule for themselves.)

---

[1] http://www.teachingenglish.org.uk/think/methodology/grammar.shtml, retrieved 26 Nov. 2005.

In other words, the former is more teacher-centered and the latter more learner-centered. Both approaches have their advantages and disadvantages. According to Tanya, the deductive approach is time saving and allows more time for practicing the language items thus making it an effective approach with lower level students. The inductive approach, on the other hand, is often more beneficial to students who already have a base in the language as it encourages them to work things out for themselves based on their existing knowledge.

Then, let's come to the PPP model.

A deductive approach often fits into a lesson structure known as PPP (Presentation, Practice, Production). The teacher presents the target language and then gives students the opportunity to practice it through very controlled activities. The final stage of the lesson gives the students the opportunity to practice the target language in freer activities that bring in other language elements.

In a 60-minute grammar class, Tanya allocates each stage approximately 20 minutes.

Presentation

In this stage the teacher presents the new language in a meaningful context. I (Tanya) find that building up stories on the board, using realia or flashcards and miming are fun ways to present the language.

For example, when presenting the subjunctive conditional, I often draw a picture of myself with thought bubbles of lots of money, a sports car, a big house and a world map.

- I ask my students what I'm thinking about and then introduce the target language. E.g. *"If I had a lot of money, I would buy a sports car and a big house."*
- I practice and drill the sentence orally before writing it on the board (positive, negative, question and short answer).
- I then focus on form by asking the students questions. E.g. *"What do we use after 'if'?"* and on meaning by asking the students questions to check that they have understood the concept (E.g. *"Do I have lots of money?"* No." *What am I doing?"* Imagining.)
- When I am satisfied that my students understand the form and the meaning, I move on to the practice stage of the lesson. During this stage of the lesson it is important to correct phonological and grammatical mistakes.

Practice

There are numerous activities which can be used for this stage including gap filling exercises, substitution drills, sentence transformations, split sentences, picture dictations, class questionnaires, reordering sentences and matching sentences to pictures.

- It is important that the activities are fairly controlled at this stage as students have only just met the new language. Many student's books and workbooks have exercises and activities which can be used at this stage.
- When teaching the subjunctive conditional, I would use split sentences as a controlled practice activity. I give students lots of sentence halves and in pairs they try and match the beginnings and ends of the sentences. E.g. *"If I won the lottery," ... "I'd travel around the world."*
- I would then do a communicative follow up game using the same sentence halves.

Production

Again there are numerous activities for this stage and what you choose will depend on the language you are teaching and on the level of your students. However, information gaps, role plays, interviews, simulations, finding someone who spots the differences between two pictures, picture cues, problem solving, personalization activities and board games are all meaningful activities which give students the opportunity to practice the language more freely.

- When teaching the subjunctive conditional, I would try to personalize the lesson at this stage by giving students a list of question prompts to ask others in the class.
- Although the questions are controlled the students are given the opportunity to answer more spontaneously using other language items and thus the activity becomes much less predictable.
- It is important to monitor and make a note of any errors so that you can build in class feedback and error analysis at the end of the lesson.

Tanya concludes the explanation by offering suggestions: When teaching grammar, there are several factors we need to take into consideration and the following are some of the questions we should ask ourselves:

- How useful and relevant is the language?
- What other language do my students need to know in order to learn the new structure effectively?

- What problems might my students face when learning the new language?
- How can I make the lesson fun, meaningful and memorable?

It is important to note that using the PPP model does not necessarily exclude using a more inductive approach since some form of learner-centered guided discovery could be built into the presentation stage.

PPP is one model for planning a lesson. Other models include TTT (Test, Teach, Test), ARC (Authentic use, Restricted use, Clarification and focus) and ESA (Engage, Study, Activate). All models have their advantages and disadvantages and teachers should use different models depending on such factors as the lesson, proficiency and learner styles.

5.4   Introduction to the teaching of vocabulary

5.4.1 Overall picture

Vocabulary instruction has been one of the most misunderstood aspects of language teaching. Research shows that most teachers deal with vocabulary in a haphazard and rather unprincipled way, and most teachers leave the selection of vocabulary to the course books (Waring, 2001)[1].

Traditionally, the teaching of vocabulary above elementary levels was mostly incidental, limited to presenting new items as they appeared in reading or sometimes listening texts. This indirect teaching of vocabulary assumes that vocabulary expansion will happen through the practice of other language skills, which has been proved not enough to ensure vocabulary expansion.

Today, it is widely accepted that vocabulary teaching should be part of the syllabus, and taught in a well-planned and regular basis. Lewis (1993) argues that vocabulary should be at the centre of language teaching, because "language consists of grammaticalized lexis, not lexicalised grammar". The importance of vocabulary can similarly be seen from comments as follows[2]:

"Without grammar very little can be conveyed; without vocabulary nothing can be conveyed." (Wilkins, 1972: 111)

---

[1] http://www1.harenet.ne.jp/~waring/papers/eltnews.html, retrieved 15 May 2005.
[2] Adapted from http://www.auburn.edu/~nunnath/, retrieved 24 May 2005.

"When students travel, they don't carry grammar books, they carry dictionaries." (Krashen in Lewis, 1993: iii)

"The more one considers the matter, the more reasonable it seems to suppose that lexis is where we need to start from, the syntax needs to be put to the service of words and not the other way round." (Widdowson in Lewis, 1993: 115)

Luckily enough for language teachers and learners, not all English words need to be learned. This is very important because it means that EVERYTHING we do as vocabulary teachers has to be focused on:

a) building the learner's "start up" or initial vocabulary, and

b) developing the learner's understanding of what learning words means, and

c) showing the learner how to learn the words effectively.

The ultimate aim, of course, is to develop the learners as independent word learners.

5.4.2 What to learn about vocabulary

FIGURE 4.10 Three factors of vocabulary[1]

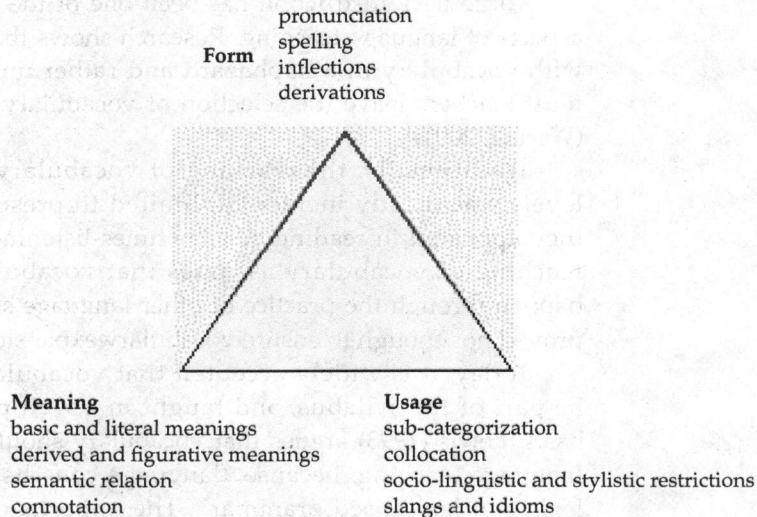

Form
pronunciation
spelling
inflections
derivations

Meaning
basic and literal meanings
derived and figurative meanings
semantic relation
connotation

Usage
sub-categorization
collocation
socio-linguistic and stylistic restrictions
slangs and idioms

From the chart we can see in vocabulary teaching and learning, there are basically three factors, namely, form, meaning and usage. To be specific, instructors of vocabulary need to consider the following

---

[1] The chart is from http://www.auburn.edu/~nunnath/engl6240/tvocabul.html. Retrieved 11 Apr. 2006

aspects (adapted from Gairns and Redman, 1986):

- *Boundaries between conceptual meaning*: knowing not only what lexis refers to, but also where the boundaries are that separate it from words of related meaning (e.g. cup, mug, bowl).
- *Pronunciation*: ability to recognise and reproduce items in speech. A word might have two opposites: the opposite of *short* might be *long* or *tall*, depending on whether we are referring to a person's hair or a person's height.
- *Polysemy*: distinguishing between the various meanings of a single word form with several but closely related meanings (e.g. head: of a person, of a pin, of an organisation).
- *Homonymy*: distinguishing between the various meanings of a single word form with several meanings which are NOT closely related (e.g. a file: used to put papers in or a tool).
- *Homophyny*: understanding words that have the same pronunciation but different spellings and meanings (e.g. flour, flower).
- *Synonymy*: distinguishing between the different shades of meaning that synonymous words have (e.g. huge, titanic, colossal).
- *Antonymy*: knowing words that are opposite to each other in meaning.
- *Affective meaning*: distinguishing between the attitudinal and emotional factors (denotation and connotation), which depend on the speakers' attitude or the situation. Socio-cultural association of lexical items is another important factor.
- *Style, register, dialect*: being able to distinguish between different levels of formality, the effect of different contexts and topics, as well as differences in geographical variation.
- *Translation*: awareness of certain differences and similarities between the native and the foreign language (e.g. false cognates).
- *Chunks of language*: multi-word verbs, idioms, strong and weak collocations, lexical phrases.
- *Grammar of vocabulary*: learning the rules that enable students to build up different forms of the word or even different words from that word (e.g. sleep, slept, sleeping; able, unable, disability).
- *Superordinates*: providing examples of words as they naturally occur in the frame, "X, Y and other/similar/related Zs" is a better way to provide hyponyms and superordinates for words.
- *Word families*: a word like *grower* is regularly derived from the verb grow, and it has other forms like grows, grew, grown,

growing. All these related words form a family.

Admittedly, the above-mentioned knowledge on vocabulary should be based on the fundamentals in morphology: the formation of words (morphemes, roots, prefixes, suffixes, borrowing, inflection, combination, etc.), the collocations, etc. We all know "human" is a word, but is "human being" one word, or two? How about "all in all" and "the day after tomorrow", and "of course"? Words are almost never found in isolation; they have partners that together form meanings in certain restricted ways. For example, we say a "beautiful woman" but not usually a "beautiful man". The same goes for "black and white" (not "white and black"), or "up and down" (not "down and up"). These collocations are very important for learners. If learners do not know these word relationships then they might sound strange and say things like "weak cheese" (mild cheese).

And another implication of the aspects mentioned is that the goals of vocabulary teaching must be more than simply covering a certain number of words on a word list. We must use teaching techniques that can help realise this global concept of what it means to know a lexical item. And we must also go beyond that, giving learner opportunities to use the items learnt and also helping them to use effective written storage systems.

5.4.3 Which words to learn?

Scholars in vocabulary studies have varying views on choices and numbers of words to learn to be effective in communication.

Some research shows that learners need about 3000 "word families" to be good at English (Waring, 1999). Teachers should concentrate on the most frequent and useful words first, as it is these words that the learners will meet very often. Many teachers, however, focus on rarer words assuming that the basic words like "get", "make" and "bring" are known. But it is these words that are among the most troublesome, with their multiple meanings and idiomatic uses. Therefore, teachers and learners should work hard on the highly frequent words.

The following table from Nation and Newton (1997: 239) shows the number of words needed for effective communication in L2[1].

---

[1] See http://www.auburn.edu, retrieved 9 Jun. 2005.

FIGURE 4.11 The number of words needed for effective communication in L2

Level	Number of Words	Text Coverage(%)
High-frequency words	2,000	87
Academic vocabulary	800	8
Technical vocabulary	2,000	3
Total to be learned	4,800	98
Low-frequency words	123,200	2
Total	128,000	100

FIGURE 4.12 Some criteria for selecting vocabularies

Criteria	Definition
Range	The extent to which a word occurs in the different types of texts
Coverage	The capacity of a word to replace other words
Frequency	The number of occurrences of a word in the target language
Learnability	The extent to which a word can be learned without difficulty
Language needs	The extent to which a word is regarded as "required" by the learner in order to communicate

5.5   Strategies and methods of vocabulary teaching (learning)

5.5.1 Memory and storage systems

In general psychology and psycholinguistics, we often come across such terms as working memory, short-term memory and long-term memory. Understanding how our memory works might help us create more effective ways to teach vocabulary. Research in the area offers us some insights into this process.

It seems that learning new items involves storing them first in our short-term memory, and afterwards in the long-term memory. We do not control this process consciously but there seems to be some important clues to consider. First, retention in short-term memory is not effective if the number of chunks of information exceeds seven. Therefore, this suggests that in a given class we should not aim at teaching more than this number. However, our long-term memory can hold any amount of information.

Research also suggests that our "mental lexicon" is highly

organised and efficient, and that semantically related items are stored together. Word frequency is another factor that affects storage, as the most frequently used items are easier to retrieve. We can use this information to attempt to facilitate the learning process, by grouping items of vocabulary in semantic fields, such as topics.

Oxford (1990) suggests memory strategies to aid learning, and these can be divided into:

- Creating mental linkages: grouping, associating, placing new words into a context;
- Applying images and sounds: using imagery, semantic mapping, using keywords and representing sounds in memory;
- Reviewing well, in a structured way;
- Employing action: physical response or sensation, using mechanical techniques.

These techniques can be used to greater advantage if we can diagnose learning style preferences (visual, aural, kinesthetic, tactile, etc.) and make students aware of different memory strategies.

Meaningful tasks, however, seem to offer the best answer to vocabulary learning, as they rely on students' experiences and reality to facilitate learning. More meaningful tasks also require learners to analyse and process language more deeply, which should help them retain information in the long-term memory.

Forgetting seems to be an inevitable process, unless learners regularly use items they have learnt. Therefore, recycling is vital, and ideally it should happen one or two days after the initial input. After that, weekly or monthly tests can check on previously taught items.

The way students store the items learned can also contribute to their success or failure in retrieving them when needed. Most learners simply list the items learnt in chronological order, indicating meaning with translation. This system is far from helpful, as items are de-contextualized, encouraging students to over-generalise usage of them. It does not allow for additions and refinements nor indicates pronunciation.

Teachers can encourage learners to use other methods, using topics and categories to organise a notebook, binder or index cards. Meaning should be stored using English as much as possible, and also giving indication for pronunciation. Diagrams and word trees can also be used within this topic/categories organisation. The class as a whole can keep a vocabulary box with cards, which can be used for revision/recycling regularly.

5.5.2 Stages in word learning

There are two main stages in learning words. The first stage is achieved when a connection is made between the meaning and the form (its spelling or pronunciation) of the word. The second stage is much more difficult and involves knowing when to use the word (and not use it), its word relationships, its shades of meanings, and so on (Waring, 1999). The first stage of learning a word is quite easy and can be done effectively by rote memorization such as by using word cards (the word on one side of a piece of paper, and its translation on the other). The second stage calls for longer practice with the words embedded in meaningful, appropriate and cultural contexts.

5.5.3 Contextualized or decontextualized learning

Many teachers insist that words be learned only in context. Typical reasons given for this are that it is more "natural", or more "enjoyable" and that words are met with their collocates and derive meaning and nuances from these relationships and thus words should be learned in the context with which they are found.

Waring (1999), however, emphasizes the importance of rote learning. Research also shows that rote learning is several times faster than learning from context and it would be a good idea if we could use this rote learning to build a quick "start up" vocabulary for our learners. The point to remember is that the rote learning part is only the initial stage and much more work should be done to deepen this knowledge. Rote learning can quickly empower learners to have a command of several hundred words within a few weeks. "Word cards" are an effective way:

"Word cards" are pieces of paper with the English on one side and a translation or picture on the other. First, the learner breaks the whole pack of word cards into manageable groups of about 8-12 words per set (words starting with the same letter, or that are similar in meaning or sound to other words in the group, should be avoided as this can interfere with learning). Secondly, the learners number each set. Then the learner learns words from set 1 by looking at one side of the card and trying to recall the other. Then the learner looks to see if the recall is correct or not. Words that are known are put in one pile; the words that are not recalled are put on the other. When he/she has gone through the full first set of words one time, the learner picks up the words that were not recalled and tries again. As before, the words that are recalled go on the "recalled" pile and those that are not go back to the "unrecalled pile". The learner works like this until the whole of set 1 is known. Then, set 1 is put to one side and the same procedure is done with set 2. Set 2 is then put to one side.

The next bit is the important but most often missed step. The learner should now *go back to set 1* and recall them again. This is essential because of the steep forgetting curve. If the learner goes to set 3 without returning to set 1, the learner will be starting to forget words in set 1. Each time a set is picked up it is important to shuffle the order of the words in the set and to learn from English to the mother tongue, and vice versa. When he/she has re-learned set 1, the learner goes back to set 2 and only then on to set 3.

As a result, in vocabulary learning, the contextualized and decontextualized modes should be flexibly combined, making them complementary to each other.

5.5.4 Foster autonomy in vocabulary learning

One of the most important goals of language education is to help students to be autonomous learners. Pavicic suggests four kinds of strategies in autonomous vocabulary learning[1].

Self-initiated independent learning

These strategies involve planned, active and motivated learning and exposure to language outside the classroom. E.g.

- Word grouping
- Making notes of vocabulary while reading for pleasure/ watching TV
- Word cards/Leafing through a dictionary
- Planning
- Recording and listening
- Regular revision

In this group cognitive strategies which include direct manipulation of lexical items are connected to meta-cognitive strategies that make the use of cognitive ones more effective. The aim is communicative use of vocabulary.

Formal practice

These strategies promote systematic learning and vocabulary practice. The aim is accurate reproduction and is often connected to the tasks of formal instruction. E.g.

---

[1] Pavicic V., Vocabulary and autonomy. http://www.teachingenglish.org.uk, retrieved 11 Oct. 2005.

- Loud repetition
- Bilingual dictionary
- Testing oneself
- Noting new items in class

Functional practice

These strategies are based on context as a vocabulary source. They also include exposure to language, but without making a conscious effort (incidental learning). They also have a social aspect, i.e. interaction. E.g.

- Remembering words while watching TV/reading
- Using known words in different contexts
- Looking for definitions
- Listening to songs and trying to understand
- Using words in conversations
- Practice with friends

Memorizing

This group includes a number of memory strategies based on inter-, intra-lingual and visual associations. E.g.

- Using pictures, illustrations
- Associations with L1 (cognates or key word method)
- Looking for similarities between words
- Visualization

5.5.5 Guessing from context

One of the most important vocabulary strategies to teach is to "guess unknown words from context". The steps are:

The first thing to do when a learner meets a new word is to ignore it. If it is important it will come again. If they meet the word a second time and communication breaks down, then they should try to guess its meaning. Initially, it is important to make them notice its part of speech, and then they should look for clues around the word to help with the meaning. If they have an idea, they should try to substitute their guess into the sentence to see if the meaning of the sentence is clear. They will soon realize if they have the wrong part of speech, or wrong meaning. Finally, they can use word affix knowledge to confirm the guess.

However, it is vital to understand when teaching learners to guess words from context that they will not be able to guess successfully until they know about 95-98% of the other words in the text. If the text is too difficult, then the large number of unknown words will make successful guessing much less likely. Therefore, it is wise not to start teaching this strategy too early in the learning process, because the learners will not know enough other words to guess successfully. Starting too early leads to too much failure and can reinforce the idea that word learning is difficult.

5.5.6 The lexical approach

The lexical approach to second language teaching has received interest in recent years as an alternative to grammar-based approaches. The lexical approach concentrates on developing learners' proficiency with lexis, or words and word combinations. It is based on the idea that an important part of language acquisition is the ability to comprehend and produce lexical phrases as unanalyzed wholes, or "chunks," and that these chunks become the raw data by which learners perceive patterns of language traditionally thought of as grammar (Lewis, 1993: 95). Instruction focuses on relatively fixed expressions that occur frequently in spoken language, such as, "I'm sorry," "I didn't mean to hurt you", rather than on originally created sentences.

Lewis (1993) puts forward the following rationales for lexis teaching:

- Lexis is the basis of language.
- Lexis is misunderstood in language teaching because of the assumption that grammar is the basis of language and that mastery of the grammatical system is a prerequisite for effective communication.
- The key principle of a lexical approach is that "language consists of grammaticalized lexis, not lexicalized grammar".
- One of the central organizing principles of any meaning-centered syllabus should be lexis.

The lexical approach makes a distinction between vocabulary—traditionally understood as a stock of individual words with fixed meanings—and lexis, which includes not only the single words but also the word combinations that we store in our mental lexicons. Lexical approach advocates argue that language consists of meaningful chunks that, when combined, produce continuous coherent text, and only a minority of spoken sentences are entirely novel creations.

Lewis insists that his lexical approach is not simply a shift of emphasis from grammar to vocabulary teaching, as "language consists not of traditional grammar and vocabulary, but often of multi-word prefabricated chunks" (Lewis, 1997). Chunks include collocations, fixed and semi-fixed expressions and idioms, and according to him, occupy a crucial role in facilitating language production, being the key to fluency.

Consequently, it is essential to make students aware of chunks, giving them opportunities to identify, organise and record these. Identifying chunks is not always easy, and at least in the beginning, students need a lot of guidance.

Hill (1999) explains that most learners with "good vocabularies" have problems with fluency because their "collocational competence" is very limited, and that, especially from intermediate level, we should aim at increasing their collocational competence with the vocabulary they have already got.

5.5.7 Definition plus collocation in vocabulary teaching (learning)

Stockdale (2004)[1] discusses the role of definition and collocation in vocabulary learning and teaching.

Definition is concerned with establishing a single word's meaning, whereas collocation takes definition for granted and is concerned with the words that typically appear with any particular word: the verbs that might occur with a noun, for example. Such collocational information often enables a word to be used.

When the focus is on definition, we might explain a verb like *dream* as follows:

"A dream is like a film in your head that you sometimes have when you are asleep." (Stockdale, 2004)

When learners hear a presentation based on definition, their main purpose is to decode the stream of words with the goal of matching an L1 translation equivalent to the new word in their minds.

When the focus is on collocation, we might say something like the following:

"An important verb for dream is *have*. Two frequently appearing modifiers for dream are *bad* and *recurrent*, and two prepositions that often occur with dream are *about* and *in*: "I had a dream about..." and "In my dream, I was .." In addition, dream can be used as a modifier in words like *dream catcher* and *dream team*. When we put a child to

---

[1] Joseph Stockdale. The Internet TESL Journal, Vol. X, No. 5, retrieved online 27 Sep. 2006 at http://iteslj.org/Articles/Stockdale-Vocabulary.html

bed at night, we often say, '*Sweet dreams!*'" (Stockdale, 2004)

Both definition and collocation have their limitations. Definition plus collocation makes for a complete presentation that allows for meaning and use.

5.5.8 IVA[1]

IVA, incidental vocabulary acquisition, is a very important and complementary way to implicit vocabulary teaching. The following chart provides a brief look at their relations.

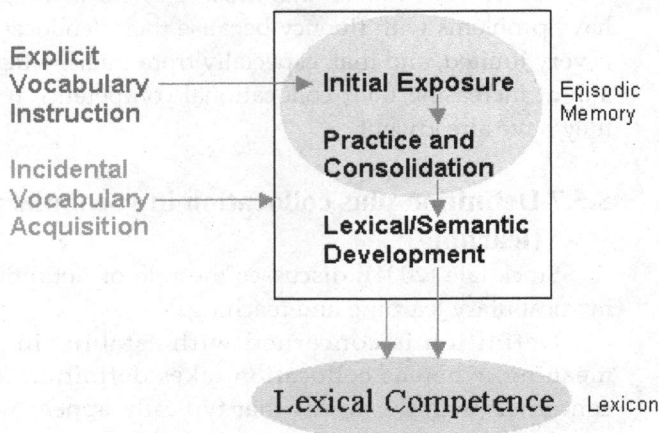

by Nan Jiang

Definition of lexical competence: Lexical information that is integrated into the mental lexicon and that can be retrieved automatically for and in natural communication.

IVA is the learning of new words as a *by-product* of a meaning-focused *communicative activity*, such as reading, listening, and interaction. It occurs through multiple exposures to a word in different contexts.

1) Learners are able to pick up vocabulary
• through extensive reading;
• through communicative interactions;
• through exposure to natural input such as movies, TV.

2) Conditions of successful IVA
a. The learners should have a sight vocabulary of 2,000 to 3,000.

---

[1] For more details, refer to http://www.auburn.edu/~ nunnath/eng/6240/tvocabul. html

b. The input should be comprehensible and interesting to the learners.

c. Input enhancement may be beneficial.

d. Guessing should be encouraged and guessing strategies be trained.

3) Advantages and disadvantages of IVA

Advantages

a. It is contextualized, giving the learner a richer sense of a word's use and meaning than can be provided in traditional paired-associate exercises;

b. It is pedagogically efficient in that it enables two activities—vocabulary acquisition and reading—to occur at the same time;

c. It is more individualized and learner-based because the vocabulary being acquired is dependent on the learner's own selection of reading materials;

d. Presentation, consolidation and lexical/semantic development occur at the same time (parallel vs. serial process of lexical development).

Disadvantages

a. IVA does not work for learning the basic core vocabulary;

b. There is no control over what is to be learned; IVL may not always occur;

c. Incorrect guessing may lead to incorrect understanding of vocabulary.

5.5.9 Summary

So far, we have introduced various strategies and methods on vocabulary teaching and learning. However, there are no universally useful strategies and they contribute to vocabulary learning in different ways. Instructors and students should use a number of strategies, and often simultaneously. The efficiency of vocabulary learning depends on how students combine individual strategies. If students combine and employ individual strategies from different groups they will be more successful in developing the target language lexicon.

In the long run, teachers should create activities and tasks (to be done both in and outside class) to help students to build their vocabulary and develop strategies to learn the vocabulary on their own. Students experiment and evaluate and then decide which to adopt or reject since strategies are not intended to be prescriptive.

It should always be remembered that "teaching does not cause learning" so teachers should expect learners not to understand sometimes and they should not expect learners to remember every word they teach. The aims of vocabulary instruction then should be to create the conditions where the learner can learn independently of the teacher. The ultimate aim of any teaching is to enable the learner to get to a position in which he/she does not need teachers anymore.

If teachers can do some of these things, learners will benefit more from their classes and will not only remember more words, but will be on the road to becoming independent vocabulary learners.

5.6   Examples of classroom activities in teaching vocabulary

Here is a selection of practical activities that direct learners towards using strategies of vocabulary learning.

The useful alphabet (self-initiated independent learning)

Each student gets a letter and has to find 5, 10 or 15 words s/he thinks would be useful for them. They then report to the class, perhaps as a mingle activity, using word cards (on one side they write the letter, on the other the information on the word—spelling, pronunciation, definition).

Word bag (formal practice)

This is to get students to write down new words they hear in class.

At the beginning of the term/course divide students into groups of about 5 and give each group a number (e.g. 1-6). At the beginning of each class give each group about 10 cards on which they write the number of their group and the new words they hear in class. At the end of each class they put their cards into the "word bag" and every 2 weeks the teacher check whether they still know those words and which group has the most cards. In the end there are two winners: the group that has the most cards, and the one that knows more words.

Especially for you (Functional practice)

The teacher prepares a list of words. Each student gets one word which is prepared especially for him or her. The trick is that each student gets a word whose initial letter is the same as the initial of the student's first name, e.g. Linda gets *listless*. Each student must look it up in the dictionary during the class and after a few minutes report to the class. E.g. "My name is Linda and I'm listless. That means that I am ... (definition)...". For homework students can do the same using their surname.

Questions for further discussion:

1. Some scholars think language should not be taught as separated skills in terms of listening, speaking, reading and writing. What is your view on this?

2. In what sense the online chatting is both oral based and written based? Are there other such examples to show the blurring between the oral and written forms of communication?

3. In the pre-listening stage, how can listeners' prior knowledge be effectively activated? How can listeners' attention be maintained during listening? And what does an effective listener usually do after listening?

4. How can schema theory be effectively used in English listening and reading?

5. Besides the listed speaking skills in the text, what other speaking skills can you think of?

6. In classroom teaching of oral English, should students' errors be corrected? Why or why not?

7. Design a 20-minute classroom speaking activity for your learners. Consider their English level, interest, and the purpose of the activity.

8. Jenkins (2004) claims that when students are learning English so that they can use it in international contexts with other non-native speakers from different first languages, they should be given the choice of acquiring a pronunciation that is more relevant to EIL intelligibility than traditional pronunciation syllabuses offer. Do you agree?

9. What reading strategies are effective to you? How can reading strategies be built into students?

10. What is SQ3R? What other reading methods do you know?

11. How is reading purpose important to reading? What are your reading purposes in intensive and extensive reading classes respectively?

12. How do you understand writing is a "communicative process" as well as "a learning process"?

13. Writing should be an interactive process between the writer and the readers. How do you understand this?

14. How can peer editing be effectively used in a large-size class in China?

15. Do you think conferencing is a good way providing students with valuable feedbacks? How can you use it in your writing class?

16. Various schools view grammar from different perspectives. How do you look at the importance of grammar in a language?

17. How can grammar be effectively learned by students? Should old and young language learners be taught differently?

18. How do you usually learn new words?

19. What aspects should a teacher focus on in presenting new words to his/her students?

20. What do you think of the role of IVA in vocabulary learning?

References:

Abbott, G. & Wingard, P. 1985. *The Teaching of English as an International Language: A Practical Guide*. Longman Nelson ELT.

Brender, A. 1993. An ethnographic study of second-language student motivation for attending writing center tutorials. Paper presented at the First National Writing Center Conference, New Orleans.

Brender, A. 1998. For more details, refer to http://www.jalt-publications.org/tlt/files/98/jul/brender.html, retrieved 27 May 2004.

Brown, H. D. 2001. *Teaching by Principles: An Interactive Approach to Language Pedagogy*. Foreign Language Teaching and Research Press.

Brown, R. S. & Nation, P. 1997. Teaching Speaking: Suggestions for the Classroom. http://www.jalt-publications.org/tlt/files/97/jan/speaking.html. Retrieved 23 Aug. 2005.

Brownell, J. 1996. *Listening: Attitudes, principles, and skills*. Allyn and Bacon.

Byrnes, H. 1998. "Reading in the beginning and intermediate college foreign language class", in Grace Stovall Burkart, (ed)., *Modules for the professional preparation of teaching assistants in foreign languages*. Center for Applied Linguistics.

Canale, M. & Swain, M. 1979. Theoretical bases of communicative approaches to second language teaching and testing. *Applied Linguistics,* (1)1.

Cassidy, J. 1996. Computer Assisted Language Arts Instruction for the ESL Learner. *English Journal* 85(9): 55-57.

Chomsky, C. 1969. Linguistics and philosophy. In S. Hook (Ed.), *Language and Philosophy*. New York University Press.

Corder, S. P. 1967. The significance of learners' errors. *IRAL*,V/4.

Corder, S. P. 1971. Idiosyncratic dialects and error analysis. *IRAL*, IX/2.

Driscoll, M. 1994. *Psychology of Learning for Instruction*. Allyn and Bacon.

Dulay, H., M. & Krashen, S. 1982. *Language Two*. Oxford University Press.

Ellis, R. 1993. The structural syllabus and second language acquisition. *TESOL Quarterly,* 27: 91-113.

Ellis, R. 1994. *The Study of Second Language Acquisition*. Oxford University Press.

Ellis, R. 2000. *Second Language Acquisition*. Shanghai Foreign Languages Publishing House.

Gairns, R. & Redman, S. 1986. *Working with Words*. Cambridge University Press.

Gaudiani, C. 1981. *Teaching Composition in the Foreign Language Curriculum*. Language in Education: Theory and Practice Series, no. 43. Center for Applied Linguistics.

Gilthrow, J. 1995. *Academic Writing*. Broadview Press, Canada.

Gudschinsky, S.C. 1973. *A manual of literacy for preliterate peoples*. Ukarumpa, Papua New Guinea: Summer Institute of Linguistics.

Halliday, M.A.K. & Hasan, R. 1989. *Language, Context, and Text: Aspects of Language in a Social-semiotic Perspective*. Oxford University Press.

Halvorson, M. A. 1992. *Literacy and lifelong learning for women*. Part of UNESCO series on literacy in development. Intermedia.

Hatch, E. 1974. Second language learning—universals? *Working Papers on Bilingualism,* 3: 1-17.

Henrichsen, L.E. 1998. Understanding Culture and Helping Students Understand Culture. *Linguistics 577* [Online], http://linguistics.byu.edu/classes/ling577lh/.

Hill, J. 1999. Collocational competence. *English Teaching Professional,* 11: 3-6.

Holemes, N. 2000. "The use of a process-oriented approach to facilitate the planning and production stages of writing for adult students of English as a foreign or second language". http://www.developingteachers.com/articles_tchtraining/.

Jenkins. 2004. Retrieved 24 Jan. 2005. For details refer to http://www.teachingenglish.org.uk/think/pron/global_english.shtml.

Kaplan, R. 1966. Cultural thought patterns in inter-cultural education. *Language Learning*, 16: 1-20.

King, M. 1984. Language and school success: Access to meaning. *Theory into Practice,* 23(3), Summer.

Kinneavy, J. L. 1971. *A Theory of Discourse: The Aims of Discourse*. Englewood Cliffs, Prentice-Hall.

Kuji, Kanagawa-ken etc. 2004. Adapted from http://www.abax.co.jp/listen/, retrieved 18 Oct. 2004.

Larsen-Freeman, D. 1983. Expanding roles of learners and teachers in learner-centered instruction. In W.A. Renandya & G.M. Jacobs (Eds.), *Learners and Language Learning Anthology Series* 39: 207-226. SEAMEO Regional Language Centre.

Larsen-Freeman, D. & Long, M. 1991. *An Introduction to Second Language Acquisition and Research*. Longman.

Legutke, M. and Thomas, H. 1991. *Process and Experience in the Language Classroom*. Longman.

Lenneberg, E. H. 1967. *Biological Foundations of Language*. Wiley.

Lewis, M. 1993. *The Lexical Approach*. Language Teaching Publications.

Littlewood, W. 1981. *Communicative Language Teaching*. Cambridge Univerity Press.

Manning, A. Writing Across Genres: Developing Competence in Stages. http://linguistics.byu.edu/classes/ling230am/writing_chapters/Types_of_Writing.html, retrieved 14 Mar. 2006.

Marshall, M. 1986. *Writing Without Tears: Advanced Writing for Academic Success*. ERIC Document Reproduction Service No. ED: 271-962.

Morley, J. 2001. Aural comprehension instruction: principles and practices, in M. Celce-Murcia (ed.), *Teaching English as a Second or Foreign Language*. 2nd edition. Newbury House.

Omaggio, A. C. 1986. Teaching language in context: Proficiency-oriented instruction. Heinle and Heinle.

Oxford, R. 1990. *Language learning strategies*. Newbury House.

Peterson, P. 1991. A Synthesis of methods for interactive listening, in M. Celce-Murcia (ed), *Teaching English as a Second or Foreign Language,* 2nd edition. Newbury House.

Pienemann, M. 1984. Psychological constraints on the teachability of languages. *Studies in Second Language Acquisition,* 6: 186-214.

Raimes, A. 1983. *Techniques in Teaching Writing*. Oxford University Press.

Richards, J. C. 1974. *Error Analysis: Perspectives on Second Language Acquisition*. Longman.

Robinson, F. P. 1970. *Effective study* (4th ed.), Harper & Row, New York.

Saricoban, A. 1999. *The Internet TESL Journal,* Vol. V, No. 12.

Schmidt, R. 1983. Interaction, acculturation, and the acquisition of communicative competence. In N. Wolfson & E. Judd (eds.), *Sociolinguistics and Language Acquisition*. Newbury House.

Selinker, L. 1972. Interlanguage, in *International Review of Applied Linguistics 10*.

SIL International. 1999. See http://www.sil.org/lingualinks/, retrieved 24 Jan. 2005.

Simpson, A. 2000. "A Process Approach to Writing by Adam Simpson". http://www.developingteachers.com/articles_tchtraining/pw1_adam.htm, retrieved 23 Apr. 2005.

Stanley, G. 1999. *Approaches to Process Writing*. British Council, Barcelona.

Temple, C. & Gillet, J. W. 1989. Language arts: Learning processes and teaching practices. Glenview, IL: Scott, Foresman and Company.

Ueno, N. 1994. Teaching English pronunciation to Japanese English majors: A comparison of suprasegmental with segmental oriented teaching approaches. Unpublished dissertation, Temple University, Japan.

Wang, Y. M. 1996. E-mail dialogue journaling in an ESL reading and writing classroom. Paper presented at the National Convention of the Association for Educational Communications and Technology, Indianapolis, IN.

Waring, R. 1999. Tasks for assessing second language receptive and productive vocabulary. Ph. D. Thesis. University of Wales.

White, R. and Valerie, A. 1991. *Process Writing*. Longman House.

Widdowson, H.G. 1978. *Teaching Language as Communication*. Oxford University Press.

Wilkins, D. A. 1972. *Lingnistics and Language Teaching*. Edward Arnold.

Xu, Q. 2000. *The Communicative Approach to English Teaching and Testing*. Shanghai Foreign Languages Education Press.

Zamel, V. 1985. Responding to student writing. *TESOL Quarterly,* 19(1): 79-97.

CHAPTER 5
Learners' Variables in English Teaching

As mentioned in Chapter 2, more and more people have come to be aware of the importance of learner differences in language learning and teaching. Even when the learning situation, the teacher, and the material remain the same, the learning results of the students vary to a great extent. The issue of differential success is, to a large degree, related to the learner differences. Learners differ according to various parameters. They may be different for the proficiency level: beginners, intermediate or advanced. They may differ in the age factor: children, adolescent or adult. They may be different for native language variable: whether they are from the western countries whose languages are similar to each other, or they are from Asia whose languages are sharply different from English. They may differ in the cognitive variable: learners use different learning strategies and have different cognitive or learning styles.

There are many factors related to learners which may influence the learning result. There are also different types of classification of the factors. In this chapter, we will mainly talk about the factors related to Chinese learners and illustrate them in the following aspects as personal difference, affective domain, cognitive styles, learning strategies, and social-cultural differences.

1. Personal differences

By personal differences, here we mean the physical innate factors related to learners, namely age, aptitude, and intelligence. These factors are born with the learners and are not easy to be changed. However, if we know the influence of these factors on language learning, we can adopt different approaches to different learners.

1.1 Age

Is age an important factor in second language acquisition? Should a foreign language be introduced in the elementary level or secondary level? What is the optimal timing for successful bilingual or immersion education programs? Do learners of different ages learn languages in different ways—should they be taught with different approaches, syllabuses or materials?

These questions have puzzled researchers and teachers for many years. The results of the studies are in favor of the priority of early studying a second language. Long and Scarcella's (1979) research got the statement that old is faster, but younger is better. Adults learn faster than children and old children faster than younger children in early morphology and syntax. However, for the ultimate attainment, only quite young (child) starters can achieve accent-free, native-like performance in a second language. Tahta, Wood and Lowenthal's (1981a, 1981b) research favored the superiority for younger over older children to imitate the pronunciation of isolated words and phrases. Lenneberg's (1977) research proved that there was a critical period or at least a sensitive period during which language acquisition is most efficient and after which complete mastery of a language is impossible.

Lenneberg proposed the critical period hypothesis. The hypothesis suggests that in child development there is a period during which language can be acquired more easily than at any other time. According to this hypothesis, the critical period lasts until puberty (around age 13), and this period is due to biological development. Lenneberg suggests that language learning may be difficult after puberty because the brain lacks the ability for adaptation. This, he believed, was because the language functions of the brain have already been established in a particular part of the brain; that is, because lateralization has already occurred by this time.

The age-related differences can be explained from the social-psychological aspect. Adult might be more inhibited than children. An adult learner may prefer to speak accented L2 speech which identifies him as a speaker of a particular L1. An adult learner may be affected by their negative attitudes toward the target language. Another explanation goes to the cognitive aspect. Adult's development of cognitive ability may influence the acquisition of the second language. They tend to think abstractly—they tend to employ problem-solving ability while child learners tend to employ language acquisition device when they are exposed to a new language. The third explanation goes to the input issue. Young learners tend to seize every opportunity to communicate with others while adults may refrain from speaking the new language for being afraid of making mistakes. So younger learners receive better and more language input than the adults and lead to better learning result. The last explanation goes to the neurological aspect. The lateralization stops prior to puberty. And this leads to the difficulty for adults to pronounce the words like the native speakers.

From the findings, we can see that starters of any age can acquire a second/foreign language, that is, the age of starting to learn a second language does not affect the order of acquisition. Even the adult learners can learn faster than younger learners. However, the age of starting to learn a second language affects the efficiency of learning a language. Young learners learn better than adult learners, particularly in the accuracy in phonetics and phonology. This implies that it is better to start to learn a second language before the puberty.

1.2   Aptitude

It seems that some learners have gifts in language learning and some are "doomed" to fail to learn a second language. Most researchers believe that this phenomenon is related to learners' different aptitudes. Aptitude refers to the natural ability to learn a language, not including intelligence, motivation, interest, etc. This ability is presumed to depend on some combination of more or less enduring characteristics of the individual (Carroll, 1981). It is hard to define what aptitude is. But we can see what aptitude includes from the multidimensional aspects of aptitude:

- Phonetic coding ability—the ability to identify and remember new sounds in a foreign or second language.
- Grammatical sensitivity—the ability to identify the

grammatical functions of different parts of sentences.
- Rote learning ability—the ability to remember words, rules, etc. in a new language.
- Inductive language learning ability—the ability to infer or induce the rules governing a language—or/and the ability to work out meanings without explanation in a new language.

There are two well-known language aptitude tests. One is the Modern Language Aptitude Test. And another is the Pimsleur Language Aptitude Battery (Pimsleur, 1966). It seems that aptitude test can select students who are likely to succeed in the classroom and bar those who are likely to fail, and stream students into different classes for levels of aptitude.

From the multidimensional aspects of aptitude, we can see that most aptitude tests predict success in L2 academic classrooms where the focus is on language forms, because aptitude breaks down into different factors such as memory and grammatical sensitivity. Therefore teachers should try to provide to students of different types of aptitude with different teaching methods and forms of evaluation (varied exercises within the class, to parallel classes, or to self-directed learning) so that students of different aptitude can all benefit from the class.

1.3 Intelligence

It is believed that intelligence is closely related to language learning and students of low IQ tend to learn a foreign language slowly. Traditionally intelligence is defined and measured in terms of linguistics and logical-mathematical abilities. Gardner recognizes more aspects of intelligence as linguistic, logical/mathematical, musical intelligence (rhythmic and pitch pattern), bodily-kinesthetic intelligence (fine motor movement), interpersonal intelligence, and intrapersonal intelligence (the ability to see oneself, to develop a sense of self-identity).

Most people have recognized the importance of intelligence. Oller (1978) considered that intelligence is as important as aptitude. But others think that intelligence is not a decisive factor in language acquisition. Cummings (1979) distinguished two types of language abilities. He held the idea that cognitive/learning language ability is related to intelligence, and basic interpersonal communicative competence has little to do with intelligence. Intelligence, as we believe, may not be an important factor in natural acquisition environment, but very important in classroom language learning, for it needs high cognitive ability when the focus is on forms and knowledge.

Teachers can change their teaching methods to suit different students. Better learning result may be achieved if different teaching methods and different learning strategies are used for learners of different intelligence. Activities focusing on language communication may be better for learners of average intelligence; and activities focusing on form analysis and memorization may be better for learners of high intelligence.

2. Affective domain

The affective domain is the emotional side of human behavior, and the development of affective states or feelings involves a variety of personality factors, feelings both about ourselves and about others with whom we come into contact. In this section, we mainly talk about extroversion, self-esteem, anxiety, risk-taking, empathy, and tolerance of ambiguity.

2.1   Introversion vs. extroversion

Extroversion and introversion are terms used to gauge two unique social styles. Extroverted characters tend to be gregarious and expressive, while the introverted tend to be private and reserved. Extroverted people are those whose conscious interests and energies are more often directed outwards towards other people and events than towards the persons themselves and their own inner experience. Introverted people refer to those who tend to avoid social contact with others and are often preoccupied with their inner feelings, thoughts and experiences.

It is not easy to say whether extroverted learners or introverted learners are better at language learning. People usually believe that extroverted people are willing to take conversational risks and are dependent on outside stimulation and interaction, and introverted people are self-sufficient and tend to concentrate, and need to process ideas before speaking so as to avoid the risks in conversation. In language learning, extroverted learners tend to be fluent while introverted learners tend to be precise.

Nowadays, psychologists no longer believe that extroversion and introversion are two distinct personality types, since many people show aspects of both. There is no evidence to show whether either extroversion or introversion is directly related to success in language learning. However, what is clear is that certain types of class activities are more appropriate for one or the other. While noticing the difference of the two characters, teachers can try to involve the introverted learners into activities needing cooperation and encourage them to express their ideas, and, on the other hand, try to make those extroverted people think about their answers before speaking them out so as to make all the students develop appropriate language skills.

2.2   Self-esteem

Self-esteem refers to the evaluation which the individual makes and customarily maintains with regard to him/herself. It expresses an attitude of approval or disapproval, and indicates the extent to which an individual believes him/herself to be capable, significant, successful and worthy. In short, self-esteem is a personal judgment of worthiness that is expressed in the attitudes that the individual holds toward him/herself. It is a subjective experience which the individual conveys to others by verbal reports and other overt expressive behavior.

Self-esteem can be described on three more specific levels: global or general self-esteem, situational self-esteem and task self-esteem. Global self-esteem is thought to be relatively stable in a mature adult and is resistant to change except by active and extended therapy. Situational or specific self-esteem refers to one's appraisals of oneself in specific situations, such as education or work. Task self-esteem has to do with particular tasks in a specific situation. In language learning, specific self-esteem refers to language learning in general, and task self-esteem might appropriately refer to one's self-evaluation of a particular aspect of the process: speaking, writing, a particular class, and even in a particular activity.

Research has shown that self-esteem correlates highly with language success, especially oral proficiency, though it's not clear whether high self-esteem leads to language success or language success leads to high self-esteem—chicken or egg question. However, it is clear that both are interacting factors. What is important for teachers is to create an environment of mutual support and care and design tasks of different levels of difficulty so as for students of different language proficiency to accomplish successfully—a sense of success. Only when students have confidence in themselves can they have higher motivation in learning.

2.3   Anxiety

Anxiety, originally belonging to the psychological domain, is associated with feelings of uneasiness, frustration, self-doubt, apprehension, or worry. It is quite possibly the affective factor that most pervasively obstructs the learning process. Like self-esteem, anxiety can be experienced at various levels. Trait anxiety is a more permanent predisposition to be anxious. It is at the deep or global level. Some people tend to be anxious about any thing at any time, while others may be relaxed. State anxiety is experienced in relation to some particular event or act.

It is generally agreed that there are two types of anxiety: **facilitating anxiety** and **debilitating anxiety**. Facilitating anxiety refers to the kind of anxiety which keeps one poised, alert, and just slightly unbalanced to the point that one can't relax entirely, which motivates the learners to "fight" the new learning task (the feeling of nervousness before giving a public speech). Debilitating anxiety, in contrast, refers to the situation that the learners got very nervous and worried to the extent that it forms a negative factor to language learning.

It is not always clear how foreign language anxiety comes into being. For some, it may be a case of having been ridiculed for a wrong answer in class; for others, it may have to do with factors unconnected to the language class itself. The root may be the repressed distress of the past—the personal hurt, particularly in the childhood.

When anxiety is present in the classroom, there is down-spiraling effect. Anxiety makes students nervous and afraid and thus contributes to poor performance; this in turn creates more anxiety and even worse performance. Language teachers should act to reduce anxiety based on the suggestions of Oxford (1999):

- Help students understand that language anxiety episodes can be transient and do not inevitably develop into a lasting problem.
- Boost the self-esteem and self-confidence of students by providing multiple opportunities for classroom success in the language.
- Reduce the competition present in the classroom.
- Give students permission to use the language with less than perfect performance.
- Encourage students to relax through music, laughter or games.
- Use fair tests with unambiguous, familiar item types.
- Help students realistically assess their performance.
- Provide activities that address varied learning styles and strategies in the classroom.

- Help students practice positive self-talk (self-encouragement) and cognitive "reframing" of negative or irrational ideas.

2.4   Risk-taking

Risk-taking refers to the personality factor which concerns the degree to which a person is willing to undertake actions that involve a significant degree of risk.

Language learning is a complex process and it is impossible not to make mistakes in communication. According to the studies in first language acquisition and second language acquisition, the process of language learning involves hypothesis making and hypothesis testing. Making guesses is a very important strategy in language learning and communicating in the foreign language. Learners should take every chance to practice and communicate even at the risk of making mistakes. Students' risk-taking behavior is a positive predictor of students' voluntary classroom participation. Learners who are sensitive to rejection—unwillingness to take risks—might avoid active participation in language class, fearing being ridiculed by their classmates or teacher. Good language learners are willing and accurate guessers who have a strong desire to communicate, and will attempt to do so even at the risk of appearing foolish.

However, it does not mean that the more risks a learner takes, the better he or she can learn a language. Research shows that learners with a high motivation to achieve are moderate, not high, risk-takers. Teachers should persuade and encourage the introverted, more anxious, and less self-confident learners to take the risk to guess the right answer or to take part in the activities in learning a language.

2.5   Empathy

Empathy refers to the quality of being able to imagine and share the thoughts, feelings, and point of view of other people. Empathy is thought to contribute to the attitudes we have towards a person or group with a different language and culture from our own, and it may contribute to the degree of success with which a person learns another language.

So far studies have shown that empathetic learners are good communicators and are potential to achieve higher levels in language and cultural learning.

2.6   Tolerance of ambiguity

Tolerance of ambiguity refers to the degree to which one can tolerate something ambiguous. Language is a very complex system and language learning is a complex process. Language learning for real communicative use, especially in situations which demand structural and lexical precision, is an extremely demanding whole-person engagement. It requires the learner to cope with information gaps, unexpected language and situations, new cultural norms, and substantial uncertainty. It is also highly interpersonal. When learning a new language, a language learner is confronted with new stimuli, many of which are ambiguous. Therefore, ambiguity is inevitable in language learning. If a language learner cannot tolerate some of the ambiguities which may be clarified in further learning, s/he will be frustrated.

It is found that tolerance/intolerance of ambiguity is significantly correlated with language success. A language learner is confronted with new stimuli, many of which are ambiguous. Clarity is not usually immediately forthcoming, and people with a low tolerance of ambiguity may experience frustration and diminished performance as a result. Teachers should help the students understand that ambiguity is inevitable in the learning process, and make the students pay attention to communicative effectiveness rather than the form. It is, however, not the case that a learner should tolerate all the ambiguities. High tolerance of ambiguity will lead to imprecise and erroneous inter-language, which may be fossilized and hard to change.

3.   Cognitive styles

3.1   Definitions and classifications of learning style

Since Herbert Thelen first used the term "learning style" to account for differences in learning in 1954, many attempts have been made to define and classify learning styles. Keefe (1979) defines learning style as the characteristic cognitive, affective and physiological behaviors that serve as relatively stable indicators of how learners perceive, interact with, and respond to the learning environment. Cook (2000) believes that "learning styles refer to an individual's natural, habitual, and preferred way(s) of absorbing, processing, and retaining new information and skills. These learning styles persist, regardless of teaching methods and content areas." Willing (1987, cited in Ellis, 1994: 499) holds that learning style reflects "the totality of psychological functioning".

Although different theorists interpret the concept of learning style in quite different ways, they all agree that the question of how a person learns is the focus of the concept. Learning style therefore relates to the general tendency towards a particular learning approach displayed by an individual.

One point to be added is that, there is a considerable confusion in the literature concerning the terms cognitive style and learning style. Numerous authors use the terms interchangeably. **Cognitive style** is generally viewed as the typical means of problem solving, thinking, perceiving, and remembering; it is a psychological term which refers to variations among individuals in preferred way of perceiving, organizing, analyzing, or recalling information and experience. The term **learning style**, on the other hand, indicates an interest in the totality of the processes undertaken during learning; it is not only involved in the cognitive field, but also connected closely with physiological and affective fields. According to Brown (2001), when cognitive styles are specifically related to an educational context, where affective and physiological factors are intermingled, they are usually more generally referred to as learning styles. In this sense, there is a broad agreement in current theoretical literature that cognitive style is part of learning style; it is one element among other elements comprising learning style.

Researchers have categorized the various learning styles in numerous ways. Among the wide composite of learning style dimensions, Oxford (1990) has put forward the following to be the most significant for language learning: global and analytic, field-dependent and field-independent, feeling and thinking, impulsive and reflective, intuitive-random and concrete-sequential, closure-oriented and open, extroverted and introverted, and visual, auditory and hands-on. However, only a few of the learning styles, such as field independence, left- and right- brain functioning, ambiguity tolerance, reflectivity and impulsivity, visual and auditory style, etc. have received the attention of second language researchers in recent years.

3.2   Review of the studies of learning style in foreign language teaching

3.2.1 Previous studies of learning style in foreign language teaching abroad

Although the study of learning style began as early as 1950s, in the field of language teaching or learning, it was not until late 1970s that studies of this domain began to attract the attention of language researchers abroad. These studies can be classified into two main types: those that investigate the basic issues involving language learners' learning style, and those that focus on the language classroom uses and implications of learning-styles information.

In the first type, some researchers probed into the influences of cultural background on language learners' learning styles, and pointed out that language teachers should attend to the cultural variation in learning styles; some explored gender differences in language learning styles and its influences on students' language achievement; some attempted to find out the similarities and differences in the ways native English learners and non-native English learners process information by comparing their learning styles.

In the second type, the researchers probed into the implication of learning styles on classroom curriculum, lesson plans, teaching techniques, strategy training, and so on by examining the relationships between learning style research and the classroom.

3.2.2 Previous studies of learning style in foreign language teaching at home

The study of learning styles by language researchers in China began in the early 1990s. Among the theoretical studies, most are introduction of western researchers' theory, attempting to identify factors hampering further development of learning styles research in Second Language Acquisition (SLA), and to point out researchers' misconception about learning style, invalidity of instruments, complexity and changeability of learning style. The empirical studies focus on the factors and characteristics of learning styles, and teaching strategies.

3.3　Relevance of learning style and teaching style

To promote students' learning and enhance teaching effectiveness, merely identifying learning style is of little value unless an attempt is made to associate it with real teaching-learning process. In the process, one factor closely related to learning style is teaching style.

Cook (2000: 173-174) views teaching style as a concept sliding among teaching methods, teaching techniques, teaching strategies and teaching approaches. Specially, he defines language teaching style as "a loosely connected set of teaching techniques believed to share the same goal of language teaching and the same views of language and of L2 learning." In general, teaching style is closely connected with a teacher's teaching attitude, knowledge structure and subjective pursuing.

There is a general agreement among many researchers that the central element of understanding teaching style is to understand the match between it and learning style. Within the field of foreign language learning or teaching, there was a great deal of theoretical support for the idea that when student and teacher styles are better matched, students are likely to work harder both in and outside the classroom and also to benefit much more from their language classes. If mismatch occurs, it often has bad effects on students' learning and attitudes to the class.

If the purpose of teaching style is to aid teachers in achieving the congruence of teaching and learning styles, then it is necessary to understand how the congruence can be achieved. There are four principles to assist teachers to match their teaching styles with students' learning styles:

1) Teachers need to guard against over-teaching by their own preferred learning styles.

It is natural for teachers to teach by their own preferred learning styles because they have an assumption that the way they learn is the most effective for everyone to learn. One big problem generated from this phenomenon is that students whose learning styles are similar to the teaching styles of the teachers benefit from the teaching, while students with opposite dimensions of the styles suffer much during class. To avoid the problem, teachers need to broaden their teaching styles to provide opportunities for students to broaden their learning styles.

2) Teachers are most helpful when they assist students in identifying and learning through their own style preferences.

By identifying the specific learning styles of students, teachers can help students understand their own strength and weakness on styles. Their guidance and counsel can encourage students to deliberately set learning goals according to their own learning style preferences so as to enable them to develop into self-aware language learners.

3) Students should have the opportunity to learn through their preferred style.

Instead of assuming that all learners will go about any particular task in the same way, teachers should recognize that individuals learn differently, and what may be an optimal learning or teaching method for one may discourage another. It is important for teachers to provide students of various learning styles an equal opportunity to learn by increasing their variety of teaching styles.

4) Students should be encouraged to diversify their style preferences.

It is not enough for students to learn only through their preferred styles. Students need to broaden their learning styles and the accompanying skills by getting practice in learning styles they are not strong in. This "style flex" is essential because by the time students have reached much higher education, they will be skilled at this adapting. Thus teachers need to utilize classroom activities which will assist students in developing flexible learning styles.

3.4 Significance of applying learning style into foreign language teaching

Learning style has been widely accepted by both teachers and researchers as one of the key factors that influence the rate and success of foreign language learning.

At practical level, applying learning style theory into foreign language teaching has at least four benefits: 1) Increase support for language learners to move from interdependence or dependence to independence. It can promote self-determination among learners, help them understand more about their own preferred learning styles and therefore, become more autonomous and less dependent on outside authority. 2) There will be greater learner-centeredness and learner direction in language classroom. Compared with traditional foreign language classroom in which teacher-centeredness pervades, students will feel that their individual differences are more respected, thus their anxiety can be reduced. 3) Knowledge of students' learning styles can help teachers to design curriculum with an equitable range of activities that enable all students to be comfortable as learners, while also stretching them to remain engaged and persist confidently with new tasks and activities. 4) The retention rate is higher than when they feel frustration and cognitive dissonance; acceptance of style as fundamental strength of each student contributes to the development of their self-esteem.

In light of the importance of learning styles to foreign language teaching, it is natural to ask if the teaching, design, delivery, and facilities take the variety of learning styles of the students into account. The following are suggestions for teachers on how to apply learning styles into foreign language teaching:

1) Diagnosing learning styles and developing self-aware language learners

Assessment of learning style is often a first step in application of learning style theory. It helps students understand their own strength and weakness on styles, guides them to broaden their self-knowledge, and develops their own learning strategies.

2) Altering the teaching styles to create teacher-student style matching

After identifying students' learning style preferences, an effective means of accommodating these learning styles that exist in the average classroom is for teachers to change their own styles and strategies, and provide a variety of learning experiences to meet the needs of different learning styles. Then all students will have at least some activities that appeal to them based on their own learning styles, and they are more likely to be successful in these activities.

Of course, in some cases, mismatches between the teacher's teaching style and the students' learning styles can be valuable because this mismatch forces students to stretch or "style-flex" as they use their non-preferred learning modes. Nevertheless, in foreign language classroom, students need encouragement and assistance in adjusting their learning style to the teaching styles of their teachers.

3) Increasing the variety of instructional techniques used in the classroom

To improve the quality of instruction and enhance foreign language teaching effectiveness, it is important for teachers to increase their variety of instructional techniques used in the foreign language classroom. If a teacher only used one single teaching style to teach the different students, the class would be very boring and not all the students could benefit from it.

4) Providing activities for different groupings

In a class made up of students with various learning styles, it is helpful for a teacher to divide students into groups by learning styles and give them activities based on their learning styles. This should appeal to them because they will enjoy themselves and be successful. On the other hand, the group made up of reflective students may need some encouragement to share ideas aloud and may want to jot down a few notes first and then share it with each other before being invited to participate in a group discussion.

In sum, learning styles theory has provided teachers with a different view of teaching-learning process. An awareness of individual differences in learning has made language educators and teachers more sensitive to their roles in teaching and learning and permitted them to match teaching and learning styles so as to develop students' potentials in foreign language learning. No matter what kinds of learning styles students have in foreign language learning, they are supposed to play an important role in the process of their learning; each dimension of learning styles is related to foreign language teaching and learning in its own way. Therefore, it is English teachers' responsibility to employ instruments to identify students' learning style preferences, provide instructional alternatives to address their differences, and plan lessons to match students' learning styles while at the same time encouraging them to diversify their learning style preferences.

4. Learning strategies

New methods of teaching turn up one after another in order to improve the efficiency of teaching. The learning result, however, is not greatly enhanced by the use of these teaching methods in the second language classroom. Teachers and researchers came to realize that teaching is a bilateral activity including teachers' teaching and students' learning. It is certainly unsuccessful if teachers only emphasize on teaching but not learning. As the knowledge of second language acquisition increased markedly during the 1970s, the focus of the research shifted from examining the teaching method to investigating the processes of learning. Most of the research was prompted by one intriguing question: why do individual learners achieve different output when everything else, including teachers, teaching method and teaching materials, remains the same? And what attributes to these differences? Therefore, the cognitive and socio-cultural factors of the learner were studied extensively. It was against this background that the issue of learning strategy in second language learning is brought into focus. Up to now, it has been widely acknowledged that language-learning strategies exist and influence two aspects of second language learning: "the rate of acquisition and the ultimate level of achievement". (Ellis, 1994: 529)

4.1   Definition of learning strategy

As one of the most important and basic issues of language learning research, strategy has been given various definitions and the literature contains conflicting views as to the meaning of the strategy. However, the definitions have a lot in common although no strong consensus yet exists. Rather than reviewing all, the following part lists some prominent ones.

Strategy is best reserved for general tendencies or overall characteristics of the approach employed by the language learner, leaving techniques as the term to refer to particular forms of observable learning behavior (Stern, 1992).

Second language strategies involve three aspects: (1) language learning behaviors learners actually engage in to learn and regulate the learning of a second language; (2) learners' knowledge about their use of strategies; (3) learners' knowledge about aspects of their language learning which may influence their choice of strategy (Wenden, 1992).

Learning strategies are operations employed by the learner to aid the acquisition, storage, retrieval, and use of information (Oxford, 1990).

Learning strategies are those processes which are consciously selected by learners and which may result in action taken to enhance the learning or use of a second or foreign language, through the storage, retention, recall, and application of information about the language (Cohen, 1990).

According to Ellis (1994), the main differences among these definitions are:

1) Are language-learning strategies a series of visible behavior or psychological activities in the brain, which cannot be observed directly, or both of them?

2) Are strategies someone's general tendencies of the approach employed in language learning or specific techniques used by second language learners to accomplish tasks in particular area of language learning?

3) Can learning strategies be seen as conscious and intentional or as subconscious?

4) Can strategies affect language-learning development directly or indirectly?

To answer the questions he raised, Ellis (1994) pointed out one of the best approaches to defining learning strategies is to list their main characteristics. The following is what he lists:

1) Strategies refer to both general approaches and specific actions or techniques used to learn a second language.

2) Strategies are problem-oriented—the learner deploys a strategy to overcome some particular learning problem.

3) Learners are generally aware of the strategies they use and can identify what they consist of if they are asked to pay attention to what they are doing/thinking.

4) Strategies involve linguistic behavior and non-linguistic.

5) Linguistic strategies can be performed in the first language and in the second language.

6) Some strategies are behavioral while others are mental. Thus some strategies are directly observable while others are not.

7) In the main, strategies contribute indirectly to learning by providing learners with data about the second language, which they can then process. However, strategies may also contribute directly (for example, memorization strategies directed at specific lexical items or grammatical rules).

8) Strategy use varies considerably as a result of both the kind of task the learner is engaged in and individual learner preference. (Ellis, 1994: 532-533)

What Ellis says is a good answer to the aforementioned questions. Strategies are both external and internal activities. They are the conscious or unconscious processes that language learners use in learning a language. It is difficult to distinguish "approach" and "techniques" in the research. According to the cognitive information processing view of human thought and action and what Ellis offered to us, language learning strategy can be defined as the special ways of processing information that efficiently enhance comprehension, learning, or retention of the information.

4.2   Classifications of learning strategy

Learning strategy classification is another disputed issue. Due to the different angles, the result is wide diversity. In the following, three popular classifications abroad have been provided based on different criteria.

(1) O'Malley and Chamot (1990) differentiated learning strategies into three categories depending on information-processing theory. They are cognitive strategies, metacognitive strategies and social/affective strategies.

Cognitive strategies refer to the steps or operations used in problem solving that require direct analysis, transformation, or synthesis of learning materials. With an operative or cognitive-processing function, cognitive strategies appear to be directly linked to the performance of particular learning tasks. Cognitive strategies include repetition, resourcing, directed physical response, translation, grouping, note-taking, deduction, recombination, imagery, auditory representation, key word, contextualization, elaboration, transfer, and inferencing.

Meta-cognitive strategies, with an executive function, make use of knowledge about the cognitive processes, and constitute an attempt to regulate language learning by means of planning, monitoring, and evaluating. Meta-cognitive strategies include advanced organizers, directed attention, selective attention, self-management, advanced preparation, self-monitoring, delayed production and self-evaluation.

Social/affective strategies entail either interaction with another person or ideational control over affect. Social/affective strategies include cooperation, question for clarification, and self-talk.

(2) Oxford (1990), in the light of the relationship between strategies and language materials, suggested two broad categories: direct strategies and indirect strategies. Direct strategies directly involve the target language, require mental processing of the language and are used to develop the four language skills: reading, speaking,

listening, and writing; indirect strategies support and manage language learning without, in many cases, directly involving the target language. They are useful in possibly all language learning situations and are applicable to all four language skills.

Direct Strategies	Indirect Strategies
Memory Strategies Creating Mental Linkage Applying Images and Sounds Reviewing Well Employing Action	*Meta-cognitive Strategies* Centering one's learning Arranging and planning one's learning Evaluating one's learning
Cognitive Strategies Practicing Receiving and Sending Messages Analyzing and Reasoning Creating Structure for Input and Output	*Affective Strategies* Lowering one's anxiety Encouraging oneself Taking one's emotional temperature
Compensation Strategies Guessing Intelligently, etc.	*Social Strategies* Asking questions Cooperating with others Empathizing with others

(3) Cohen (1990) thought that strategies in specific stage in processing—that is before, during, or after the performance of some language behavior—are different. Due to that, Cohen divided strategies into two types: language learning strategies and language using strategies.

Language learning strategies refer to strategies that are employed to learn language. Language learning strategies include strategies for identifying the material that needs to be learned, distinguishing it from other materials if necessary, grouping it for easier learning, having repeated contact with the material through classroom tasks or the completion of homework assignments and formally committing the material to memory when it does not seem to be acquired naturally.

Language using strategies refer to strategies that are employed to use the language. Strategies for using the material include four subsets of strategies: retrieval, rehearsal, cover and communication strategies. Retrieval strategies are those strategies used to call up language material from storage through whatever memory searching strategies the learner can muster; rehearsal strategies refer to the strategies for rehearsing target language structures; cover strategies are those strategies that learners use to create the impression that they have control over material when they do not; and communication strategies focus on approaches to conveying a message that is both meaningful and informative for the listener or reader.

4.3　Research issues

Based on the theoretical studies, empirical research was carried out mainly focusing on the following issues.

4.3.1 The strategies that effective language learners use

The empirical research began from the study of good language learners (Rubin, 1975). According to Rubin, good language learners are willing and accurate guessers who have a strong desire to communicate, and will attempt to do so even at the risk of appearing foolish. Even though they are highly motivated to communicate, they also attend to form and meaning. Moreover, good language learners practice and monitor their own speech and the speech of others.

4.3.2 The differences of strategies that effective learners and non-effective learners use

Since the 1980s, a lot of empirical research tended to be on the strategic differences between successful and less successful learners. According to O'Malley and Chamot (1990), successful learners used more strategies and used them in ways that helped these learners complete the language tasks successfully; while less successful learners had fewer strategies and used them inappropriately in the learning task, which cannot lead to success in language learning. In their study, successful language learners, much more than less successful learners, were more purposeful in their approach to a task, monitored their comprehension and production for meaningfulness rather than only for individual components, and effectively used their prior general knowledge and their linguistic knowledge while working on a task.

4.3.3 The relationship between strategies use and the achievement of second language learning

A number of studies have sought to examine whether there are specific strategies that are statistically related to second language proficiency. But the results obtained by these studies are not always clear due to the different tests and different questionnaires.

4.3.4 The factors affecting language learning strategies

Many empirical studies have been done to investigate the factors affecting the use of language learning strategies. The factors can be divided into two types:

External factors: national origin, teaching method, language learning environment, task requirement and so on.

Internal factors: language proficiency, age, gender, motivation, belief, cognitive style and so on.

The studies all shed light on the complex phenomenon of the factors affecting the learning strategy. However, the empirical research on the effect of personality and learning style has been still insufficient.

4.3.5 The method and effect of language learning strategies training

Considerable research has been conducted on how to improve students' learning strategies. The following are three influencing training models:

1) Oxford et al.'s Seven-step Strategy Training Model

The model stresses explicit strategy awareness, instruction, training, and demonstrating the transferability of the strategy to new language tasks.

The sequence is as follows:

a.   Ask learners to do a language activity without any strategy training.

b.   Have them discuss how they did it, praise any useful strategies and self-directed attitudes that they mention, and ask them to reflect on how the strategies they selected may have facilitated the learning process.

c.   Suggest and demonstrate other helpful strategies, mentioning the need for greater self-directed and expected benefits, and making sure that the students are aware of the rationale for strategy use. Learners can also be asked to identify those strategies that they do not currently use, and consider ways that they could include new strategies in their learning repertoires.

d.   Allow learners plenty of time to practice the new strategies with language tasks.

e.   Show how the strategies can be transferred to other tasks.

f.   Provide practice using the techniques with new tasks and allow learners to make choices about the strategies they will use to complete the language learning tasks.

g.   Help students understand how to evaluate the success of their strategy use and to gauge their process as more responsible and self-directed learners.

2) O'Malley and Chamot's Four-step Strategy Training Model

In 1994, O'Malley and Chamot put forward the four-step model which is centered on solving problems. In this model, learners selected their strategies while learning and also monitoring, evaluating their strategy use to achieve the aim of transferring of the strategy to new tasks.

a.   Planning: the instructor presents the students with a language task and explains the rationale behind it. Students are then asked to plan their own approaches to the task, choosing strategies that they think will facilitate its completion.

b.   Monitoring: during the task, the students are asked to self-monitor their performance by paying attention to their strategy use and checking comprehension.

c.   Problem-solving: as they encounter difficulties, the students are expected to find their own solutions.

d.   Evaluation: after the task has been completed, the learners are then given time to debrief the activity, i.e. evaluate the effectiveness of the strategies they used during the task.

3) Cohen's Five-step Strategy Training Model

The five-step student-centered strategy training model was stated by Cohen in 1998. This model emphasizes students' choices, so it is easy for students to form the autonomy learning habit and develop students' personalities. Combining closely the strategies with the daily materials is beneficial to developing and strengthening students' learning strategies.

a.   Teachers describe, demonstrate, and give examples to students on the likely employed strategy completing a certain learning tasks.

b.   Ask students to illustrate more examples according to their own experience.

c.   Discuss the strategies in groups or in class.

d.   Encourage students to practice using different strategies and seek for their own proper strategies.

e.   Combine strategies with the everyday language learning materials and use strategies in the course of learning language materials by means of definition or concealing.

5.   Learning motivation

Besides metacognitive and cognitive strategies, affective strategy has also been put under close scrutiny. In this part, we look at the studies on motivation, as an exemplification.

Motivation refers to the inner drive, impulse, emotion, or desire that moves one to a particular action. Or in more technical terms, motivation refers to the choice people make as to what experiences or goals they will approach or avoid, and the degree of effort they will exert in that respect (Brown, 2001).

5.1   Types of motivation

Gardner and Lambert (1972) introduced the notions of **instrumental** and **integrative motivation**. In the context of language learning, instrumental motivation refers to the learner's desire to learn a language for utilitarian purposes (such as employment or travel, or to pass the examination), whereas integrative motivation refers to the desire to learn a language to integrate successfully into the target language community.

Many theorists and researchers have found that it is important to recognize the construct of motivation not as a single entity but as a multi-factorial one. Researchers like Oxford, identified various factors that impact motivation in language learning (1990):

- Attitudes (i.e. sentiments toward the learning community and the target language)
- Beliefs about self (i.e. expectancies about one's attitudes to success, self-efficacy, and anxiety)
- Goals (perceived clarity and relevance of learning goals as reasons for learning)
- Involvement (i.e. extent to which the learner actively and consciously participates in the language learning process)
- Environmental support (i.e. extent of teacher and peer support, and the integration of cultural and outside-of-class support into learning experience)

People also distinguish another two types of motivation: **intrinsic motivation** and **extrinsic motivation**, considering the source of the drive. Intrinsic motivation refers to the learner's own inner drive to the language: *I want to learn*; whereas extrinsic motivation refers to external wish or requirement exerted on the learners: *I am asked and required to learn.*

People usually agreed that integrative motivation and intrinsic motivation play a more important function than instrumental motivation and extrinsic motivation on language learning. However, we should be aware that they are not static, that is, instrumental motivation can sometimes turn into integrative motivation and extrinsic motivation can sometimes turn into intrinsic motivation, and vice versa.

5.2 Dynamic feature of motivation

Not until recently did researchers begin to notice and study the dynamic features of motivation. Traditional research on motivation focused on its components: integrative or instrumental; intrinsic or extrinsic; attitude, interest, etc. Tremblay and Gardner's (1995) model of L2 motivation is a typical example:

(Simplified)

FIGURE 5.1 Tremblay and Gardner's (1995) model of L2 motivation

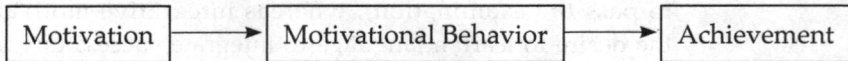

At the same time, many researchers including Tremblay and Gardner themselves proposed the counter-hypothesis that success in language learning promoted motivation and attitude which started the study of the reciprocal relationship between linguistic outcomes and attitudinal-motivational variables. Other researchers emphasized the role of classroom factors by including them in the components of L2 learning motivation (Crookes & Schmidt, 1991). Based on these studies and teaching experience in China, Tian (2005) proposed a model of the dynamic features of FL learning motivation (FIGURE 5.2).

FIGURE 5.2 Dynamic features of FL learning motivation

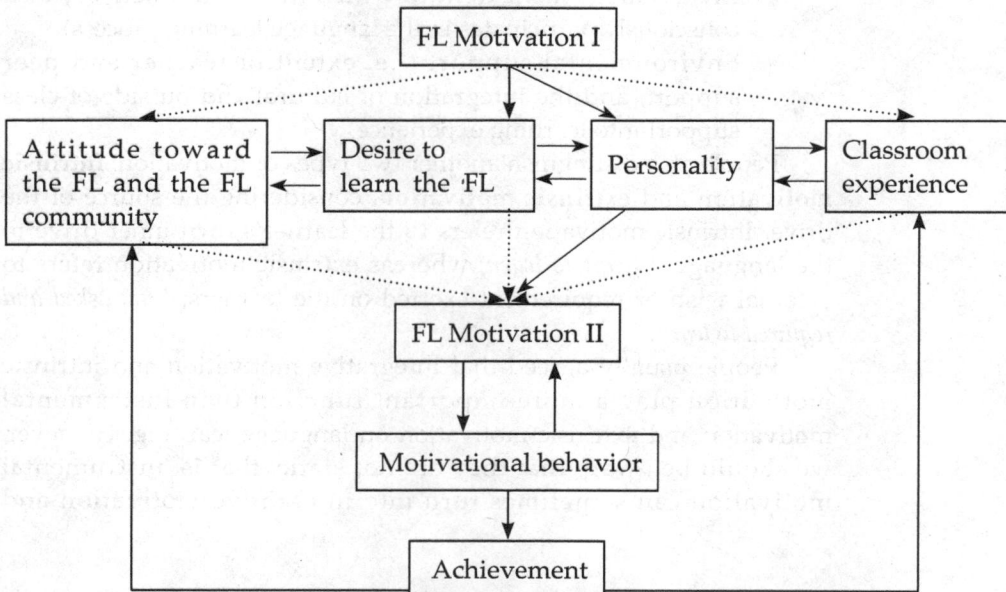

In this figure, FL Motivation I refers to students' original motive or/and interest of learning a FL. It may include attitude toward the language or/and the language community (integrative vs. instrumental); desire to learn the language as a result of either interest or requirement (intrinsic vs. extrinsic) and desire for achievement. After the students learn the language for a period of time, this motivation becomes the either decreased or increased FL Motivation II either in strength, in quality, or in both because of the change of attitude or/and desire, the learner's personality, the influence of classroom experience, and the interactive influence among them. This somewhat changed motivation influences the actual effort the students make in learning the language, their readiness in engaging actively in the work, their persistence in accomplishing the task of learning the language and their activity level which, in turn, may influence FL Motivation II and the final achievement (examination here). The achievement along with other factors influences, in a way, the attitude, desire, personality and classroom experience, which in turn affect FL Motivation II.

5.3   Classroom factors and students' learning motivation

Among the factors influencing motivation, classroom factors are more important. One reason is that, to most students in China, classroom is the most important and the only source of input. Another reason is that attitude factors—the language level, the desire and personality factors tend to be more generalized and established and, therefore, do not lend themselves easily to manipulation or modifications. Classroom factors, on the other hand, are more specific, dynamic, thus more easily to be manipulated and modified. Therefore studies should be conducted in this area to increase the learners' motivation in learning a FL.

The study of classroom factors in relation to learners' motivation can be made at the following levels, namely: the teacher, material, approach, classroom climate, and examination. In some research, syllabus is listed as one of the levels (Crookes & Schmidt, 1991). It is not mentioned here for the authors think that syllabus can be reflected at all the other levels.

5.3.1 The teacher level

Most students are highly motivated to learn a course if they like the teacher—an affiliation drive. Teacher's personality, attitude toward teaching and students, teaching style, language proficiency, teaching competence, etc. are all related to and, in fact, have great influence on students' motivation of learning a FL. To ensure a high teacher-specific motivation of the students, a teacher should make great efforts in the following aspects:

1) Be sensitive to students' needs, feelings. Have a non-judgmental, positive regard to each student. Understand them as complex human being with both virtues and faults.

2) Be a facilitator rather than an authority figure. Develop a warm rapport with the students to reduce their anxiety.

3) Promote learner autonomy by acknowledging different ways to goal attainment and learning styles, minimizing external pressure and control and fostering an intrinsic motivation, sharing responsibility with the students in the learning process.

4) Promote learner curiosity by using varieties of teaching methods and activities. Change is an essential part of maintaining attention because otherwise habituation will set in (Crookes & Schmidt, 1991).

5.3.2 The material level

Authenticity and interest are the most important factors of materials in terms of learning motivation. Research and language teachers' experience show that authentic materials increase the learners' level of on-task behavior, concentration and involvement in the target activity more than artificial materials. However, authentic materials are not necessarily interesting. In fact, students' report to authentic materials was significantly less than artificial materials.

In the current situation of English teaching in China where the materials for textbook are mainly authentic for communicative purpose, the authors suggest the use of interesting materials as supplementary materials together with recording, visual aids and other facilities.

5.3.3 The approach level

Traditional approach to English teaching in classroom in China is teacher-front talking. Students are passive in class and unmotivated to involve themselves in the learning process. In communicative language teaching classroom, where various activities and tasks are provided, students are more voluntarily involved to accomplish the task, to achieve a goal through language.

Tasks in class should be interesting, attracting, motivating and attainable. Tasks should provide certain amount of uncertainty and unpredictability to increase students' interest and involvement in them. Tasks should be challenging enough to motivate students to make efforts in accomplishing and attainable enough to accomplish after the students have worked hard to strengthen their beliefs that they have the ability to learn the target language. Even if they fail, the failure may be due to their not making enough effort or not in the "right" way instead of their ability. This is very important, though very difficult to manipulate. When the level of challenge is perceived as higher than the individual's level of ability, the result is anxiety; and when the level of challenge is perceived as lower than the individual's ability, the result is boredom (Crookes & Schmidt, 1991).

5.3.4 The classroom climate

By "classroom climate", we mean whether the classroom atmosphere is co-operative or competitive or individualistic. We will concentrate our discussion on co-operative and competitive climate, since, in individualistic situation, emphasizing individualistic effort and no interdependence among the students does not appeal to many people in terms of motivation.

Traditionally in the English classrooms in China, teachers adore competitive climate where students are believed to be highly motivated to learn since they are motivated to do better than others as a result of peer pressure. However, research has shown only the few who have strong self-confidence and do actually outperform others are motivated. Most students' motivation decreases owing to competition.

In the cooperative situation, on the other hand, where a student can achieve his/her goals only with mutual cooperation and help from all the members of the group, collaborative group effort serves the need for affiliation, and makes it easier for a feeling of achievement to be attained. The more cooperative students' attitudes are, the more they are intrinsically motivated, the more they tend to ascribe academic success to effort rather than luck, the more effort they will make to achieve the goal, and the more perseverance they will show in pursuing the learning task.

To foster cooperative climate, teachers should give more emphasis on mastery performance than on relative performance. When mastery is the goal, students are concerned with developing new skills, and tend to develop positive attitudes toward the subject studied and toward the activities involved, contributing to high task persistence.

5.3.5 The examination level

There seems to be an agreement on the reciprocal relationship between motivation and achievement, mainly the result of examination. Achievement is not only the effect but also a cause of motivation. Generally speaking, success in examination enhances a sense of self-confidence which in turn contributes to success. Failure in examination, on the other hand, will either increase or reduce motivation.

Students are usually success-oriented or failure-oriented. The former tends to attribute success to internal, stable causes (e.g. ability) and failure to external, unstable causes as well as lack of effort. This attitude maximizes the experience of positive feelings and minimizes negative feelings. In contrast, failure-oriented students are inclined to ascribe failure to internal, stable and uncontrollable causes and success to external, unstable and uncontrollable causes (luck, easy task). This attitude maximizes negative feelings, which results in low success expectancy in future learning and low motivation.

Figure 5.3 Failure and motivation: success-oriented

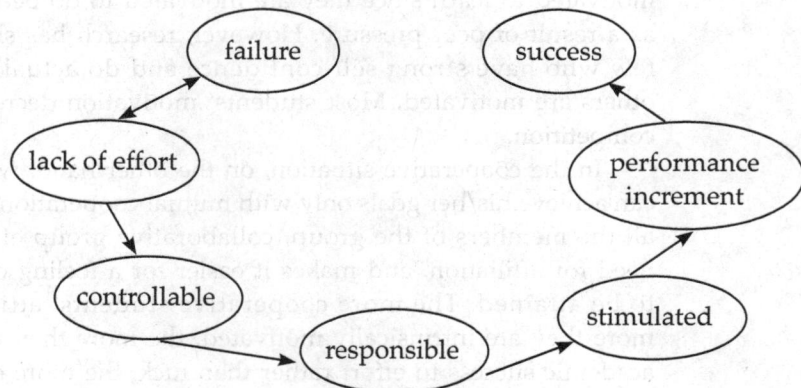

Figure 5.4 Failure and motivation: failure-oriented

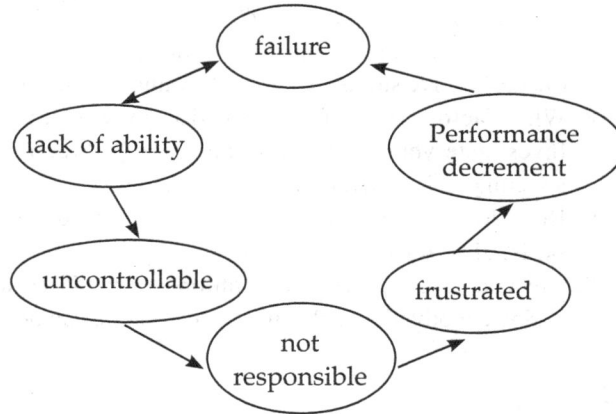

To minimize the negative influence of examination on motivation, teachers should, on the one hand, emphasize task achievement—mastery goal, instead of examination achievement—high score, to increase students' self-confidence and higher self-expectancy in future work. On the other hand, teachers should help their students analyze the cause of their failure to develop an appropriate self-concept of themselves and to motivate them to work harder.

This section analyzes the influence of classroom factors on students' learning motivation and provides some suggestions to highly motivated students in classroom. Further empirical studies are needed to verify and prove what the authors suggest.

Questions for further discussion:

1. Do you think age plays a key role in language learning? What implications can we get from Lenneberg's Critical Period Hypothesis?
2. Identify a few introverted and extroverted learners in your class. Compare their language learning styles and strategies.
3. Research shows that learners with a high motivation to achieve are moderate, not high, risk-takers. What is your view on this?
4. What is the relationship between students' learning style and teachers' teaching style? How can the two be combined for effective teaching and learning?
5. What are the differences between learning style and learning strategy?

6. How many learning strategies can you list in learning English listening, speaking, reading and writing?
7. Explain the importance of planning, monitoring, and evaluating (metacognitive strategies) in the learning of English.
8. What factors influence motivation in learning a foreign language? Investigate your classmates and identify three most important factors affecting their motivation in learning English.
9. How does anxiety influence your learning of listening and speaking skills? How do you deal with it?
10. Are you success-oriented or failure-oriented? How do you understand intrinsic motivation and extrinsic motivation can be mutually converted?

References:

Brown, H. D. 2001. *Teaching by Principles: An Interactive Approach to Language Pedagogy.* Foreign Language Teaching and Research Press.

Carroll, B. J. 1981. Specification for an English language service. Issues in Language Testing. *ELT Documents III.* British Council.

Cohen, A. 1990. *Language Learning: Insights for Learners, Teachers, and Researchers.* Newbury House.

Cook, V. 2000. *Second Language Learning and Language Teaching.* Cambridge University Press.

Crookes, G. & Schmidt, R. W. 1991. Motivation: Reopening the Research Agenda. *Language Learning,* 41(4): 469-512.

Cummings, J. 1979. Cognitive/academic language proficiency, linguistic interdependence, the optimal age question and some other matters. *Working Papers on Bilingualism*, 19: 197-205.

Ellis, R. 1994. *The Study of Second Language Acquisition.* Oxford University Press.

Gardner, R. C. & Lambert, W. E. 1972. *Attitudes and Motivation in Second Language Learning.* Newbury House.

Keefe, J. W. 1979. Learning style: An overview. In JW Keefe (Ed.). *Student Learning Styles.*

Lenneberg, E. H. 1977. *Thinking: Readings in Cognitive Science.* Cambridge University Press.

Long, M., & Scarcella, R. 1979. Age, rate, and eventual attainment in second language. acquisition. *TESOL Quarterly*, 13: 573-582.

Oller, J. W & Perkins, K. (Eds). 1978. *Language in Education: Testing the Tests.* Newbury House.

O'Malley, J. M. & Chamot, A. U. 1990. *Learning Strategies in Second Language Acquisition.* Cambridge University Press.

Oxford, R. 1990. *Language Learning Strategies.* Newbury House.

Oxford, R.1999. Anxiety and Language Learner. In J. Arnold (Ed.). *Affect in Language Learning*. Cambridge University Press.

Pimsleur, P. 1966. *Pimsleur Language Aptitude Battery*. Harcourt Brace Jovanovich.

Rubin, J. 1975. What the 'good language learner' can teach us. *TESOL Quarterly* 9: 41-51.

Stern, H. H. 1992. *Issues and Options in Language Teaching*. Oxford University Press.

Tahta, S., Wood, M., & Lowenthal, K. 1981a. Foreign accents: Factors relating to transfer of accent from the first language to a second language. *Language and Speech,* 24: 265-272.

Tahta, S., Wood, M., & Lowenthal, K. 1981b. Age changes in the ability to replicate foreign pronunciation and intonation. *Language and Speech,* 24(4): 363-372.

Tremblay, P. F. & Gardner, R. C. 1995. Expanding the motivation construction in language learning. *The Modern Language Journal* 79/4: 502-520.

Wenden, A. 1992. *Learner Strategies for Learner Autonomy*. Prentice Hall.

田金平. 2005. 课堂教学与学生外语学习动机. 中国英语教学 Vol.28 No.2.

CHAPTER 6
Cultural Awareness and English Language Teaching

In this chapter, we will examine the relationship between language and culture and see why the teaching of culture should constitute an integral part of the English language curriculum. To begin, we'd like to quote Hinkel (1999a):

"The relationship between language and culture has been a focus of attention from a variety of disciplinary perspectives for many years. Linguists, anthropologists, sociologists, psychologists, and others have sought to understand whether and how cultural factors influence aspects of human behavior such as perception, cognition, language, and communication.

Within language teaching, cultural factors have occasionally attracted the interest of both theoreticians and practitioners. Robert Lado was one of the first to suggest that cultural systems in the native culture could be compared with those in the target culture and serve as a source of transfer or interference in much the way other types of contrasting linguistic systems do. Others have examined a range of different aspects of second language use that are subject to culturally based influences, including classroom interaction, roles of teachers and students, and teaching styles."

1. Relationship between culture and language

1.1   What came first: language or culture?

The relationship between language and thought has been an ages-old chicken or egg debate. In much the same way, language and culture also pose a thorny issue. On the one hand, language seems to be woven into the very fabric of human culture; and to such an extent that it is hard to imagine what human culture would be like without language. For instance, most myths about the origin of humanity—whether religious or otherwise—seem to suggest that humans had language from the very beginning. On the other hand, what use would there be for human languages if they were not topics to talk about? Living in groups of highly intricate social interactions provides an endless amount of possible discussion material. Some sort of shared culture would seem to be a plausible component as a necessary pre-requisite for language.

This problematic feature can be best manifested by Sapir; in a more extreme opinion, he held that the worldview of a culture is subtly conditioned by the structure of its language. Language can mold and "determine" human thought, and in turn, further mold human culture (known as the Sapir-Whorf Hypothesis). In his milder version, however, Sapir (1921) states that:

Language has a setting. The people that speak it belong to a race (or a number of races), that is, to a group which is set off by physical characteristics from other groups. Again, language does not exist apart from culture, that is, from the socially inherited assemblage of practices and beliefs that determines the texture of our lives. Anthropologists have been in the habit of studying man under the three rubrics of race, language, and culture.

This statement points out clearly the dependence of language on human culture.

Donald (1998) argues for a culture-first theory in which the prior emergence of a mimetic adaptation provides scaffolding for the subsequent evolution of language. The cornerstone of Donald's theory of language evolution is *mimesis*, an evolved cognitive capacity unique to humans. The concept of mimesis involves the reduplication of action sequences for the purpose of social communication, such as when a child stamps his/her feet to communicate his/her disagreement with some decision made by the parents.

A set of domain-general cognitive skills is suggested to have evolved in early hominids, allowing rudimental knowledge sharing across individuals in a nonverbal manner. The selective advantage of such information exchange would then provide a pressure toward improving communication, leading to the emergence of language as an efficient system for sharing cultural knowledge (Donald, 1998).

Nonetheless, the approach to language evolution, according to some other scholars (like Christiansen 1994), suggests a possible third alternative, one in which language and culture evolved together in a spiral fashion, feeding on each other and constrained by the learning and processing mechanisms of early hominids.

In this sense, the issue of culture first or language first is of less importance. Instead, we can focus on the interplay between culture and language in hominid evolution, and how this interplay may have been constrained by the various cognitive mechanisms in the evolving hominid brain.

1.2   Language as expression of culture

Throughout the world, human beings use thousands of languages to communicate with one another. Yet besides being the most important communications tool, language is also an expression of culture.

One feature that distinguishes languages from other communications systems like the artificial electronic communications is that people, as members of a community, may have a *sentimental attachment* to a language because it is a vital means of expressing their culture.

The reason for people's attachment to their language is that, as sort of a *human currency*, it is an essential component of the consumption system of cultural products. For products such as literature, song and film, language is an integral part of the message that is sent. It makes little difference whether one views a film with Realone or Windows software, but it does make a difference if one views a film that has been translated rather than in its original language. These products of a cultural nature represent a significant proportion of a consumer's budget, and great importance is therefore attached to their linguistic component. For most people, language is a means of identifying with a community or a nation. In fact, many countries throughout the world are defined by a national language. Other countries include various regions identified with a linguistic community. For these communities, it is a matter of national pride to speak their own language, regardless of its effectiveness as a means of communication.

Each individual initially has his/her mother tongue. For some, this is widely sufficient to perform every desired task. But for many, learning a second language is necessary at some point in their life to broaden their communications horizons in dealing with other cultures. Language, as both a communications tool and a means of expressing a culture, is a collective *good*. If a language is used in a given environment, those who know it can fully benefit from it without costing them anything.

1.3　Language as part of culture

Language is also thought of as a part of culture, which provides a useful link between inner thought and public behavior. Saville-Troike states that cultures are systems of symbols, and language is only one of the symbolic systems in this network (1996). Duranti (1997) makes a step further by saying "one should think of language in culture and not just of language and culture. The linguistic system interpenetrates all other systems within the culture... By connecting people to their past, present and future, language becomes their past, present and future" (336-337).

Language is a social institution, both shaping and shaped by society at large, in which it plays an important role. Language is social practice both creating and created by "the structures and forces of [the] social institutions within which we live and function" (Duranti, 1997). Certainly, language cannot exist in a vacuum; there is a kind of "transfusion" at work between language and culture. Among those who have dilated upon the affinity between language and culture, Duranti succinctly encapsulates how these two interpenetrate:

To be part of a culture means to share the propositional knowledge and the rules of inference necessary to understand whether certain propositions are true (given certain premises). To the propositional knowledge, one might add the procedural knowledge to carry out tasks such as cooking, weaving, farming, fishing, giving a formal speech, answering the phone, asking for a favor, writing a letter for a job application (Duranti, 1997: 28-29).

More and more experts in ELT now believe that "cultural learning has to take place as an integral part of language learning, and vice versa. The mere acquisition of information about a foreign country, without the psychological demands of integrated language and culture learning, is inadequate as a basis for education through foreign language teaching" (Byram et al, 1994: 5).

Clearly, everyday language is "tinged" with cultural bits and pieces. By the very act of talking, we assume social and cultural roles, which are so deeply entrenched in our thought processes as to go unnoticed. Culture defines not only what its members should think or learn but also what they should ignore or treat as irrelevant.

1.4   Language learning style and culture

In learning a language, learning styles are very important. Learning styles involve cognitive, affective, and physiological characteristics, which enable us to individually perceive and interact with our learning environment. Cognitive factors are psychological (left brain/right brain, analytic/relational, reflective/impulsive) and sociological (concept of self, partner, group); affective factors include the emotional (motivation, persistence, self-confidence); and the physiological factors are environmental (light, sound, temperature, design structure) and physical (perception, time, posture, mobility, food intake). Any combination of the above preferences affects learning; as a result, learning style preferences are varied and complex.

Studies show that learning style preferences are shaped by culture, which provides the "mold" through which we obtain, process, and use information. Culture, as a common social norm, here refers to what the group generally shares through learned behavior in similar environments. Thus, learning styles have a dimension of socialization through interaction with family, friends, and others in the community.

Learners from different cultures perceive reality differently. They obtain information, solve problems, and create on the basis of both culturally and individually unique perspectives and experiences. Misunderstanding cultural behavioral styles or assuming learning can happen with just one fixed style of teaching and can create a dissonance between teacher and student and lead to mistreating, mislabeling, and misplacing learners. Such teaching can be undemocratic and inequitable and fosters academic difficulty, tracking, and, eventually, limited options for future learner success. Learning style diversity must be considered in a social-cultural context.

1.5   Summary

Both language and culture have been "adequately" and "inadequately" defined up till now. Both terms have enjoyed definitions of hundreds, yet none of them have ever been acknowledged as a norm. For example:

Language is defined as a tool man uses to encapsulate thoughts, symbols, and emotion (Giles et al., 1977), or as social history of a people, structuring social perceptions of the past and interpreting the future, that is, creating consciousness (Khleif, 1979), or ....

On culture, Kramsch (1998: 127) offers three definitions:

a. Membership in a discourse community that shares a common social space and history, and a common system of standards for perceiving, believing, evaluating, and acting.

b. The discourse community itself.

c. The system of standards itself.

Rose (2001)[1] thinks culture is: A way of life; a set of social practices; a system of beliefs; a shared history or set of experiences. A culture may be synonymous with a country, or a region, or a nationality or it may cross several countries or regions. Tylor (1920) states that culture is a compound including knowledge, belief, art, law, morals, customs and any other capabilities and habits acquired by man as a member of society (see Lustig and Koester, 1999).

No matter how many definitions have been put forward on language or culture, and regardless of the complex and even controversial state of their relations, the two are definitely inter-knotted. At any rate, to speak means choosing a particular way of entering the world and a particular way of sustaining relationships with those we come in contact with. It is often through language use that we, to a large extent, are members of a community of ideas and practices. In social contexts, they are co-influenced and co-influencing each other. Language is the presentation of culture and without cultural knowledge, it is almost impossible to learn language well.

2.   Culture in foreign language teaching

Since culture can be broadly defined as an integrated pattern of human behavior that includes thoughts, languages, practices, values,

---

[1] See http://www.teachingenglish.org.uk/think/methodology/intercultural2.shtml, retrieved 28 Nov. 2006.

customs, manners of interacting, etc. and roles, relationships and expected behaviors of a racial, ethnic, religious or social group; and language is not only part of the way culture is defined; it also reflects culture (Peterson & Coltrane, 2003)[1], then, one question arises, that if language and culture are so intricately intertwined, why should we overtly focus on culture when there are other aspects of the curriculum that need more attention?

There are a number of reasons. First of all, to believe that whoever is learning the foreign language is also learning the cultural knowledge and skills required to be a competent L2/FL speaker "denies the complexity of culture, language learning, and communication" (Lessard-Clouston, 1997). Second, it is deemed important to include culture in the foreign language curriculum because it helps correct stereotypes learners might have toward certain cultures and helps enhance students' awareness in learning them. The third reason for expressly teaching culture in the foreign language classroom is to enable students to take control of their own learning as well as to achieve autonomy by evaluating and questioning the wider context within which the learning of the target language is embedded. Tomalin & Stempleski (1993: 7-8) consider that the teaching of culture has the following goals:

1) To help students understand that all people exhibit culturally-conditioned behaviors.
2) To help students understand that social variables such as age, sex, social class, and place of residence influence the ways in which people speak and behave.
3) To help students become more aware of conventional behavior in common situations in the target culture.
4) To help students increase their awareness of the cultural connotations of words and phrases in the target language.
5) To help students develop the ability to evaluate and refine generalizations about the target culture, in terms of supporting evidence.
6) To help students develop the necessary skills to locate and organize information about the target culture.
7) To stimulate students' intellectual curiosity about the target culture, and to encourage empathy towards its people.

Thus, the culture associated with a language cannot be learned in

---

[1] Peterson & Coltrane. 2003. Culture in Second Language Teaching, retrieved online 4 Nov., 2006 at http://www.cal.org/resources/Digest/0309peterson.html.

a few lessons about holidays, a few songs, or costumes. Culture is a much broader concept that is inherently tied to many of the linguistic concepts taught in second language classes.

2.1　Importance of culture in language teaching

Linguists, anthropologists and education experts have long recognized that the forms and uses of a given language reflect the cultural values of the society in which the language is spoken. And culture is not a static phenomenon. Robinson (1988: 11) sees culture as a dynamic "system of symbols and meanings" whereby "past experience influences meaning, which in turn affects future experience, which in turn affects subsequent meaning, and so on"

Language learners need to be aware of the culturally appropriate ways to address people, express gratitude, make requests, and agree or disagree with someone. They should know that behaviors and intonation patterns that are appropriate in their own speech community may be perceived differently by members of the target language speech community. They have to understand that, in order for communication to be successful, language use must be associated with other culturally appropriate behavior. Moreover, cultural awareness should be viewed as an important component informing and enriching communicative competence.

As a result, teaching a foreign language is not tantamount to giving a homily on syntactic structures or learning new vocabulary and expressions, but mainly incorporates cultural elements, which are intertwined with language itself, in that effective communication is more than a matter of language proficiency and that, apart from enhancing and enriching communicative competence, cultural competence can also lead to empathy and respect toward different cultures as well as promote objectivity and cultural perspicacity.

Culture teaching allows learners to increase their knowledge of the target culture in terms of people's way of life, values, attitudes, and beliefs, and how these manifest themselves or are couched in linguistic categories and forms. More specifically, the teaching of culture can make learners aware of speech acts, connotations, etiquette, i.e. appropriate or inappropriate behavior, as well as provide them with the opportunity to act out being a member of the target culture.

2.2   Implicitness and explicitness in culture teaching

For many years, culture has been mainly taught implicitly in foreign language teaching classrooms; it's embedded in the linguistic forms that students are learning. With more awareness of the cultural features reflected in the language, some language teaching programs are opening culture courses and teachers are paying more attention to making those cultural features explicit topics of discussion in relation to the linguistic forms being studied. For example, an English as a second language (ESL) teacher can help students understand socially appropriate communication, such as making requests that show respect such as, "Hey guy, come here" may be a linguistically correct request, but it is not a culturally appropriate way for a student to address a professor. And it is often culturally inappropriate to evade tips on some occasions. Students will master a language only when they learn both its linguistic and cultural norms.

Cultural information should not be presented in a judgmental, even a biased fashion, but in a way that does not place value or judgment on distinctions between the students' native culture and the culture explored in the classroom. Some teachers and researchers have found it effective to present students with objects or ideas that are specific to the culture of study but are unfamiliar to the students. The students are given clues or background information about the objects and ideas so that they can incorporate the new information into their own worldview.

It is also important to teach students not to be stereotyped and help them understand that cultures are not monolithic. A variety of successful behaviors are possible for any type of interaction in any particular culture. Teachers must allow students to observe and explore cultural interactions from their own perspectives to enable them to find their own voices in the second language speech community. In a word, implicit and explicit methods should both be used in introducing culture to language learners.

2.3   Culture teaching in language syllabi

Foreign language learning is comprised of several components, including grammatical competence, communicative strategies, socio-cultural competence, etc. Cultural competence, i.e. the knowledge of the conventions, customs, beliefs, and systems of meaning of another country, is indisputably an integral part of foreign language learning, and many teachers have seen it as their goal to incorporate the teaching of culture into the foreign language curriculum.

However, many language teachers believe that language teaching consists of teaching the four skills "plus" culture. This dichotomy of language and culture is an entrenched feature of language teaching around the world. It is part of the linguistic heritage of the profession: Culture is seen as mere information conveyed by the language, not as a feature of language itself; cultural awareness becomes an educational object on itself, separate from language.

Buttjes (1990: 55) has attempted to show that language and culture are from the start inseparably connected. He summarizes the reasons why this should be the case:

1. language acquisition does not follow a universal sequence, but differs across cultures;
2. the process of becoming a competent member of society is realized through exchanges of language in particular social situations;
3. every society orchestrates the ways in which children participate in particular situations, and this, in turn, affects the form, the function and the content of children's utterances;
4. caregivers' primary concern is not with grammatical input, but with the transmission of socio-cultural knowledge;
5. the native learner, in addition to language, acquires also the paralinguistic patterns and the kinesics of his or her culture.

The implications of Buttjes' findings for the teaching of culture are evident. Language teaching is culture teaching as Buttjes notes, "language teachers need to go beyond monitoring linguistic production in the classroom and become aware of the complex and numerous processes of intercultural mediation that any foreign language learner undergoes…"(Buttjes, 1990: 55)

Foreign language learning is meanwhile foreign culture learning and to learn a foreign language is not merely to learn how to communicate but also to discover how much leeway the target language allows learners to manipulate grammatical forms, sounds, and meanings, and to reflect upon, or even flout, socially accepted norms at work both in their own or the target culture. And this notion should be clearly reflected in syllabus/curriculum design.

Although there is still a long way to go in effectively incorporating culture not only into the foreign language curriculum but also into learners' repertoire and outlook on life, we have seen signs in this regard in ELT in China. Admittedly, this trend goes in line with better understanding of language teaching and learning. Communication is viewed not only as an exchange of information but also a highly cognitive as well as affective and value-laden activity. By virtue of the increasing multi-cultural trend of various societies, in syllabi design, learners should be helped to be aware of certain cultural factors at work, such as age, gender, and social class, etc.

3. Instructional strategies for teaching culture

As discussed above, cultural activities and objectives should be carefully organized and incorporated into lesson plans to enrich and deepen the teaching content. In this regard, Rose (2001) dwells on the notion of **intercultural communicative competence.**

Intercultural communicative competence is an attempt to raise students' awareness of their own culture, and in so doing, help them to interpret and understand other cultures. It is not just a body of knowledge, but a set of practices requiring knowledge, skills and attitudes (Rose, 2001).

Chris Rose further lists the components of **intercultural awareness skills**[1]:

- observing, identifying and recognizing
- comparing and contrasting
- negotiating meaning
- dealing with or tolerating ambiguity
- effectively interpreting messages
- limiting the possibility of misinterpretation
- defending one's own point of view while acknowledging the legitimacy of others
- accepting difference

But how can we incorporate culture into the foreign language curriculum, with a view to fostering cultural awareness and communicating insight into the target civilization?

The usual practice is through discoursing upon the geographical environment and historical or political development of the foreign culture, its institutions and customs, its literary achievements, even the minute details of the everyday life of its members. At other times, insights into the target community have taken the form of small

---

[1] Adapted from http://www.teachingenglish.org.uk/think/methodology/intercultural2.shtml, retrieved 10 May 2006.

lectures on such issues as marriage customs and ceremonies, festivals, Sunday excursions, and so forth. To teach culture more efficiently, we should take more elements into consideration:

- Culture teaching must be commensurate with the dynamic aspects of culture. Students' knowledge of and about the L2/FL culture through receptive channel is not sufficient. Learners will also need to master some skills in culturally appropriate communication and behavior for the target culture.
- Cultural awareness is necessary if students are to develop an understanding of the dynamic nature of the target culture, and this calls for culture teaching in a systematic and structured way.
- Evaluation of culture learning is a necessary component of the foreign culture curriculum, providing students with feedback and keeping teachers accountable in their teaching.

In the following sections, we have a look at some practical considerations in culture teaching.

3.1 Using authentic materials

Using authentic sources from the native speech community helps to engage students in authentic cultural experiences. The authentic materials can include movies, TV documentaries, sit-coms, ads, news broadcasts, web sites, photographs, magazines, newspapers, restaurant menus, travel brochures, and other audio-visual or printed materials. Teachers can adapt their use of authentic materials to suit the age and language proficiency level of the students. For example, beginning language students can watch pictures, scrapbooks, cartoons, listen to music, and even watch and listen to video clips taken from a television show in the target language and focus on such cultural conventions as greetings. The teacher might supply students with a detailed translation or give them a chart, diagram, or outline to complete while they listen to a dialogue or watch a video. After the class has viewed the relevant segments, the teacher can engage the students in discussion of the cultural norms represented in the segments and what these norms might say about the values of the culture. Discussion topics might include nonverbal behaviors (e.g. the physical distance between speakers, gestures, eye contact, societal roles, and how people in different social roles relate to each other). Students might describe the behaviors they observe and discuss which of them are similar to their native culture and which are not and determine strategies for effective communication in the target language.

With the help of multi-media equipments, film and television segments offer students opportunities to witness behaviors that are not as vivid or obvious in text forms. Film (also termed as light and shadow) is often one of the more current and comprehensive ways to encapsulate the look, feel, and rhythm of a culture. Film also connects students with language and cultural issues simultaneously (Stephens, 2001), such as depicting conversational timing or turn taking in conversation. Studies show that students achieved significant gains in overall cultural knowledge after watching videos from the target culture in the classroom.

Proverbs and saying can be brought into the language classroom. Common proverbs in the target language could focus on how the proverbs are different from or similar to proverbs in the students' native language and how differences might underscore historical and cultural background. Using proverbs as a way to explore culture can also provide a way to analyze the stereotypes about and misperceptions of the culture, as well as a way for students to explore the values that are often represented in the proverbs of their native culture.

Literary texts are often replete with cultural information and evoke memorable reactions for readers. Rather than being a fifth adjunct to the four skills (reading, writing, speaking, and listening), culture can best find its expression through the medium of literature. Texts that are carefully selected for a given group of students and with specific goals in mind can be very helpful in allowing students to acquire insight into a culture. As Valdes (1986: 137) notes, literature is a viable component of second language programs at the appropriate level and…one of [its] major functions …is to serve as a medium to transmit the culture of the people who speak the language in which it is written.

First of all, literary texts are an important resource of authentic language that learners can avail themselves of. Exposure to literary works can help them to expand their language awareness and develop their language competence. Moreover, trying to interpret and account for the values, assumptions, and beliefs infusing the literary texts of the target culture is instrumental in defining and redefining those obtaining in the home culture.

3.2   Designing effective activities

Role Play

The task of language teacher, as observed by Ellis, is to stimulate students' interest in the target culture, and to help establish the foreign language classroom "not so much as a place where the language is taught, but as one where opportunities for learning of various kinds are provided through the interactions that take place between the participants" (Ellis, 1992: 171).

Role playing can be made use of to stimulate students' interest and enhance their awareness of culture. In role plays, students can act out inappropriate language use or a miscommunication that is based on cultural differences. For example, after learning about ways of addressing different groups of people in the target culture, such as people of the same age and older people, students could role play a situation in which an inappropriate greeting is used. Other students observe the role play and try to identify the reason for the miscommunication. They then role play the same situation using a culturally appropriate form of address.

Kodotchigova (2002) suggests a step-by-step guide to making a role play in cultural teaching. The steps are as follows:

Step 1 A situation for a role play

To begin with, choose a situation for a role play, keeping in mind students' needs and interests. Teachers should select role plays that will give the students an opportunity to practice what they have learned. To make sure the role play is interesting, the teacher can let the students choose the situation themselves. They might either suggest themes that intrigue them or select a topic from a list of given situations.

Step 2 Role play design

After choosing a context for a role play, the next step is to come up with ideas on how this situation may develop. Students' level of language proficiency should be taken into consideration. If you feel that your role play requires more profound linguistic competence than the students possess, it would probably be better to simplify it or to leave it until appropriate.

Step 3 Linguistic preparation

Once you have selected a suitable role play, predict the language needed for it. At the beginning level, the language needed is almost completely predictable. The higher the level of students the more difficult it is to prefigure accurately what language students will need, but some prediction is possible anyway. It is recommended to introduce any new vocabulary before the role play.

At the beginning level, you might want to elicit the development of the role play scenario from your students and then enrich it. For example, the situation of the role play is returning an item of clothing back to the store. The teacher asks questions, such as, "In this situation what will you say to the salesperson?", "What will the salesperson say?" and writes what the students dictate on the right side of the board. When this is done, on the left side of the board the instructor writes down useful expressions, asking the students, "Can the customer say it in another way?", "What else can the salesperson say?" This way of introducing new vocabulary makes the students more confident acting out a role play.

Step 4 Factual preparation

This step implies providing the students with concrete information and clear role descriptions so that they could play their roles with confidence. For example, in the situation at a railway station, the person giving the information should have relevant information: the times and destination of the trains, prices of tickets, etc. In a more advanced class and in a more elaborate situation include on a cue card a fictitious name, status, age, personality, and fictitious interests and desires.

Describe each role in a manner that will let the students identify with the characters. Use the second person "you" rather than the third person "he" or "she". If your role presents a problem, just state the problem without giving any solutions.

At the beginning level cue cards might contain detailed instructions. For example,

Cue Card A:

YOU ARE A TAXI-DRIVER

1. Greet the passenger and ask him/her where he/she wants to go.
2. Say the price. Make some comments on the weather. Ask the passenger if he/she likes this weather.
3. Answer the passenger's question. Boast that your son has won the school swimming competition. Ask if the passenger likes swimming.

Cue Card B:

> **YOU ARE A PASSENGER IN A TAXI**
>
> 1. Greet the taxi driver and say where you want to go. Ask what the price will be.
> 2. Answer the taxi-driver's question and ask what kind of weather he/she likes.
> 3. Say that you like swimming a lot and that you learned to swim 10 years ago when you went to Spain with your family.

Step 5 Assigning the roles

Some instructors ask for volunteers to act out a role play in front of the class, though it might be a good idea to plan in advance what roles to assign to which students. At the beginning level the teacher can take one of the roles and act it out as a model. Sometimes, the students have role play exercises for the home task. They learn useful words and expressions, think about what they can say and then act out the role play in the next class. There can be one or several role play groups. Very often, optimum interaction can be reached by letting the students work in one group with their friends.

Whether taking any part in the role play or not, the teacher should be as unobtrusive as possible. He or she is listening for students' errors and making notes. Mistakes noted during the role play will provide the teacher with feedback for further practice and revision. It is recommended that the instructor avoid intervening in a role play with error corrections.

Step 6 Follow-up

Once the role play is finished, spend some time on debriefing. This does not mean pointing out and correcting mistakes. After the role play, the students are satisfied with themselves, they feel that they have used their knowledge of the language for something concrete and useful. This feeling of satisfaction will disappear if every mistake is analyzed. It might also make the students less confident and less willing to do the other role plays.

Follow-up means asking every student's opinion about the role play and welcoming their comments. The aim is to discuss what has happened in the role play and what they have learned. In addition to group discussion, an evaluation questionnaire can be used.

Problem solving

Cultural problem solving is an important way to provide cultural information (Singhal, 1998). In this case, learners are presented with some information but they are on the horns of a dilemma; learners are given the opportunity to step into the shoes of a member of the target culture. And they need to learn culture in experiencing culture.

Indisputably, conventional behavior in common situations is a subject with which students should acquaint themselves. For instance, in the US, it is not common for a student who is late for class to knock on the door and apologize to the teacher. Rather, this behavior is most likely to be frowned upon and have the opposite effect, even though it is common behavior in some other cultures. As a result, students need to learn the correct attitude and action to tackle such a problem (like explaining and apologizing after class).

Culture realia

Knowing how to say something with correct pronunciation, grammar, and vocabulary is not sufficient for effective communication in an FL/SL. Learners need to understand the culture and society and must know what to say and what not to say, when to say it, and how to adjust what they say for the occasion. Foreign/second language students, especially "Beginning foreign language students want to feel, touch, smell, and see the foreign peoples and not just hear their language" (Peck, 1998). At any rate, the foreign language classroom should become a "cultural island" (Peck, 1998), and teachers are expected to bring in the class posters, pictures, maps, and other realia in order to help students develop "a mental image" of the target culture (Peck, 1998).

Students can be presented with objects (e.g. figurines, tools, etc.) or images that originate from the target culture. The students can then be responsible for finding information about the item in question, either by conducting research or by being given clues to investigate. They can either write a brief summary or make an oral presentation to the class about the cultural relevance of the item. Such activities can also serve as a foundation from which teachers can go on to discuss larger cultural, historical, and linguistic factors that tie in with the objects. Such contextualization is, in fact, important to the success of using culture capsules.

Native speakers as cultural resources

According to Straub (1999), the teaching of culture is to foster understanding of the target culture from an insider's perspective—an empathetic view that permits students to accurately interpret foreign cultural behaviors. Contact with native speakers is good for fostering empathy in culture learning.

In the present world, cultural and economic exchanges are getting more and more frequent. In many places, schools are more culturally and ethnically diverse than they have ever been. Native language teachers, exchange students, immigrant students, and even foreign visitors can be invited to the classroom as expert sources. These students can share authentic insights into the home and cultural life of native speakers of the language. Through these activities, students can better understand the cultural context of day-to-day conversational conventions such as greetings, farewells, forms of address, thanking, making requests, and giving or receiving compliments. And this means more than just being able to produce grammatical sentences. It means knowing what is appropriate to say to whom, and in what situations, and it means understanding the beliefs and values represented by the various forms and usages of the language.

Group work

Another insightful activity is to divide the class into groups of three or four and have them draw up a list of those characteristics and traits that supposedly distinguish the home and target cultures.

Once major differences (between the home and target cultures) have been established, students can be introduced to more words or expressions like "marriage", "euthanasia", "homosexuality", etc., and thus be assisted in taking an insider's view of the connotations of these words and concepts.

For instance, in English culture, both animals and humans have feelings, get sick, and are buried in cemeteries. In Indian culture, bull is regarded as a sacred animal, which calls for "respect". In Hispanic culture, however, the distinction between humans and animals is great, and bullfighting is unlikely to be seen as a cruelty. For Spanish people, a bull is not equal to the man who kills it—a belief that has the effect of exonerating, so to speak, the bullfighter from all responsibility; a bull can be strong but not intelligent or skilful; these are qualities attributed to human beings. In this light, notions such as "cruel", "slaughter", carry vastly different undertones in the two cultures (Lado, 1986).

Culture assimilators and cultoons

Henrichsen (1998)[1] proposes two interesting methods: culture assimilators and cultoons. Culture assimilators comprise short descriptions of various situations where one person from the target culture interacts with persons from the home culture. Then follow four possible interpretations of the meaning of the behavior and speech of the interactants, especially those from the target culture. Once the students have read the description, they choose one of the four options they think is the correct interpretation of the situation. When every single student has made his choice, they discuss why some options are correct or incorrect.

On the other hand, cultoons are visual culture assimilators. Students are provided with a series of four pictures highlighting points of misunderstanding or culture shock experienced by persons in contact with the target culture. Here, students are asked to evaluate the characters' reactions in terms of appropriateness (within the target culture). Once misunderstandings are dissipated, learners read short texts explaining what was happening in the cultoons and why there was misunderstanding.

The premises of using culture assimilators and cultoons are: when teaching language use, teachers are teaching not only a rule-governed structural system, whose usage is sanctioned by society, but the actualization of meaning potential associated with particular situation types. By teaching grammar teachers are teaching contextual shaping, contour. What's more, language use has its own social grammar or roles, settings, rules of speaking, and norms of interpretation. The meaningful context is critical for language learning has been widely recognized.

3.3 The role of the teacher

In the language classroom that integrates culture teaching and learning, what are teachers? Are they activities managers, language facilitators or resource providers? In line with Rose (2001)[2], intercultural learning gives the teacher a role not only as one or more

---

[1] Henrichsen, L.E. 1998. Understanding Culture and Helping Students Understand Culture. Linguistics 577 (Online), http://linguistics.byu.edu/classes/ling577lh, retrieved 9 Mar. 2004.

[2] See http://www.teachingenglish.org.uk/think/methodology/intercultural2.shtml, retrieved 8 May 2005.

of these, but also as an educator.

Teachers are helping language learners to become more aware of the world around them, and to better interact with that world. These are the crucial roles of the teacher. Moreover, some FL teachers tend to have a wide variety of different backgrounds in different disciplines. They have different experiences, and in many cases may have traveled extensively and got to know several different cultures. They may have undergone the experience of living in, adjusting to and understanding a different culture. There is a lot that they can bring to the job. They are unique mediators of cultural relativity.

Concerning the timing for language teachers to introduce "cultural awareness", Chris Rose is against the traditional practice: Seeing cultural awareness as something for advanced learners, an extension exercise that can be "tacked on" to an ordinary lesson, which is partly due to "the all-too frequent error of assuming that students with a low level of English also have a low intellect generally, or that it is impossible to explain intellectual concepts in level one English" (Rose, 2001). Intercultural awareness, as a fundamental feature of language and an integral part of language learning, is important at all levels.

4. Problems faced by Chinese learners in English culture learning and recommendations

4.1 Major problems

From our experience as English teachers, we find that Chinese English learners tend to be shy. With the presence of teachers and during group discussions, they tend to be over-anxious. And as for oral discussions, debates, speech presentations and essay writing they have the habit of "beating around the bush": not going to point directly but describe a lot of background information, histories, and only mention their point of view briefly at the end.

Young (1996) mentions there are different expectations and norms between Chinese and English native speakers regarding where the argument is going and where it is coming from. In a similar way, Green (1996) finds that in writing argumentative essays, Chinese students tend to state their viewpoint at the end which is "foreign" to most from English-speaking cultures.

More problems lie in time concept and reasoning. As observed by Wu (2004)[1], a common complaint by westerners in communicating with Chinese is that they always do not focus on getting things done in an efficient manner. Part of the reason is the huge difference in the Chinese and western worldviews. Scollon & Scollon (1995) differentiate between the western Utopian and eastern Confucian Golden Age concepts of time. The Utopian concept of time is based on a belief in progress and we have yet to reach our greatest accomplishments. In addition, there is always the idea of time urgency to reach our goals as soon as possible. The Golden Age concept of time, on the contrary, is based on the idea that the present time is worse than the past. Therefore, there is no hurry to rush forward because moving forward is getting away from the better conditions of the past. One obvious intercultural communication (ICC) problem from this difference is that those holding the Utopian concept have a negative evaluation of the slower counterparts from the Golden Age.

The inclination of Chinese to be more inductive in reasoning as compared to the deductive reasoning which is more common in the west causes differences in the expectations of the flow of arguments (Scollon & Scollon, 1995). These two characteristics contribute to a totally different set of expectations and norms of Chinese learners in their logic of arguments compared to that of native speakers of English. At the same time, they explain why Chinese learners have the tendency of giving a lot of background information before stating their points of views at the end in introducing their arguments.

Wu (2004) also mentions the organization of society as a factor contributing to the difficulty for Chinese students to learn English culture, according to whom, the lack of initiatives in participating in classroom activities is caused by Chinese learners' concept of the roles of teachers and students, in which teachers should be dominating, authoritative while students should be obedient and respect teachers who are at a higher level in the social hierarchy. Confucianism emphasizes the hierarchy of relationships and collectivism. Each individual in the society has a set of responsibilities and obligations to fulfill in the hierarchy which is based on kinship, age, experience, education, gender, geographical region, political affiliation, etc. In contrast to the western individualistic and egalitarian culture, Chinese

---

[1] Manfred Wu Man Fat. 2004. "Problems Faced by Chinese Learners in L2 English Learning and Pedagogic Recommendations from an Inter-Cultural Communication Perspective". See http://www3.telus.net/linguisticsissues/problemschinese.html, retrieved 7 Oct. 2006.

perceive themselves not as biological individuals but are intimately related to immediate kinship. The hierarchical organization of Chinese society results in differences in pragmatic issues. For example, Chinese are less likely to express their emotion, either positive or negative through jokes or invectives especially in the workplace. Another example given by Brick (1991) is the difficulty of young Chinese in addressing older Australians by their first names and expressing their own opinions to authorities. The emphasis on the interests of groups rather than that of individuals means that one will employ different rhetorical strategies in communicating with those of own group (ingroup) and others (outgroup). Brick (1991) mentions that in addressing friends and those in subordinate position, Chinese tend to be direct or even rude when translated into English.

In terms of non-verbal communication, Scollon & Scollon (1995) point out the importance of kinesics and proxemics. The former is the movement of our bodies while the latter refers to the use of space. One example they mention is that Chinese tend to smile more easily than westerners when they feel difficulty or embarrassment. Smile because of embarrassment by a Chinese might be interpreted as being friendly by a westerner and cause problems in intercultural communication. Another example is that Chinese tend to avoid direct eye-contact in face-to-face interaction out of respect while they might be perceived as not paying attention or even disrespectful by westerners. With regard to space, Scollon & Scollon (1995) point out Asians in general have a smaller sphere of personal space than westerners. With different expectations of personal space, a Chinese speaking to an American might find that he or she is trying to keep a distance while on the other hand the American might feel that the Chinese is intruding into his or her personal space. This inevitably affects the evaluation of each other and interpretations of interactions.

Chan (1992)[1] provides a summary of contrast in communicating styles between Asian and western cultures as follows:

Asian	Western
Indirect	Direct
Implicit, nonverbal	Explicit, verbal
Formal	Informal
Goal oriented	Spontaneous
Emotionally controlled	Emotionally expressive
Self-effacing, modest	Self-promoting, egocentric

[1] See http://www3.telus.net/linguisticsissues/problemschinese.html, retrieved 6 Dec. 2005.

4.2   Recommendations for English cultural teaching in China

Socio-cultural awareness

The most direct way of raising intercultural communication awareness is to share the cultural differences explicitly with learners (Wu, 2004). Dirven and Putz (1993) equate the aim of foreign language learning as to an awareness of cultural communicative differences, followed by increased tolerance and finally accommodation. Dunnett et al. (1986) point out the importance of asking inter-cultural questions, choosing ICC topics for discussion and problem solving to raise learners' awareness of intercultural differences. For instance, they suggest learners list down stereotypes with teachers leading discussions on the stereotypes. They give the following specific suggestions on how to achieve greater cultural awareness among learners:

- Giving more emphasis on ICC elements in curriculum, select materials and course books with stronger emphasis on ICC issues, as well as incorporating contents and developing specific strategies for teaching culture.
- Providing learners with a comprehensive program of extra-curricular activities on English-speaking cultures.
- Hiring teachers with a strong background in comparative culture or ICC and those with overseas training experience.
- Providing in-service training in ICC to teachers and orientation to new teachers.

Another way of raising the cultural awareness for teachers is to conduct simple comparison between L2 culture and learners' cultures. Lado (1986) provides some general guidelines for such comparison, in which teachers can look for *form, meaning, distribution, misinformation* and *linguistic evidence* with learners. *Form* is the physical setting and objects of a event; *Meaning* refers to the meaning of a event to members of the culture; *Distribution* is the frequency which the event occurs; *Misinformation* is the wrong misinterpretation of people of another culture towards the event; and finally *Linguistic Evidence* is the differences in languages the two cultures in describing the same event.

Wu (2004) uses a western wedding dinner as an illustration of the application of Lado's guidelines. The differences in *Form* can be easily recognized, with buffet food distinctively different from Chinese food. Other differences in *Form* include the clothes of couple, guests, etc., how food is placed, decorations and how people eat. Teachers can ask learners how a western wedding dinner is different from a

Chinese wedding dinner. More matured learners might be able to tell the differences in the *Meanings* attached to marriage between Chinese and western cultures. In discussing *Distribution*, teachers can point out the importance of the selection of wedding date and time for Chinese wedding. It is because a good wedding date and time will bring good luck and prosperity not only to the couple but also to its immediate families, ancestors and offspring.

Tomalin and Stempleski (1993) list out the guidelines for ICC activities of general knowledge of people, knowledge of the English speaking cultures, cultural behaviors, patterns of communication, values and attitudes, etc. They provide language teachers with the following practical teaching principles:

1. Use the target language to access the culture.
2. Incorporate cultural behaviors as an integral part of lesson.
3. Achieve the socio-economic competence learners feel they need.
4. Make the awareness of one's own and target cultures as the aim for all levels of learners.
5. Let learners know teaching about culture does not necessarily result in changes in behaviors but increased awareness and tolerance towards other cultures.

As culture learning should be in tandem with language learning, teachers should make sure there is a balance between the two elements (Wu, 2004). In his teaching model which consists of four components, namely, language learning, language awareness, cultural awareness and cultural experience, Byram (1990) emphasizes the mutually supportiveness of the components and the balance in the proportion allocated to each component in different learning stages.

Non-verbal communication

Teachers should raise Chinese learners' awareness of their non-verbal and paralinguistic features such as kinesics, proxemics and differences in communication styles as summarized by Chan (1992) discussed above.

Raising meta-pragmatic awareness, which refers to speakers' capacity to comment on language use and give off signals about social relationships (Roberts, 1998: 111) should not be neglected too. Since meta-pragmatic activity is implicit and suggestive in language and non-verbal communication, there is a high chance of misunderstanding as meta-pragmatic assessments are based on inferences. This is especially true in ICC because of the differences of worldviews, concepts on the organization of society, etc., of different cultures.

Linguistic competence

In teaching English culture, teachers should minimize learners' transference of linguistics and paralinguistic features of their own Chinese culture (Wu, 2004). Comparison of Chinese and western cultures can help learners to be more aware of the differences thus improve their grammatical accuracy. Linguistic relativity theory implies that teachers should raise learners' sensitivity towards the linguistic aspects of English which do not exist or are not emphasized in the Chinese culture. Moreover, teacher's focus on training pronunciation and intonation should be on intelligibility rather than the achievement of native standard (Walker, 2001)[1]. This is especially true for native teachers who might easily set unrealistic standards for learners.

4.3 Summary

To sum up, sharing of knowledge and skills, comparative analysis of cultures conducted by learners and teachers themselves, providing ICC experiences through visits and activities, comparative analysis of the linguistics aspects are effective means to develop Chinese learners' intercultural competence as well as to raise the tolerance of both learners and teachers towards other cultures (Wu, 2004).

The ultimate goal of ICC learning is for learners to achieve "intercultural communicative competence" (Widdowson, 1992). L2 English teachers should also take this into account in order to allow learners to develop not only grammatical but also discoursal competence. Examples of activities to be conducted include case studies, contrastive analysis, culture capsules, culture quizzes, dialogues, problem solving, readings, visits and cultural exchange program, etc.

At a wider scale, education authorities in China can carry out "community languages" by incorporating ICC learning as one of the core component in curriculum. However, most educational institutions do not see the value of cultural awareness training and do not put resources into the ICC development of both teachers and learners. More effort should be put to raise the awareness of policy makers and the public at large. Recently, there has been a shift in the

---

[1] Walker, R. (2001). Pronunciation for intercultural intelligibility. Retrieved online 4 Dec. 2006 from http://www3.telus.net/linguisticsissues/internationalintelligibility.html.

goal of language learning towards cultural learning and competence in participating in multilingual communities and global society.

A more ambitious way is to develop cultural-specific approaches to suit the need of learners of a particular culture (Wu, 2004). Holliday (1994) advocates the use of action research to develop cultural-sensitive teaching methodology. Therefore, with the same time borrowing directly from the above suggestions, Chinese teachers can with also develop their own methodology against the larger backdrop of Chinese culture.

Questions for further discussion:

1. What is your view on the relationship between language and culture?
2. Studies show that learning style preferences are shaped by culture, which provides the "mold" through which we obtain, process, and use information. Do you agree? Then what is the typical Chinese students' learning style?
3. Should culture be taught/learned explicitly or implicitly?
4. In what ways can language teachers bring authentic materials into their classroom?
5. Create a 20-mininute language task for your students, embodying culture teaching in it.
6. What factors should a teacher take into consideration in designing a culture-learning task for students?
7. In terms of cultural influence on language learning, "face" is often mentioned as an important factor. Discuss with your partners how face influences your English language learning.

References:

Brick, J. 1991. *China: A Handbook in Intercultural Communication.* NCELTR.

Buttjes, D. 1990. Teaching foreign language and culture: Social impact and political significance. *Language Learning Journal, (2)*: 53-57.

Byram, M., Morgan, C. et al. 1994. *Teaching and Learning Language and Culture.* Multilingual Matters.

Christiansen, M. H. 1994. Infinite languages, finite minds: Connectionism, learning and linguistic structure. Unpublished PhD dissertation. University of Edinburgh, Scotland.

Dirven, R. and Putz, M. 1993. Intercultural communication, *Language Teaching*, 26: 144-156.

Donald, M. 1998. Mimesis and the executive suite: Missing links in language evolution. In J. R. Hurtford, M. Strddert-Kennedy, and C. Knight (Eds.), *Approaches to the Evolution of Language.* Cambridge University Press.

Dunnett, S., Dubin, F. & Lezberg, A. 1986. *English Language Teaching from an Intercultural Perspective.* Valdes.

Duranti, A. 1997. *Linguistic Anthropology.* Cambridge University Press.

Ellis, R. 1992. Second Language Acquisition and Language Pedagogy. *Multilingual Matters*, Philadelphia.

Giles, Howard, Richard, Bourhis, and Donald. 1977. Towards a theory of language in ethnic group relations. In Giles, H (ed.) *Language, Ethnicity, and Inter-group Relations.* Academic Press.

Green, C. F. 1996. The origins and effects of topic-prominence in Chinese-English interlanguage. *IRAL, 34*(2).

Hinkel, E. 1999a. Introduction: Culture in research and second language pedagogy. In Hinkel, E. (Ed.) *Culture in Second Language Teaching and Learning.* Cambridge University Press.

Holliday, A. 1994. *Appropriate Methodology and Social Context.* Cambridge University Press.

Khleif, B. B. 1979. Language as an ethnic boundary in Welsh-English relations. *IJSL* 20: 59-74.

Kodotchigova, M. A. 2002. Role play in teaching culture: Six quick steps for classroom implementation. *The Internet TESL Journal, Vol. VIII*, No. 7, July 2002. Retrieved on November 16, 2006 from http://iteslj.org./Techniques/Kodatchigova-Roleplay.html.

Kramsch, C. 1998. *Language and Culture.* Oxford University Press.

Lado, R. 1986. How to compare two cultures. In Valdes, J. M. (ed.). *Culture Bound: Bridging the Cultural Gap in Language Teaching.* Cambridge University Press.

Lessard-Clouston, M. 1997. Towards an Understanding of Culture in L2/FL Education. In Ronko, K. G. *Studies in English*, 25: 131-150. Kwansei Gakuin University Press.

Lustig, M. and Koester, J. 1999. *Intercultural Competence: Interpersonal Communication Across Cultures*, Longman.

Peck, D. 1998. *Teaching Culture: Beyond Language.* New Haven Teachers Institute.

Peterson & Coltrane. 2003. *Culture in Second Language Teaching*, retrieved online 4 Nov. 2006 at http://www.cal.org/resources/Digest/0309peterson.html.

Roberts, C. 1998. Awareness in intercultural communications, *Language Awareness, 7*: 109-127.

Robinson, G. 1988. *Cross-cultural Understanding*. Prentice-Hall.

Sapir, E. 1921. *An Introduction to the Study of Speech*. Rupert Hart-Davis.

Saville-Troike, M. 1984. The place of silence in an integrated theory of communication. In D. Tannen & M. Saville-Troike (Eds.), *Perspectives in Silence*. Ablex Publishing Co.

Scollon, R. & Scollon, S. 1995. *Intercultural Communication*. Basil Blackwell.

Singhal, M. 1998. Teaching Culture in the Foreign Language Classroom. *Thai TESOL Bulletin*, Vol. 11.

Stephens, J. L. 2001. Teaching culture and improving language skills through a cinematic lens: A course on Spanish film in the undergraduate Spanish curriculum. *ADFL Bulletin, 33*(1): 22-25.

Straub, H. 1999. Designing a Cross-Cultural Course. *English Forum, 37*: 3, July, 1999.

Tomalin, B. & Stempleski, S. 1993. *Cultural Awareness*. Oxford University Press.

Valdes, J. M. (ed.). 1986. *Culture Bound: Bridging the Cultural Gap in Language Teaching*. Cambridge University Press.

Widdowson, H. G. 1992. *Aspects of the Relationship Between Culture and Language*. Ahren and Antor.

Wu, M. M. F. 2004. "Problems Faced by Chinese Learners in L2 English Learning and Pedagogic Recommendations from an Inter-Cultural Communication Perspective". See http://www3.telus.net/linguisticsissues/problemschinese.html, retrieved 7 Oct. 2006.

Young, R. 1996. *Intercultural Communication*. Multilingual Matters.

CHAPTER 7
Classroom Practice

In the foregoing chapters, we talked about the theories and some practicalities concerning English educology. However, for those faced with the reality that tomorrow they will step into a classroom and will be putting the theoretical and practical knowledge into application, a battery of questions comes to their mind: How to plan a lesson? How to manage the classroom? How to judge whether a lesson is successful or not?

This chapter will cast light on these issues. And the word "lesson", following Brown (2001: 395), is considered to be a unified set of activities that cover a period of classroom time, which provides a rhythm to a course of study.

1. Lesson plan

Making a good plan plays a significant role in carrying out a task successfully. In classroom teaching, lesson plans are the blueprint for the following activities in classrooms.

1.1　Format of a lesson plan

There exist plentiful variations of lesson plans. However, seasoned teachers generally agree on what are the essential elements of a lesson plan.

1.1.1 Goals

A goal refers to an overall purpose that a teacher should attempt to accomplish by the end of the class period. This goal might be quite generalized, but it serves as a unifying theme for the lesson. For example, "understanding conversations at an airport" and "learn to greet people properly" generally identify the lesson topic.

1.1.2 Objectives

For teachers, it is very important to state explicitly what they want students to gain from the lesson. Explicit statements help to:

a. make sure that the teachers know what they want to accomplish;
b. preserve the unity of the lesson;
c. predetermine whether the teachers are trying to accomplish too much;
d. evaluate students' success at the end of, or after the lesson. (Brown, 2001: 396)

Compared with the general goal(s), objectives are most clearly captured in terms of stating what students will do. As a result, vague, unverifiable statements like "Students will practice some sentence patterns" or "Students will do the writing section" should be avoided. Brown (2001) holds that in stating objectives, **terminal** and **enabling** objectives should be distinguished. Terminal objectives are final learning outcomes that the teachers will need to measure and evaluate. Enabling objectives are interim steps that build upon each other and lead to a terminal objective. Consider the following examples:

Terminal lesson objective:

- Students will successfully request information about airplane arrivals and departures.

Enabling objectives:

- Students will comprehend and produce the following six new words.
- Students will read and understand the airline schedule.
- Students will produce questions with when, where and what time.
- Students will produce appropriate polite forms of requesting.

Of course, more enabling objectives can be listed depending upon students' proficiency level. Whatever the students' level, the objectives must be specific and clear.

1.1.3 Materials and teaching aids

Teaching materials and aiding equipment are very important for a lesson. Are you going to use multimedia or just the blackboard? Good planning tactics always indicate the importance of knowing what the teachers need to take to and arrange in the classroom. It is often easy to forget to bring a tape recorder or a poster or some handouts for the students in the harried life of a language teacher.

1.1.4 Procedures

Obviously for the classroom activities, no two are identical. Lessons have endless variations. But as a general set of guidelines, the following steps should be considered:

a. an **opening statement** or activity as a "warm-up", which addresses:
   - How will you introduce the ideas and objectives of this lesson?
   - How will you get students' attention and motivate them?
   - How can you tie lesson objectives with student interests and past classroom activities?
   - What will be expected of students?
b. a set of **activities and techniques** in which the teacher has considered appropriate proportions of time for:
   i)   whole class work
   ii) small group and pair work
   iii) teacher talk
   iv) student talk
   - At this point, the following questions should be considered:
   - What is the focus of the lesson?
   - What will you do to facilitate learning and manage the various

activities?

– What are some good and bad examples to illustrate what you are presenting?

– How can materials be presented to ensure each student will benefit from the learning experience?

c. closure/conclusion

– What will you use to draw the ideas together for students at the end?

– How will you provide feedback to students to correct their misunderstandings and reinforce their learning?

1.1.5 Evaluation

The next question concerning a lesson plan is: How can a teacher determine whether the objectives have been accomplished? If the lesson has no evaluative component, it is just a set of assumptions not verified by observation and measurement. Meanwhile, it must be borne in mind that evaluation can take place in the course of regular classroom activities. Evaluation can be formal or informal, following the students' learning.

1.1.6 Homework/Follow-up Activities

Homework also needs careful planning, especially for the input-poor language environment in China. With good and effective homework, students' interest in learning English can be maintained and their knowledge and ability consolidated.

– What activities might you suggest for enrichment and remediation?

– What lessons might follow as a result of this lesson?

1.1.7 Prerequisites

We put prerequisites here because although prerequisites are not necessarily written down in the lesson plans, teachers need to be very clear about what their students have already known and what not. Prerequisites can be useful when considering the readiness state of students. Prerequisites allow you, and other teachers replicating your lesson plan, to factor in necessary prep activities to make sure that students can meet the lesson objectives.

– What must students already be able to do before this lesson?

– What concepts have to be mastered in advance to accomplish the lesson objectives?

1.2   Guide for lesson planning

1.2.1 How to draft a lesson plan

Begin with three basic questions: Where are your students going? (Outcome of learning) How are they going to get there? (Rate and route of learning) How will you know when they've arrived? (Evaluation) These questions are the general guide for the next steps.

In many circumstances, teachers have been given a textbook and told to teach from it. Assuming that they are already familiar with the curriculum students have to follow, the teacher should look over the textbook chapter and get familiar with the contents and arrangement.

a.   Determine the topic and purpose of the lesson, based on the curriculum and the language needs of the students, and write down the overall goal: What are your goals for this lesson? What do you expect students to be able to do by the end of this unit?

b.   Consider the curriculum and the students' needs, and draft out one to three explicitly stated terminal objectives for the lesson. The objectives for the daily lesson plan are drawn from the broader aims of the unit plan but are achieved over a well defined time period.

c.   Of the exercises that are in the textbook, decide which ones to include in the teaching process and how to change, adapt, and delete them, based on the objectives of the lesson.

d.   Draft out a skeletal outline of what the lesson will look like.

e.   Make step-by-step procedures for carrying out all techniques, and state the purposes of each technique and activity as enabling objectives.

For the new hands, it is very useful to write script of the lesson plan in which the exact anticipated words are written down and followed by exactly what the teacher anticipates the students to say in return. Scripting out a lesson plan helps a teacher to be more specific and often prevents classroom pitfalls.

1.2.2 Variety, sequencing, pacing, and timing

The draft plan provides a detailed, step-by-step description of how to conduct the lesson and achieve lesson objectives. This is usually intended for the teacher to proceed with implementation of the lesson plan. As the step-by-step procedures are drafted out, the teacher needs to look at how the lesson plan holds together as a whole. Brown (2001: 399) suggests four considerations:

a.   Is there sufficient variety in techniques to keep the lesson lively and interesting? This keeps minds alert and enthusiasm high.

b.   Are the techniques or activities sequenced logically? Easier aspects should be better placed at the beginning of a lesson.

c.   Is the lesson as a whole paced adequately? Pacing can mean several things: first, it means that activities are neither too long nor too short; second, it means various activities and techniques flow tighter; third, it means a proper transition from one activity to the next.

d.   Is the lesson appropriately timed, considering the number of minutes in the class hour? It is not unusual for new teachers to plan a lesson so tightly that they actually complete their lesson plan early, but after just a little experience the most common occurrence is that the planned lessons cannot be finished within the time allotment. Timing is very important for a lesson plan: if the planned lesson ends early, have some backup activity to insert; if the lesson is not completed as planned, be ready to gracefully end a class on time and on the next day pick up where you left off.

1.2.3 Gauging difficulty and focal points

Figuring out how easy or difficult certain techniques will be is something that usually must be learned by experience. It requires the teacher to put him/herself in his/her students' shoes and anticipate their problems. Thus, for lesson plans, it is very helpful to list out the difficult points in advance; writing them ahead of time provides teachers with a chance to be more objective in determining if everything is clear.

It is similar for the focal points. If the main target of a lesson is passive voice, the structure of passive voice must be clearly pointed out. Of course, very often the difficult point and the focal point overlap.

1.2.4 Student talk and teacher talk

Give careful consideration in the lesson plan to the balance between student talk and teacher talk. As teachers, our natural inclination is to talk too much. We must learn to refrain from dominating the class time and give students chances to talk, interact, produce language and initiate their own topics and ideas.

1.2.5 Learner differences

As discussed in former chapters, students are different from each other in terms of their aptitude, intelligence, affect, personality etc. And they tend to use different strategies and styles in learning a language. For the most part a lesson plan should cater to the majority of students in the class who comprise the average ability range. But the lesson plan should also take into consideration the different demands and needs of the top and low range students by:

a. designing techniques that have easy and difficult aspects of items;

b. trying to design techniques that involve all learners;

c. encouraging group and pair work.

1.2.6 Lesson "tips"

In delivering a speech, some speakers take a note card with them. In classroom, this note/tip card is equally useful. But if a note is too detailed and complicated, the lecture may become too stiff and lack spontaneity. Most teachers work well with no more than one page of a lesson outline and notes, as long as the notes are clearly sequenced and well organized.

1.3 Sample lesson plans

In this section, we selected two sample lesson plans for readers' reference in planning a lesson.

1.3.1 A listening lesson plan

Listening: Telephone Conversation[1]

Grade Level: Vocational Education, Adult/Continuing Education

Subject(s):

- Foreign Language/English Second Language
- Vocational Education/Business

Duration: 50 minutes

Description: Students use telephone conversation as a listening/speaking activity to practice conversation.

---

1 Retrieved and adapted online on 27 of July 2007. For more details refer to http://www.eduref.org/cgi-bin/printlessons.cgi/Virtual/Lessons/Foreign_Language/English_Second_Language/ESL0203.html

Goals:
1. To improve students' listening skills.
2. To practice telephone conversations and greetings.

Objectives:
1. Students will be able to identify various job titles used in companies.
2. Students will be able to respond to questions asked in mock telephone conversations.

Materials:
- Prepared note cards containing different job titles found in a company (i.e. president, general manager, CEO, sales manager, secretary, accountant, assistant, vice-financial manager, etc.)
- Tape recorders with blank tapes

Procedure:

Warm-up/Review: (10 minutes)

Students are currently learning new vocabulary about job titles and departments within companies. During this period, students will practice identifying the job titles through listening. First, show students the note cards of the job titles and ask them to describe the job titles. For example, show them *sales manager* and ask, "What department does he work for?" Students will reply, "The sales and marketing department." Then ask, "What does this department do?" The students will reply, "Sell goods/company products to the market/customers." This serves as a check to see if students know the new vocabulary.

Pre-activity: (15 minutes)

Pass out note cards to each student; everyone should have a job title. Then demonstrate the telephone conversation practice (of course, the opening/ending greetings of telephone conversation should be mentioned.) First say, "Hello, this is Kimberly from ABC Inc. May I speak to the general manager, please?" Then the student who has the job title *general manager* will stand up and answer, "Yes, this is general manager Tom speaking. May I help you?" Check to make sure all students know their job titles and practice simple conversation for greetings.

Listening Activity: (20 minutes)

Continue to call on students as during the pre-activity, but this time add more message information, such as checking the date/place for the meeting, giving a telephone number, an invitation for dinner, etc. Students should be able to get the message accurately and then repeat/reconfirm the message to the teacher—to check for understanding. If students don't understand or feel unclear, they can give response, "Pardon me?" or "Can you repeat again more slowly?" During the conversation, the teacher should also note if students are using the polite form of conversation.

Conclusion/Assignment: (5 minutes)
The teacher can give students some suggestions and comments based on the outcomes of the listening activities.

Assignment/Follow-up: Ask students to find a partner. Assign the task of designing their own telephone conversation. Students should use a tape recorder to record their conversation. Students should bring the recordings to the next class so that they can be used for whole class listening practice. Ideas for listening practice:

1. Call General Manager: to set up the time for Monday's meeting.
2. Call Secretary: to cancel the conference for tomorrow afternoon.
3. Call Security Guard: to reserve four visitors' parking spots for next Wednesday, 9:00 a.m.
4. Call Marketing Manager: to change the time schedule for presenting the proposal in Nissan Inc.
5. Call President's Assistant: to give the president his wife's new cellular phone number and ask him to return her call.

1.3.2 A reading lesson plan

Introducing Electronic Newspapers (e-paper)
in the ESL Reading Classroom[1]

Grade Level: Vocational Education, Adult/Continuing Education
Subject(s):
- Foreign Language/English Second Language
- Language Arts/Reading
- Computer Science

Duration: 50 minutes

---

[1] Retrieved and adapted online on 27 of July 2007. For more details refer to http://www.eduref.org/cgi-bin/printlessons.cgi/Virtual/Lessons/Foreign_Language/ English_Second_Language/ESL0204.html

Description: In this activity, ESL students use online newspapers to practice their reading skills, specifically skimming and scanning.

Goals: Students will be able to improve their reading skills, enrich their vocabulary, gain some cultural knowledge, and be up-to-date with current situations in the world.

Objectives:

1. Students will be able to identify the various sections of a newspaper.
2. Students will be able to skim, scan, and summarize newspaper articles.

Materials:

- today's newspaper (English version, such as USA Today or local newspaper)
- multimedia language lab (computers with Internet access)
- teacher-prepared copies of selected articles from e-paper

Procedure:

Warm-up: (10 minutes)

To begin, discuss techniques for "how to read a newspaper," and introduce the elements of a newspaper, such as headlines, pictures, topic sentences, body, etc. Next, talk about the definitions and importance of "skimming" and "scanning." Then use today's local newspaper to demonstrate these two techniques. Ask students when and why they need to use these techniques (have students brainstorm). *Skimming:* Quickly running one's eyes across a whole text to get the gist. It gives readers the advantage of being able to predicate the purpose of the passage, the main topic. *Scanning:* Quickly searching for some particular pieces of information in a text. Scanning exercises may ask students to look for names, dates, to find a definition of a key concept, or to list a certain number of supporting details. The purpose of scanning is to extract specific information without reading through the whole text.

Communicative Activity: (15 minutes)

Introduce and show the web site, "Online Newspapers—thousands of world newspapers at your fingertips" (http://www.onlinenewspapers.com/index.htm). After making sure every student's computer is at the web site, ask students to locate different topic areas—front page, weather, sports, classified, entertainment, etc. Next, go back to the news section; assign well-known headline international news and ask students to find information about the news by looking through different countries/newspapers. Then ask students to select one article, use skimming and scanning techniques, and summarize the article. Finally, select several students to report their summaries and then compare theirs with other students' summaries.

Focus Practice: (25 minutes)

Activity I: Pass out a selected e-paper article to each pair of students. Students will discover that the first sentence from each paragraph has been deleted. Ask students to put the sentences back into the correct places in the text. When finished, have each pair of students discuss their answers with another pair.

Activity II: Give each pair of students another article—this time jumble the paragraphs for the students to reorder.

Activity III: Give each pair a third article. Highlight some words in the text and ask students to deduce their meanings from the context.

Assessment/Assignment: As a follow-up assignment, have students locate an article from e-paper to practice skimming and scanning skills. Then students should summarize the article. They need to print out the original article from e-paper and then turn in the assignment for the next class.

2. Classroom management

Brown (2001: 411) raises questions like "Is teaching an art or a science?" and "Are teachers born or made?" and further regards these questions as "both-and" questions rather than "either-or" questions. The coexistence of art and science in the profession of teaching lies in one important issue: classroom management.

Classroom management encompasses a wide range of factors: discipline, physical layout, teaching styles, learning atmosphere, activities and techniques, etc. Understanding these variables can help classroom teachers to be more effective in the process of teaching.

2.1 The classroom itself

The first factor for classroom management is the physical environment for teaching and learning.

2.1.1 Sound, light and comfort

Although it seems to be trivial, the physical environment for learning plays a significant role. Students can be profoundly affected by what they see, hear and feel when they enter the classroom. The teacher should see to it that:

- The classroom is neat, clean and orderly.
- The blackboard is erased.
- The light is appropriate for reading and watching.
- The chairs are appropriately arranged.
- The room is free from external noises.
- If necessary, the cooling or heating systems are operating.

Of course, you may find yourself powerless to control some of the above. But as far as possible, make the classroom as physically comfortable for learning.

2.1.2 Seating arrangement

In the English classrooms of China, the seats are lined and rowed, and some are even fixed onto the ground. To most language educators, this military-formation is not conducive to language learning, but just good for controlling. If you have movable chairs, consider patterns of circles, U-shapes, semicircles, etc.

The variation of classroom layout can help to maintain students' interest in learning; it can also facilitate interaction and communication between students.

2.1.3 Visual aids and equipment

Are you going to use the blackboard, the whiteboard or the screen? Make sure they work well and help you auditory. And try to be neat and orderly in your blackboard/whiteboard use, erasing as often as appropriate; a messy, confusing blackboard drives the students crazy. For those visual aids like realia, do not show them if you are not using them; otherwise the students' attention will be distracted.

If you are using computer or other multimedia equipment, make sure the equipment fits well in the room, all students can see/hear it, and you know how to operate it.

2.2   Voice and body language

Among the qualities and qualifications of a good teacher, voice control and body language play a very important role through which language teachers send messages to their students.

A good teacher needs first to be heard clearly by all the students in the classroom. When speaking, remember the students are just learning English. And the speaking rate should not be too slow, (slowing down a bit is good for low-level students). Clear articulation is usually more of a key to comprehension than slowed speech (Brown, 2001: 414).

Non-verbal messages are equally helpful. In language classes, where students may not have all the skills they need to decipher verbal language, their attention is drawn to nonverbal communication. Some tips:

- Let your body posture exhibit an air of confidence.
- Your face should reflect optimism, brightness and warmth.
- Use facial and hand gestures to enhance meanings of involved words and sentences.
- Make eye contact with all the students in the class.
- Move around the classroom, but not to distraction.
- Follow the conventional rules of proxemics and kinesthetics that apply for the culture of the students.
- Dress appropriately considering the expectations of your students. (Brown, 2001)

2.3   Flexibility in teaching

Since the rules and rubrics are mentioned above concerning classroom teaching, it seems that procedures of teaching are quite mechanic. This is wrong. A good teacher should always prepare for the unexpectedness in classroom. We have to engage in what we call unplanned teaching in the process. One of the initiation rites that new teachers go through is experiencing these unexpected events and learning how to deal with them gracefully. And very often we need to adjust our plans and allow the lesson to move on.

2.4   Empowerment in teaching

Teacher empowerment has been a recent topic in fields like sociolinguistics and sociology. Teachers need to empower themselves in various adverse circumstances:

2.4.1 Teaching large classes

Ideally, language classes should have no more than a dozen people or so: large enough to provide diversity and student interaction and small enough to give students plenty of opportunity to participate and get attention. Unfortunately, in China English classes with 50 or so learners are very common. Consider the following solutions:

- Try to make each student feel important by learning and using their names.
- Get students interactive with group work and pair work.
- Set up some small learning centers or clubs in the class.
- Do more listening and use peer-learning in writing.
- Give students a range of extra-class work.

2.4.2 Compromising with the authority

In China, teaching policies are usually enhanced through top-down direction. Teachers have sometimes, to deal with institutional conditions and find themselves helpless in the professional work. Regarding this, the handling of such situations almost always demands some sort of compromise on the teachers' part. As teachers, we must be ready to bring professional diplomacy and efficiency to bear on the varying degrees of hardship.

Moreover, in current China, under the "publish or perish" drive, many teachers are under great pressure to teach and research. Although this has long been a controversial issue, it is no doubt teachers need to learn and improve themselves consistently.

2.4.3 Discipline

This discipline not only means disciplines for the students, but also for teachers in work. Classroom discipline has been a frequent topic in ELT. Even if all the students were hard-working, active, and dedicated, a teacher still faces discipline problems: how to be comfortable with the learners, how to gain respect from them, how firm to be with them, how to resolve disciplinary matters, etc.

At the same time, teachers, as role models, should teach discipline by following disciplines themselves like being punctual, to be honest, etc.

2.5   Creating a positive and harmonious classroom

The roles a teacher plays and the styles a teacher develops will merge to give some tools for creating a classroom atmosphere. As far as possible, teachers should create a positive, harmonious, stimulating and energizing classroom.

1. Rapport

To create a harmonious and conducive classroom learning environment, rapport is very important. Rapport is the close relationship that is built on trust and respect between the teacher and students. This trust can lead to students' feeling capable, competent, and creative.

By showing interest in each student as a person, giving them feedback on their progress, valuing and respecting what they think and say, laughing with them and not at them, working with and facilitating them can rapport be slowly established.

2. Praise and criticism

Part of the rapport created is based on the delicate balance that the teacher sets between praise and criticism. Genuine praise, appropriately delivered, enables students to welcome criticism and to put it to use.

3. Dynamo

Brown prefers the term *classroom energy*. But where does the energy come from? Following Brown (2001), the teacher is the key and dynamo, because students initially look to their teacher for leadership and guidance. And through whatever role or style the teacher accomplishes this, the teacher needs solid preparation, confidence and a sense of joy in doing the job.

3.   Reflection and evaluation

To make sure a lesson has been successful, a teacher needs to reflect on and evaluate the whole teaching process. Although any one lesson is uniquely different from others, the key elements to be reflected should include the following.

1. The introduction

A sound lesson should have a good introduction, which serves to bridge the preceding lesson with the present lesson, arouse learners' interest and which functions as advance organizer. As a result, the teacher should check the introduction or the lead-in part both before preparing for and after conducting the actual teaching.

2. Demonstration and illustration

A teacher should also reflect on the examples, realia, and activities designed before and during the lesson to see if they are appropriate, adequate, and clear enough. Demonstration and illustration are meant to make things and issues simpler, not more complicated. The teacher should always bear in mind the importance of selecting proper realia and classroom activities to facilitate students' understanding and mastery of involved concepts and issues.

3. Organization

A lesson should be a united whole, with one task naturally leading to another. At the same time, the time allocation for different tasks should be considered beforehand, to avoid the situation that on one task the arrangement is too loose and on another the time is too tight. Of course, for different age groups, rest time, lecture time and activity time should take different formats. For instance, younger learners have shorter attention span; and for them, rest and activities are very important between teacher's talk.

4. Gestures and voice control

A good teacher should use appropriate gestures and other body language to help him or her get across. Meanwhile, good gestures can help to maintain an interactive atmosphere between the teacher and the learners. Of course, too much body language can sometimes distract students from their attention.

A good teacher should assess his or her voice, and if necessary make some adjustment. Too low, too soft or too high, too harsh voices will lead to learners' dislike of the teacher. Too flat or too monotonous voices will cause similar result. So a good teacher should constantly "listen to him/herself" and make sure the voice is powerful and attractive enough.

5. Questioning

Asking witty and proper questions is a prerequisite for a good teacher. A good lesson should be woven not only by teachers' talk, but more importantly, the interaction between teachers' asking and students' responding and vice versa. The teacher should often reflect on how consolidating, or checking, or provocative, thought-provoking questions can be asked and when these questions can be asked.

The teacher should avoid asking meaningless, self-evident questions and refrain from hasting forward the answer to the question by him/herself.

6. Language

In classroom teaching, language is the major means by which information gets exchanged. In an English lesson, some experts maintain that teachers speak English as much as possible and speak Chinese only when necessary. Although there is no general agreement on the percentage of mother tongue in a foreign language lesson, too much mother tongue is not good for the cultivation of students' language feel (of that specific foreign language).

Code-switching, though, is important for clear instructions, abstract ideas, or other involved meta-language.

7. Conclusion

Following introduction of a lesson, interaction between students and the teacher, a conclusion follows. A good conclusion sums up what has been covered in the whole lesson, checks students' understanding and looks forward to the next lesson.

With the modern classroom teaching emphasizing more and more the teaching process, continual assessment has gradually been built into classroom teaching. The wrap-up often serves such an assessing function.

To build good lessons, a teacher needs constant reflection on his/her own teaching, learning from others', and creative thinking in improving his/her job. Teaching is both science and art. A good teacher is both born and made. And education is to light a fire, not just to fill in a bucket.

Questions for further discussion:

1. The following are some curricular goals:
   Understanding academic lectures
   Writing a business letter
   Understanding a travel brochure
   For each of them, briefly describe a specific audience for which the goal might be appropriate, and then transform the goals into terminal objectives and list a few enabling objectives.
2. Look at the sample lesson plans in this chapter and evaluate them.
3. Write a lesson plan for either a writing, reading, speaking or listening class.
4. According to your observation, list some bad nonverbal communication—what you should not do in your classroom. Discuss these points with your classmates.
5. What are the common problems encountered in large classrooms? What suggestions do you have to solve the problem and make learning efficient?
6. What other "adverse circumstances" are there in classroom teaching? How would you deal with them?
7. How can teachers maintain classroom energy? How to strike a balance between discipline and energy?

References:

Brown, H. D. 2001. *Teaching by Principles: An Interactive Approach to Language Pedagogy.* Foreign Language Teaching and Research Press.
Web sources:
http://www.eduref.org/cgi-bin/printlessons.cgi/Virtual/Lessons/Foreign_Language/English_Second_Language/ESL0203.html
http://www.eduref.org/cgi-bin/printlessons.cgi/Virtual/Lessons/Foreign_Language/English_Second_Language/ESL0204.html

CHAPTER **8**
English Testing

Testing is a way of life in the educational world. In almost every learning experience there comes a time to pause and take stock, to put our focal processes to their best use and to demonstrate—either to self or others—accumulated skills or knowledge. Tests can serve positive, intrinsically motivating aims as they spur one to muster one's abilities for a particular performance and then provide feedback on one's progress toward goals.

These comments on the merits of testing made by H. D. Brown (2001) are definitely true. But in various contexts of education, testing serves as a double-edged sword. And as teachers of English, they may have considerable control over the way language is taught in the classrooms, and may use this autonomy to tap methodologies which they feel will benefit learners. However, they have much less say, in the way that learners will eventually be tested, especially for some high-stakes tests.

Should language testing be part of the pleasant student life or part of nightmare for students? In this chapter we look at language testing theories and practice.

1. Ways of assessing students

1.1 Distinctions of testing, measurement, assessment, and evaluation

In line with Airasian's (1994: 5-6) observation, the following distinctions can be made:

- Assessment is a general term that includes all the ways teachers gather information in their teaching processes.
- A test is a formal, systematic, usually paper-and-pencil procedure used to gather information about learners' behavior. Tests are only one of many types of assessment information teachers deal with, and thus, tests are a subcategory in the general domain of assessment approaches. (Other evidence-gathering strategies that also fit within the general domain of assessment are observations, interviews, and projects etc.)
- Measurement is the process of quantifying or assigning a number to performance. The most common example of measurement in the classroom occurs when a teacher scores a quiz or test. Scoring produces a numerical description of performance: Kitty got 28 out of 40 items correct on the grammar test. Other common measurements are made of pupils' height and weight. In these examples, a numerical score is used to represent the individual's performance.
- Evaluation involves making judgments about the quality of pupils' performance or a possible course of action. It is an activity after assessment information has been collected for decisions to be made on pupils, instruction, or classroom climate. For instance, when the assessment information collected has been synthesized and thought about, the teacher is in a position to judge the quality of a pupil's performance during a term or a year.

Nunan (1991) defines assessment as the set of processes through which we make statements about a learner's level of skills and knowledge. Here, Nunan's "a set of processes" includes activities done in class and outside. Tests, homework, projects, class participation, portfolio, quizzes, etc. are all factors which can be counted in learner assessment.

In this book, assessment includes the full range of information teachers gather in and outside their classrooms: information that helps them understand their pupils, monitor their instruction, and establish a variable classroom culture. It also includes the variety of ways teachers gather, synthesize, and interpret that information.

Then what is "authentic assessment"? In order to provide authentic assessment of students' grammar proficiency, for example, an evaluation must reflect real-life uses of grammar in context. This means that the activity must have a purpose other than assessment and require students to demonstrate their level of grammar proficiency by completing some task.

Authentic assessment activities should begin with the types of tasks that students will actually need to do using the language. Assessment can then take the form of communicative activities like those used in the teaching process.

To further exemplify the difference between assessment and testing, look at the following table:

FIGURE 8.1 Assessment scale used at Shanghai Theatre Academy[1]

ASSESSMENT SCALE			
Components	Weight (%)	Pupil's mark	Teacher's mark
Homework	10	9	8
Class attendance	10	10	10
Quizzes	10	7	7
Class performance	15	12	11
Individual progress	10	8	9
Project	15	10	12
Test results	30	24	24
Total score	100	80	81
Teacher's signature: Student's signature:			
This assessment scale is adapted from Kari Smith (1999). The scale reflects the importance of ongoing work at home and in class. Tests are an important part of the assessment but not the only source of information.			

The table not only illustrates the difference between assessment and testing, but also the usual components of an assessment scale.

1.2 "Informal" ways utilized in the assessment process

Teachers of a foreign language need to assess their students'

---

[1] The assessment scale is used by the author in his teaching practice at Shanghai Theatre Academy in the first academic term of 2004-2005. In the process, both the student and the teacher gave scores on various factors. This is a trial program. The biggest benefit from it is students get involved in the program and their anxiety in English tests gets lowered. Admittedly, some students dislike the idea and there are some big disparities between the students' scores and the teacher's scores.

language performance informally on a continuous basis. This is necessary in order to determine whether the students have acquired the language skill they need to keep up with their instruction and to use the language effectively when communicating with target language users (Genesee & Upsher, 1996). In communicative teaching approaches, the perspective of multi-dimensional assessment is valued. Information is gathered through observation of student behavior during routine lessons, from student's self-evaluation, from comments by students during individual conferences, or from entries in students' journals. All of these can divulge important data about student learning and the effectiveness of instruction, as can information from school records, parents, and fellow students. The following is a detailed explanation of some of the commonly used methods.

1) Observation

As the term implies, observation involves watching learners carry out various tasks, such as speaking, reading, and discussing.

Observation is one important approach classroom teachers use to collect assessment data (Heaton, 1990). Richard J. Stiggins[1], who founded the online Assessment Training Institute to provide professional support to teachers and school leaders as they face the challenges of day-to-day classroom assessment, strongly insists on the use of observation as an essential way for assessing students' performance in classroom. He has been committed to helping teachers gather accurate information through observation about students and use that information to benefit (not just grade and the sort) their students.

Observation is particularly useful in interactive and communicative classes. Since a lot of interactive tasks are organized during the teaching process, there exist correspondingly lots of live and ongoing opportunities for the teacher to observe. When students mispronounce words in oral reading, interact in groups, speak out in class, lose their concentration, have puzzled looks on their faces, patiently wait their turn, raise their hands in class, and fail to sit still for more than five minutes, teachers become aware of these behaviors through visual and aural observation. Much of the information that is essential for minute-to-minute decision making in classrooms comes from teacher observation, not from paper-pencil procedures. What a teacher needs to do is to set up an observation log in which students'

---

[1] See http://www.assessmentinst.com/meetati.html, adapted 2 Sep. 2005.

daily activities can be recorded as a reference to form descriptive evaluations on their performance.

2) Self-assessment and Peer assessment

Genesee & Upsher (1996) suggest another important means of continuous assessment in language classes: student self-assessment. Students are asked to assess themselves regularly according to appropriate grades listed on a simple form. Of course, rules should be rigid and clear and examples can be provided to make these listed points fully understood by the students. For example, as a weekly assessment, the students assess themselves in the learning process during the week and then show the teacher their forms at the end of the week and briefly discuss their results individually with the teacher. The weekly self-assessment may include all the skills (reflecting all the learning that has taken place) or may concentrate on only one skill or area of language, depending on the type of course given. If it concentrates on only one skill, the teacher should make sure that progress in a different skill is evaluated by students each week e.g. Week 1 listening; Week 2 writing; Week 3 speaking.

The following is an example of forms which can be used for student self-assessment of listening.

FIGURE 8.2 Student self-assessment of listening (adapted from Genesee & Upsher, 1996)

9-10	I understood everything the first time. All my answers to the exercises were correct.
8-9	I understood almost everything the first time and found it easy after repetition. Almost all my answers were correct.
7-8	I understood a lot the first time and almost everything after repetition. I got a few wrong answers.
6-7	I understood a lot after repetition but I still have a few doubts. I got several wrong answers.
Below 5	I found it difficult to understand even after repetition. Most of my answers were wrong.

Peer assessment can be conducted in much the same way. The only difference is that the assessment of one student is fulfilled by his/her classmates with ready-made assessing scales.

3) Student portfolio & Processfolio

A portfolio is a purposeful collection of students' work that demonstrates to students and others their efforts, progress, and achievements in given areas. Student portfolios have been inspired by professionals such as photographers and architects as a means of keeping a record of their accomplishments to show to others. In countries like the UK and US, many teachers have used portfolio assessment, in which a student collects all of his/her best work in a class and presents it at the end of the semester as part of his/her final grade (Genesee & Upsher, 1996). Portfolios offer a simple and fairly effective way of assessing a student's work without the typical multiple-choice, end-of-term tests.

Foreign language portfolios can have a very specific focus, such as writing, or a broad focus that includes examples of all aspects of language development. Students can keep the portfolios in various ways: a file folder, or a small cardboard box. The primary value of portfolios is in the assessment of student achievement. They are particularly useful in this respect because they provide a continuous record of students' language development that can be shared with others:

FIGURE 8.3 Benefits of portfolios (Genesee & Upsher, 1996: 99-100)

Portfolios provide:
A continuous and cumulative record of language development A holistic view of student learning Insight about progress of individual students Opportunities for collaborative assessment and goal-setting with students Tangible evidence of student learning to be shared with parents, other educators and other students Opportunities to use meta-language to talk about language
Portfolios promote:
Student involvement in assessment Responsibility for self-assessment Interaction with teachers, parents, and students about learning Student ownership of and responsibility for their own learning Excitement about learning Students' ability to think critically about schoolwork Collaborative, sharing classrooms

The positive effects of portfolios on student learning arise from the opportunities they afford students to become actively involved in assessment and learning. This does not happen automatically, however, simply by having students keep portfolios of their own work. Rather, it depends critically on teacher's conscious efforts to use portfolios as a collaborative assessment process. "They must be used actively and interactively, and they must be an integral part of instruction and instructional planning" (Genesee & Upsher, 1996: 99-100).

Gardner, as well as some other researchers, agrees that classroom assessment should focus primarily on day-to-day evaluation, feedback and improvement. True assessment of a student's skills must be personal and intensive, not a periodic test which is gauged against the standard norm for similar students (Gardner, 1994). Gardner takes this ideal one step further and refines it into what he calls a processfolio. Unlike a portfolio, a processfolio includes every single creative step towards some particular goal. In the case of a major report, a student would include all comments and criticisms made by the teacher and other students. He/She would also include his/her own personal interpretations of that criticism—in other words, a meta-assessment of his/her work in progress. In the end, the processfolio would demonstrate the student's growth, as well as his/her completion of the work.

Of course, another important and even "indispensable" way for gathering information about students' language knowledge and ability is language tests. Although formal instruments can not tell us about all aspects of student achievement and they cannot tell us much about the other factors (such as motivation, persistence, affect, strategy and efforts) that often figure in second language evaluation, they are an important component of assessment. It is especially true for English language teaching in the context of China with some practical considerations like its large population. The following section discusses ways to design an effective English test.

2. Testing systems

2.1 Theoretical trends of testing practice in the world

2.1.1 Gardner's Multiple Intelligences (MI) Theory on testing

1) A brief introduction to MI

Mentioned earlier in this book, intelligence is traditionally defined operationally as the ability to answer test items of intelligence, which includes exclusively linguistic competence and mathematical-logical reasoning. The inference from the test scores to some underlying ability is supported by statistical techniques that compare responses of subjects.

Multiple intelligences theory, on the other hand, pluralizes the traditional concept. According to Gardner (1993: 15), instead of a single dimension called intellect, on which individuals can be rank-ordered, there are vast differences among individuals in their intellectual strengths and weaknesses as well as cognitive styles, human cognitive competence is better described in terms of a set of abilities, talents, or mental skills, which he names "intelligences". Gardner and his colleagues have so far distinguished nine kinds of intelligences: verbal/linguistic intelligence, logical/mathematical intelligence, visual/spatial intelligence, musical/rhythmic intelligence, bodily/kinesthetic intelligence, interpersonal intelligence, intrapersonal intelligence, naturalistic intelligence, and existential intelligence. According to Gardner, "multiple" is to stress an unknown number of separate human capacities; "intelligences" to underscore that these capacities are as fundamental as those historically captured within the IQ test.

2) Gardner's view on testing and assessment

Assessment is clearly distinguished from testing in Gardner's works. The former is defined as the obtaining of information about the skills and potential of individuals, with the dual goals of providing useful feedback to the individuals and useful data to the surrounding community. The latter is conceived as an objective, decontextualized form of assessment. What differentiates assessment from "formal testing" is the former favors techniques that elicit information in the course of ordinary performance and its uneasiness with the use of formal instruments administered in a neural, decontextualized setting. Gardner believes that "standard pencil-and-paper short-answer tests sample only a small proportion of intellectual abilities and often reward a certain kind of decontextualized facility. The means of assessment we favor should search for genuine problem-solving or product-fashioning skills in individuals across a range of materials" (1993: 15). In contrast to formal testing, Gardner analyzes the other extreme of assessment—the "apprenticeship" method, which demands the assessment of learners be implemented within a naturally occurring context in which the particularities of a craft are embedded.

To many, Gardner's ideals seem to be sweet lofty dreams. But actually Gardner and his collaborators are not simplistic, whimsical dreamers. As Gardner puts it, "most observers today do not lament the passage of the obligatory apprenticeship system, with its frequent excesses and blatant sexism; from several points of view, contemporary formal testing represents a fairer and more easily justifiable form of assessment" (Gardner, 1993: 162). However, he points out that the modern society has embraced the formal testing mode to an excessive degree and certain aspects of the apprentice mode of learning and assessment could be reintroduced into the educational system.

To sum up, the tenets of Gardner's proposition on testing reform are:

a) Assessment, rather than tests, ought to be practiced. Instead of designing only short-answer, timed measures of the static knowledge, test developers should adopt a multi-dimensional perspective and assess learners in the close-to-nature, dynamic context.

b) Assessment should focus on the students' success, rather than failure. In cases where tests have to be used, they should be designed to allow students to show their strengths and to perform optimally, rather than to intimidate them and expose only their weaknesses. Tests are not merely to discriminate and screen people, but more to help and enhance learning.

c) It is necessary to have a developmental perspective in the process of assessment, that is, the process should reflect the individual's development in cognition, learning and creativity in terms of multiple faculties or intelligences.

d) Assessment programs should be sensitive to individual differences, their developmental levels and fields of expertise. Standard formal tests are technically objective and non-bias, but meanwhile they are skewed because they are "especially friendly to those who are comfortable in being assessed in a decontextualized setting under timed and impersonal conditions" (Gardner, 1993: 180).

e) Decisions ought to be made on basis of all-round assessment of an individual, because "few practices are more nefarious in education than the drawing of widespread educational implications from the score of a single test" (Gardner, 1993: 176). One-dimensional thinking in education and assessment needs an urgent overhaul.

2.1.2 Bachman & Palmer's testing theory

Tenets of Bachman & Palmer's testing usefulness theory:

1) Bachman & Palmer (1996) break down the "myth" held by many: There exists the best test for every test situation and test developers have the magical power to develop such a test. And in turn, they usher in a new concept: test usefulness, which includes six test qualities—construct validity, reliability, authenticity, interactiveness, impact, and practicality. "When we design a language test we need to consider the characteristics of the language use situation and tasks and of the language users and test takers" (Bachman & Palmer, 1996: 11).

FIGURE 8.4 Correspondences between language use and language test performance

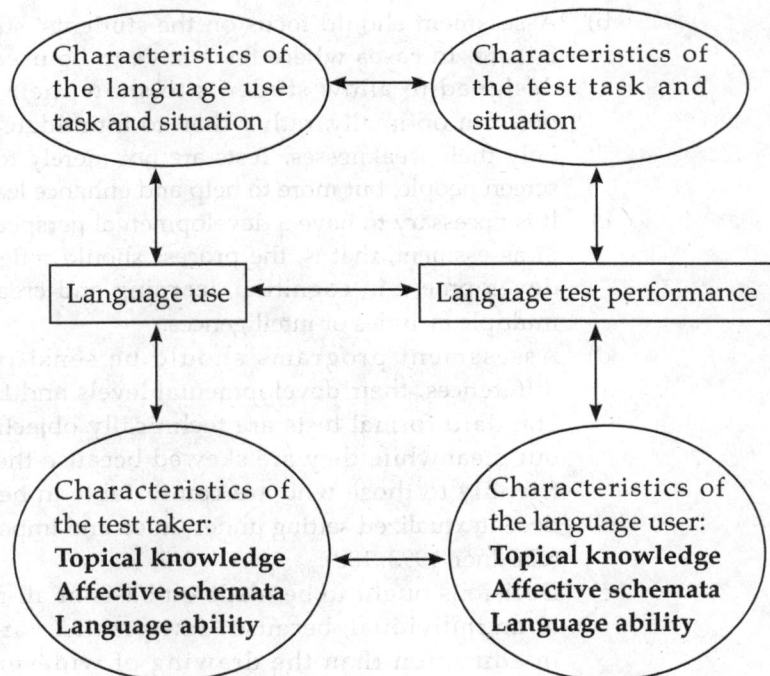

Characteristics of the language use task and situation ↔ Characteristics of the test task and situation

Language use ↔ Language test performance

Characteristics of the test taker:
Topical knowledge
Affective schemata
Language ability
↔
Characteristics of the language user:
Topical knowledge
Affective schemata
Language ability

2) The traditional approach to describing test qualities (focusing mainly on validity and reliability) has been to discuss them as more or less independent characteristics, emphasizing the need to pursue the maximum of these qualities. This approach

has led to the result of maximizing one or two qualities at the expense of others. Bachman & Palmer (1996: 18) insist that the test developers find an appropriate balance among the qualities they have listed, and emphasize their complementarity. They regard test usefulness as a whole system in a specific test situation and that it is the overall usefulness of the test that is to be maximized.

3) Another point is that Bachman & Palmer introduce the concept of degree into their theory. Since situation of tests differs, qualities of tests vary in line with the purpose, construct, test takers, criterion and resources of each test. For instance, they adopt the terms like "relatively more" or "relatively less" authentic or interactive, rather than simply "authentic" and "inauthentic", or "interactive" and "non-interactive".

4) The fourth point is that Bachman & Palmer's test development theory puts more emphasis on the process to guarantee a satisfactory outcome. They point out in the test development process, especially for large-scale, formal tests, the determination of usefulness is cyclical. Take their considerations of practicality as an example. They are likely to affect the decisions made on a test at every stage along the way, and may lead test developers to reconsider and perhaps revise some of the earlier specifications.

5) Another point is their emphasis on meaningful "interactiveness" and humanism. Bachman & Palmer (1996) mention in the statement of their philosophy on language testing:

① Tests must be developed so as to encourage test takers to perform at their highest level of ability.

② Test-developers must build considerations of fairness into test design.

③ The testing process should be humanized: seeking ways to involve test takers more directly in the testing process; treating test takers as responsible individuals; providing them with as complete information about the entire testing procedure as possible.

④ It must be recognized that decisions based on test scores are fraught with dilemmas, and that there are no universal answers to these. As a result, people concerned should seek for more balanced and fairer ways to tackle these problems in a persistent and continuous manner.

Gardner's and Bachman & Palmer's theories are similar in many ways. Both of them emphasize the importance of direct, meaningful and close-to-life assessment; both prioritize the assessment process;

both advocate the multi-dimensional view and both highlight the role of assessment on the individual's overall development.

2.2　Developing an effective test

2.2.1 Procedures involved

Since every test is unique in terms of its test purpose and situation, it is realistic to discuss test development based on the concrete context of a specific test. In Bachman & Palmer's *Language Testing in Practice*, the authors make a detailed illustration of various tests. However, for all tests, certain general procedures should be followed. The following discussion mainly focuses on an EFL progress test.

As a full exemplification, readers can refer to Bachman & Palmer's *Language Testing in Practice*, "Project 10: Portions of a syllabus-based EFL progress test for primary school children" (1996: 355).

Stage 1: Design
1) Test purpose

Constructing language tests means selecting a task or tasks that will elicit the kind(s) of language knowledge or skills test developers and organizers are interested in assessing. First of all, the purpose of the test should be decided upon. For instance, the purposes of Project 10 (Bachman & Palmer, 1996) are to help the teachers to: Understand how their students are progressing; find out students' strengths and weaknesses; work out ways of helping the students; use information from the assessment as a basis for future lesson planning.

2) Description of the target language use (TLU) domain and tasks

The classroom setting and the teaching/learning tasks that are used constitute the TLU domain and tasks for EFL progress tests. Teaching syllabi are of great help in designing classroom progress tests or tests of achievement. Such tests should be based on the skills and language areas from the teaching syllabus or from what a teacher has actually taught. If there is no syllabus, make a note of the communicative functions and as well as the grammar and vocabulary points which the course-book has covered. Think about what skills are required in the students' practical use of the language. These learning tasks are intended to correspond to situations outside the classroom in which students might possibly use English.

3) Characteristics of test takers

These include:

a. Personal characteristics: for instance, boys and girls in primary grades 1 through 3, ages seven through nine. They come from a wide range of socio-economical backgrounds. The majority are native Cantonese speakers.

b. Topical knowledge: the children, having just begun their academic careers, will have relatively little "academic" knowledge.

c. General level and profile of language ability: Some students come from homes in which English is spoken by one or both parents, and thus will have moderate English ability. The majority, however, will have very little working knowledge of English.

4) Definition of the construct to be measured

This activity makes explicit the precise nature of the ability to be measured, by defining it abstractly. These are usually grouped into three categories: dimension targets, language skills, language items and communicative functions. Dimension targets include:

a. Interpersonal dimension: To develop an ever-improving capacity to use English to establish and maintain relationship, to exchange ideas and information.

b. Knowledge dimension: To develop an ever-improving capability to use English to provide or find out, interpret, and use information, to explore, express, and apply ideas, to solve problems.

c. Experience dimension: To develop an ever-improving capability to use English to respond and give expression to real and imaginative experience.

Language skills include listening, speaking, reading, and writing.

Language items include the major categories of grammar in English and communicative functions include items such as greetings and bidding farewell, etc.

5) Plan for evaluating qualities of usefulness

In Bachman's words, test usefulness is an essential consideration in all stages of test development, which should be evaluated from six perspectives: reliability, construct validity, authenticity, interactiveness, impact and practicality.

For high-stakes (often characterized by being large-scale and very important to testees) tests, reliability and construct validity should be set rather high. To collect evidence for evaluating reliability, two common ways are used: several examiners give the same test to a group of test takers and calculate the consistency of scores across the different test administrations; several raters score the same tests and calculate the consistency of scores across the different raters. To collect evidence for construct validity, the test-takers' test performance and language performance in later study or work are kept and compared. The minimum levels (low, moderate, high) of authenticity, interactiveness and impact are also set according to various test situations and purposes. However, for evaluation of them, test takers and others concerned are interviewed to collect information. Given the relative low-stakes nature of classroom ELT tests, a high level of reliability is not absolutely essential compared with the importance of test validity, which is individually the most important factor.

Practicality involves the resources available and allocation, which is discussed in the coming section.

6) Inventory of available resources and plan for their allocation

This activity makes explicit the resources (human, material, time) that will be required and that will be available for various activities during test development and provides a plan for how to allocate and manage them throughout the development process.

Stage 2: Operationalization

Operationalization involves: **a**. developing test task specifications for the types of test tasks to be included in the test; **b**. making a blueprint that describes how test tasks will be organized to form actual tests; **c**. developing and writing the actual test tasks, instructions; **d**. specifying the procedures for scoring the test.

To develop actual test tasks, the test developer may either modify TLU tasks or create original test tasks whose characteristics correspond to TLT tasks. To develop test tasks from TLU tasks, the developer starts by using needs analysis to identify and select those TLU tasks that test users consider most important. These tasks should meet the minimum requirements for authenticity and interactiveness specified in the plan for evaluating usefulness. The test developer makes the second cut by evaluating this pool of TLU tasks against the minimum levels of usefulness for the remaining qualities of usefulness: reliability, validity, impact and practicality. Some of the TLU tasks in the pool may need very little modification to satisfy these minimum requirements, and these tasks would be retained. Other TLU tasks may need so much modification that the initial qualities of authenticity and interactiveness may suffer, and these tasks would be rejected. The final step in the operationalization is to modify the characteristics of the retained TLU tasks for use as test tasks, so as to satisfy minimal levels that have been set for the qualities of usefulness, or to develop original test tasks whose characteristics correspond to those of TLU tasks and also satisfy minimum levels on the qualities of usefulness (Bachman & Palmer, 1996: 178).

A blueprint is a detailed plan that provides a basis for developing an entire test. In addition, the blueprint is used to evaluate the intentions of the test developers, to permit the development of other tests or parallel forms of the test with the same characteristics, to evaluate the correspondence between test as developed and the blueprint from which it was developed, and to evaluate the authenticity of the test.

Writing instructions involves describing fully and explicitly the structure of the test, the nature of the task the test takers will be presented, and how they are expected to respond.

Specifying the scoring method involves two steps: a. defining the criteria by which the quality of the test takers' responses will be evaluated and b. determining the procedures that will be followed to arrive at a score (Bachman & Palmer, 1996: 91).

Stage 3: Test administration

The test administration stage involves giving the test to a group of individuals, collecting information, and analyzing this information. Administration typically takes place in two phases: try-out and operational testing.

Try-out involves administering the test for the purpose of collecting information about the usefulness of the test itself, and for the improvement of the test and testing procedures. And **operational test** use involves administering the test primarily in order to accomplish the specified use of the test, but also for collecting information about test usefulness.

Analyzing and archiving test scores are integral parts of test development. They help to evaluate the present test in both qualitative and quantitative ways, and build up a large pool of test tasks so as to facilitate the development of subsequent tests.

As mentioned earlier, test developers must base their judgment and decisions on concrete test situations. This does not contradict that they should organize test development following the three stages: design, operationalization and administration. Meanwhile, although test development is generally linear, with one step following another, the process is also an iterative one in which reconsideration, repetition, revision, even abortion may happen.

2.2.2 Common types of tests

1) Multiple choice questions

Probably the most common way of testing language is the multiple choice test. These tests have the advantage of being easy to grade and being able to cover a lot of grammatical points quickly.

The most common type of multiple choice item is one in which the test maker gives the testee a sentence with a blank and four or five choices of a word or phrase which completes the sentence correctly. For example,

Because my father was seriously ill, I _____ to go home last week.
A) had   B) have   C) has   D) hadn't

To give slightly more context, this type of question sometimes makes use of a short dialogue, with one person saying something and the other person responding.

A way of testing short answers and responses is to give the testees an utterance, and have them decide which of four or five utterances is an appropriate response. This can be either a test of comprehension or a test of grammar. For example,

— I think that the life here has too high a tempo.
— _____.
A) I do so.   B) Do I so.   C) I so do.   D) So do I.

Another way of using multiple choice items is to give testees a sentence and ask them to choose which of four or five alternatives has the same meaning. For example,
The school should have expelled him.
A) The school didn't expel him, which was wrong.
B) The school expelled him, because it was necessary.
C) The school might have expelled him, if it had known.
D) The school will probably expel him in the near future.

Again this is a test of reading comprehension as well as grammar, but in order to understand the meaning of the sentence, the reader does have to understand the grammar.

The test maker must find a balance between giving enough context and giving too much. One way to give more context and make the language more natural is to give the items in the form of a short reading passage rather than individual sentences. This gives the testees more context and, if the passage is chosen carefully, is also much more interesting than reading individual, uncontextualized sentences. However, it may be more difficult to test a range of grammatical points, since the grammatical points are restricted by the content of the passage.

2) True or false

True or false judgment is a very common way to check students' comprehension of the main idea or some details. For instance:

Judge, after reading the passage, whether the following statements are true or false.
1.   The author was a happy boy without worry or sorrow before his friend suffered from AIDS.
2.   One day David told the author the truth, and he believed David without any doubt.

In recent years, with more voices on the reliability of this test form (since it has only two possibilities and one can be either right or wrong with a 50-50), many tests have added a third choice: not mentioned by the passage/author.

3) Error correction

Error correction items are also useful for testing language points, especially vocabulary and grammar. An error correction item is one in which the testee is given a sentence with an error. Four words or phrases in the sentence marked with letters, and the testee needs to decide which of the words or phrases has the error and sometimes also correct the error. For example,

(a) **Most athletes** in this game (b) **believe** that they (c) **should have got** better scores (d) **than they are.**

The teacher may also mix in some sentences that have no errors, and students are required to indicate that there is no error. In addition, the students might be required to correct the error. Errors from students' actual writing are a good source of ideas for this type of exercise.

4) Matching

Match making is a common exercise and test form on vocabulary. Students are provided with two columns of words or expressions, and they are required to match the corresponding terms close in meaning, in translation, or in interpretation. For example:

Find in column B a word which has close meaning to words in column A.

A	B
assist	drop
fall	help

5) Items to test knowledge of word/sentence order

Other types of items can be used to test testees' knowledge of word order. The possibility is to give testees the four (or many) words and ask them to put the words in order, or to form a complete sentence. For example,

I wonder how my wife knows _____.
A. how B. it C. much D. costs
/ __/ __/ __/ __/

This can also be done in a way that actually requires the writer to do some writing. For example,

I / wonder /she /how / it /much / costs /how /knows

_____ .

Understanding of appropriate sentence order can also be tested in a similar way by giving testees several sentences and asking them to put them in order. This type of test tests knowledge of references, cohesive devices, etc.

6) Cloze or completion items

Completion items are items in which the testees are asked to fill in blanks in sentences. For the purpose of a grammar test, the words which fit in the blanks should be function words, such as articles and prepositions. (Completion items intended to test reading ability or vocabulary knowledge, in contrast, use content words.) For example,

Please fill in each blank with one suitable word.

I saw my grandfather's tears. I had never seen him cry before. His 36. _____ became hoarse.

"One day a terrible war came, and my 37. _____, like so many sons, went away to fight a great evil. He and I went to the train station 38. _____. Three months later a telegram came. My son had 39. _____ in some tiny village in Italy. 40. _____ I could think of was 41. _____ the last thing I said to him in this life was goodbye."

42. _____ slowly stood up. Don't ever say goodbye, Billy. Don't ever 43. _____ in to the sadness and the loneliness of that word. I want you to remember instead the joy and the 44._____ of those times when you first said hello to a friend. Take that special hello and 45._____ it away within you—in that place in your heart where summer is an always time. When you and your friends must part, I want you to reach deep within you and bring back that first hello.

The advantage of completion items is that they test production, not just recognition. The disadvantage is that they need to be marked by hand and there will be some cases where the marker needs to make judgments about whether a response is correct. It is not always easy to write items for which there is only one possible answer. Using a piece of continuous prose rather than disconnected sentences is one way of cutting down on possible different interpretations of what goes into a particular blank, but it is probably impossible to entirely eliminate the possibility of different answers.

Also, it is possible to require a phrase instead of a word in each blank. However, while this method presents a more realistic situation, it does become more difficult to mark. While it is probably not realistic for large-scale testing situations, it is something that is useful for classroom teachers who want to help their students develop an ability to produce appropriate grammatical forms in context.

7) Transformation items

Another type of testing item makes use of transformations. In this type of item, testees are given a sentence and the first few words of another sentence to change the original sentence without changing the meaning. For example,

1. Jack hasn't been home in a long time.
    It's been a long time _____.
2. We don't need to go to the grocery store this week.
    It isn't _____.

Again, this type of test is difficult to grade because the teacher has to be aware of the variety of possible answers. Another problem is that it does not in any way test the testees' knowledge of when each of the possible transformations would be most appropriate. For example, the testee might be perfectly able to transform an active sentence to a passive sentence but not know when to use passive rather than active. However, it is still sometimes a useful test of grammatical knowledge.

8) Word changing items

Another type of item is one in which the testees are given a sentence and a word which they need to fit into the sentence by changing the form of the word. For example,

1.   We have never _____ to Europe. (be)
2.   Nobody wants to live in the _____ part of the city. (industry)

This type of test item tests students' knowledge of different word forms and how they are used in sentences.

9) Sentence combining

Sentence combining exercises can play a part in testing grammar as well as its more traditional use as part of composition testing and training. For example, testees might be instructed to combine the following sentences using a relative pronoun.

I met a sport star.
The sport star went to the same college I did.
I met a sport star who went to the same college I did.

10) Writing and translation

Writing and translation are also very popular language test forms. The former tests students' ability in planning, organizing and editing a foreign language while the latter tests the students' knowledge and proficiency in both L1 and L2.

Of course, the above forms of language test by no means exhaust the ways or forms of language testing. With such notions as "authenticity" and "interactiveness" counting more in test design, we are seeing more test forms.

2.3   Testing students' communicative competence

Testing language has traditionally taken the form of testing knowledge about language, usually the testing of knowledge of vocabulary and grammar. However, there is much more involved in the use of language than simply knowledge about it. Dell Hymes coined in 1966 and formally used in 1971 the term *communicative competence*. He argued that a speaker "can" be able to produce grammatical sentences that are completely inappropriate. In communicative competence, he included not only the ability to form correct sentences but to use them at appropriate times (Hymes, 1971). Since then, it has been expanded considerably, and various types of competencies have been proposed. However, the basic idea of communicative competence remains the ability to use language appropriately, both receptively and productively, in real situations. Let's first have a look at the communicative approach to testing.

2.3.1 The Communicative Approach to testing

Communicative language tests are intended to be a measure of how the testees are able to use language in real life situations. In testing productive skills, emphasis is placed more on appropriateness than on ability to form grammatically correct sentences. In testing receptive skills, emphasis is placed on understanding the communicative intent of the speaker or writer rather than on picking out specific details (Kathleen & Kitao, 1996)[1]. And, in fact, the two are often combined in communicative testing, so that the testee must both comprehend and respond in real time.

In real life, the different skills are not often used in isolation. Students in a class may listen to a lecture, but they later need to use information from the lecture in a paper. In taking part in a group discussion, they need to use both listening and speaking skills. Even watching a TV series for pleasure may very well be followed by recommending it to a friend or colleague and telling him/her why you liked it.

A continuum

The "communicativeness" of a test might be seen as being on a continuum:

Few tests are completely communicative; many tests have some element of communicativeness; and a few ones are rather "incommunicative". For example, a test in which testees listen to

---

[1] S. Kathleen, & Kenji Kitao. 1996. http://iteslj.org/Articles/Kitao-Testing.html retrieved online 18 April 2004.

an utterance on a tape and then choose from among three or four choices the most appropriate response is more communicative than one in which the testees answer a question about the meaning of the utterance. However, it is less communicative than one in which the testees are face-to-face with the interlocutor (rather than listening to a tape) and are required to produce an appropriate response.

Tasks

Communicative tests are often very context-specific. A test for testees who are going to American universities as students would be very different from one for testees who are going to their company's branch office in Singapore. If at all possible, a communicative language test should be based a description of the language that the testees need to use. Though communicative testing is not limited to English for Specific Purposes situations, the test should reflect the communicative situation in which the testees are likely to find themselves. In cases where the testees do not have a specific purpose, the language that they are tested on can be directed toward general social situations where they might be in a position to use English.

This basic assumption influences the tasks chosen to test language in communicative situations. A communicative test of listening, then, would test not whether the testee could understand what the utterance, "Would you mind switching off the lights before you leave" means, but place it in a context and see if the testee can respond appropriately to it.

If students are going to be tested over communicative tasks in an achievement test situation, it is necessary that they be prepared for that kind of test, that is, the course material cover the sorts of tasks they are being asked to perform. For example, you cannot expect testees to correctly perform such functions as requests and apologies appropriately and evaluate them on it if they have been studying from a structural syllabus. Similarly, if they have not been studying writing business letters, you cannot expect them to write a business letter for a test.

Tests intended to test communicative language are judged, then, on the extent to which they simulate real life communicative situations rather than on how reliable the results are. In fact, there is an almost inevitable loss of reliability as a result of the loss of control in a communicative testing situation. If, for example, a test is intended to test the ability to participate in a group discussion for students who are going to a British university, it is impossible to control what the other participants in the discussion will say, so not every testee will be observed in the same situation, which would be ideal for test reliability. However, according to the basic assumptions of communicative language testing, this is compensated for by the realism of the situation.

Evaluation

There is necessarily a subjective element to the evaluation of communicative tests. Real life situations don't always have objectively right or wrong answers, and so band scales need to be developed to evaluate the results. Each band has a description of the quality (and sometimes quantity) of the receptive or productive performance of the testee.

To give a clearer picture of communicative test tasks, we adapt the following examples from (Kathleen & Kitao, 1996).

2.3.2 Examples of communicative test tasks

1) Testing speaking and listening
Information gap activity

An information gap activity is one in which two or more testees work together, though it is possible for a confederate of the examiner rather than a testee to take one of the parts. Each testee is given certain information but also lacks some necessary information. The task requires the testees to ask for and give information. The task should provide a context in which it is logical for the testees to be sharing information, e.g.:

Student A: You are planning to buy a tape recorder. You don't want to spend more than 60 pounds, but you think that a tape recorder that costs less than 40 pounds is probably not of good quality. You definitely want a tape recorder with auto reverse, and one with a radio built in would be nice. You have investigated three models of tape recorder and your friend has investigated three models. Get the information from him/her and share your information. You should start the conversation and make the final decision, but you must get his/her opinion, too. (information about three kinds of tape recorders)

Student B: Your friend is planning to buy a tape recorder, and each of you investigated three types of tape recorder. You think it is best to get a small, light tape recorder. Share your information with your friend, and find out about the three tape recorders that your friend investigated. Let him/her begin the conversation and make the final decision, but don't hesitate to express your opinion.(information about three kinds of tape recorders)

This kind of task would be evaluated using a system of band scales. The band scales would emphasize the testee's ability to give and receive information, express and elicit opinions, etc. If its intention were communicative, it would probably not emphasize pronunciation, grammatical correctness, etc., except to the extent that these might interfere with communication. The examiner should be an observer and not take part in the activity, since it is difficult to both take part in the activity and evaluate it. Also, the activity should be tape recorded, if possible, so that it could be evaluated later and it does not have to be evaluated in real time.

Role play

In a role play, the testee is given a situation to play out with another person. The testee is given in advance information about what his/her role is, what specific functions he/she needs to carry out, etc. A role play task would be similar to the above information gap activity, except that it would not involve an information gap. Usually the examiner or a confederate takes one part of the role play.

The following is an example of a role play activity.

Student: You missed class yesterday. Go to the teacher's office and apologize for having missed the class. Ask for the handout from the class. Find out what the homework was.

Examiner: You are a teacher. A student who missed your class yesterday comes to your office. Accept his/her apology, but emphasize the importance of attending classes. You do not have any extra handouts from the class, so suggest that he/she copy one from a friend. Tell her/him what the homework was.

Again, if the intention of this test were to test communicative language, the testee would be assessed on his/her ability to carry out the functions (apologizing, requesting, asking for information, responding to a suggestion, etc.) required by the role.

2) Testing reading and writing

Some tests combine reading and writing in communicative situations. Testees can be given a task in which they are presented with instructions to write a letter, memo, summary, etc., answering certain questions, based on information that they are given.

In many situations, testees might have to write business letters, letters asking for information, etc.

Letter writing

The following is an example of such a task.

Your boss has received a letter from a customer complaining about problems with a coffee maker that he bought six months ago. Your boss has instructed you to check the company policy on returns and repairs and reply to the letter. Read the letter from the customer and the statement of the company policy about returns and repairs below and write a formal business letter to the customer. (the customer's complaint letter; the company policy)

The letter would be evaluated using a band scale, based on compliance with formal letter writing layout, the content of the letter, inclusion of correct and relevant information, etc.

Summarizing

Testees might be given a long passage—for example, 400 words—and be asked to summarize the main points in less than 100 words. To make this task communicative, the testees should be given realistic reasons for doing such a task. For example, the longer text might be an article that their boss would like to have summarized so that he/she can incorporate the main points into a talk.

The summary would be evaluated, based on the inclusion of the main points of the longer text.

3) Testing listening and writing/Note taking

Listening and writing may also be tested in combination. In this case, testees are given a listening text and they are instructed to write down certain information from the text. Again, although this is not interactive, it should somehow simulate a situation where information would be written down from a spoken text.

An example of such a test is as follows:

You and two friends would like to see a movie. You call the local theaters. Listen to their recording and fill in the missing information in the chart so that you can discuss it with your friends later.

Theater Number	Movie	Starting Time
1	KING KONG	
2		4:00, 6:10, 8:20
3		4:35, 6:45, 8:55
4	Godfather III	

3. Relationship between language teaching and testing

3.1   Influence on each other

3.1.1 Interaction under common theoretical and practical influences

Firstly, a brief review of the history of testing shows that language testing is closely related to language teaching in terms of their development. Put it another way, the developing stages of language testing roughly match those of the language teaching. At different stages, people in the field of language teaching take different views on language and correspondingly, they adopt different language testing methods. Generally speaking, the development of language testing experiences four stages (Shao Yongzhen, see Robert Wood, 2001: F24):

- *Pre-scientific stage* (before 1960, during which essay-writing and translation are the main forms of language tests)
- *Psychometric-structural stage* (from 1961, marked by the publication of Robert Lado's article *Language Testing* to the mid 1970s)
- *Psycho-linguistic and socio-linguistic stage* (from the mid 1970s to the 1980s)
- *Communicative language testing stage* (from the 1980s till now)

Second, it is an established fact that language teaching is based on linguistic and educational theories. The same story for language testing. Wharton (2002: 155-157) believes that it is impossible to write a test without consciously or unconsciously bringing in the views about the nature of language and also the nature of learning. The change of views on language ability in linguistics, for instance, underlies the recent development of language tests considerably—broadening from the traditional focus on grammar and lexis to include the value of actual utterances in context. Test attendants may be asked, for instance, to listen to a conversation and answer questions which focus not only on the understanding of content, but also of speaker attitude and intention.

Third, foreign language teaching (and learning), lays the knowledge and skills foundation in language learners for language testing to evaluate. Language testing research tends to focus on the complexities of the language proficiency that are the result of language teaching and learning. Since language testing is the procedure to assess the effect of this result, it was and is still regarded by many as a part of language teaching. Fred and Johna (1996: 154-167) define language test as a set of tasks requiring observable responses to language or in language that can be scored and interpreted with reference to norms, domains, or instructional objectives. Norm-referenced tests provide interpretations of test scores relative to other learners and criterion-referenced tests provide interpretation of test scores relative to an identified domain of language knowledge or skill. Although the types of language tests vary along different dimensions (for instance, according to use of the information from tests, there are achievement, proficiency, diagnostic, placement tests), embodiment of the effect of language teaching is almost ubiquitous.

Meanwhile, the importance of language testing on FLT is hard to be neglected. The following discussion focuses on this issue.

3.1.2 Backwash effect

The term *Backwash* is commonly used in the field of language testing. Hughes (2000) provides the following definition: The effect of testing on teaching and learning is known as backwash which can be harmful or beneficial.

However, many experts, like Heaton, prefer to use the term *washback* effect:

This is the phrase used to refer to the way an exam or test influences teaching and learning in the classroom. In the effort to enable their students to pass certain exams, teachers will gear their teaching very closely to the examination. If it is a good examination, it will have a useful effect on teaching; if bad, then it will have a damaging effect on teaching. (Heaton 1990)

Bachman & Palmer (1996: 30-35) point out that washback is an effect that has been of particular interest to both language testing researchers and practitioners and most discussions of this have focused on processes of learning and instruction (teaching). They think these processes take place in and are implemented by individuals, as well as educational and social systems. As a result, the effect of washback should be considered within the scope of impact on individuals (mainly on test takers and teachers), educational systems, and society at large.

The following table lists Bachman & Palmer's analysis of washback (or backwash) effect:

FIGURE 8.5 Bachman & Palmer's analysis of washback

Impact on test takers	Impact on language teachers	Impact on society and educational systems
Test takers can be affected by three aspects of the testing procedure: 1) the experience of taking and, in some cases, of preparing for the test 2) the feedback they receive about their performance on the test 3) the decisions that may be made about them on the basis of their test scores	In an instructional program, the test users that are most directly influenced by test use are teachers: 1) impact on the program of instruction 2) impact on the decisions made on language learners or test takers by teachers 3) impact on award for good performance or punishment for poor performance of their students in tests	This impact is of particular concern with high-stakes tests, which are used to make major decisions about large numbers of individuals: (e.g.) 1) the impact on the FLT practice in a country of using a certain type of test task, like multiple-choice item on a national level 2) the impact on societal values and goals of using language tests for particular purposes

As an important way for collecting information for language teaching, language testing at the end of certain units or at the end of a course is very important to teachers for reflecting on their previous teaching and for planning ongoing instruction, to students for organizing and adjusting their own learning activities. And also, these results can be used by people outside the classroom: to school authorities for accountability, and to parents who are interested in their children's education and to the national even international society at large. In order to ensure good washback, some considerations on classroom test use ought to be kept in mind:

- Frequency of formal and informal tests should be kept at a balance. Formal tests, used primarily to compare students' performances can be given to students every term, once a year or even a longer time. Informal classroom tests, on the other hand, can be set a bit more often. They can be used to diagnose difficulties as well as to encourage students.

- Classroom tests should be designed to reflect the development of all language skills. If classroom tests dwell only on reading abilities and not speaking skills, the effect on teaching and learning can be very harmful indeed. Although oral tests can be time-consuming, regular tests of speaking ability can be made and should be made by the teacher in more flexible ways.

- Teachers should try to lower the anxiety of students when giving them a test. If classroom language tests are conducted in a tense and formal atmosphere, students will be negatively affected mentally and emotionally. And meanwhile, teachers should make sure that the test is proper to their current level, enjoyable and useful. A good classroom test is one which students actually enjoy doing and do not regard as being a test (Fred & Johna, 1996).

Unfortunately, a lot of tests are harmful because they create too much anxiety in students. An advantage of short informal tests should be that they help students overcome such feelings of anxiety (Fred & Johna, 1996). Moreover, if the class teacher is the test writer, students will soon become familiar with the type of test usually set and will feel reassured because the test contents will be based on the course contents.

3.2　A discussion on their conflicts

Many a language teacher harbors a deep mistrust of tests (Hughes, 2000: 1). One important cause is that a lot of language tests are of poor quality and thus have a very harmful effect on teaching and learning. Most teachers are familiar with the amount of impact testing can have on their instruction. In spite of the fact that teachers may want to try some innovative teaching methods, if they find they have to use a specific test they may find "teaching to the test" almost unavoidable. The term "teaching to the test" indicates doing something in teaching that may not be compatible with teachers' own values and goals, or with the values and goals of the instructional program (Bachman & Palmer, 1996: 33). If teachers feel what they teach is not relevant to the test, the test may probably have harmful impact on the instruction.

In ELT in China today, students' language use ability is prioritized and in classroom instructions, educators emphasize the use of communicative and interactive approaches like TBLT; the process of communication and interaction is highlighted. But if we look at English tests, we find they are overwhelmingly individualistic. Most test tasks require students to respond without collaboration and this is reflected both in rubrics and in task design. Collaboration in exam practice may therefore, not be regarded as legitimate by students; a sense of competition comes to dominate the class instead. This is an apparent mismatch between language teaching and testing (Wharton, 2002: 157).

The second cause for mistrusting tests is that very often they fail to measure what they are intended to measure. Students' ability is not always reflected accurately in the test scores that they get. Admittedly, language ability is not easy to measure and as a result this inaccuracy is inevitable to some extent. However, we can expect greater accuracy than is frequently achieved (Hughes, 2000: 2). According to Hughes, there are two major causes leading to this inaccuracy. The first concerns test content and test techniques. Both pose problems for the test results to be desired. Professional testers have expended great effort and money, in attempts to improve the accuracy, but the best is only to get an approximate measure and that is all. "When testing is carried out on a large scale, when the scoring of tens and thousands of compositions might seem not to be a practical proposition, it is understandable that potentially greater accuracy is sacrificed for reason of economy and convenience. But it does not give testing a good name and it does set a bad example" (Hughes, 2000: 2).

Of course, the opposite situation also exists. That is, those responsible for the instructional program (especially teachers) may not be satisfied with the quality of the teaching program and the results it produces. This dissatisfaction may arise because various aspects of the program (teaching materials, types of learning activities etc.) may be out of touch with what teachers currently believe promotes effective learning. Many language testers have argued that, in situations such as this, one effective way to bring instructional practice in line with current thinking in the field is to develop or adopt a testing procedure that reflects this thinking.

The hypothesis in this situation is that improvement in language instruction can be brought about through the use of tests that incorporate or are compatible with what are believed to be principles of effective teaching and learning (Bachman & Palmer, 1996: 34). This implies that language testing can also go ahead of language teaching and learning at certain stages.

But on the whole, it is not realistic to expect the public examination bodies to do all, or even very much of the work for development and change. Testing bodies are conservative for good reason (Skehan, 1991): Candidates and teachers need to be informed of change well in advance, which means a considerable time lag in the implementation of change. Testing bodies are also commercial operations, whose success depends on public familiarity with, and confidence in, their product. This is not a situation that is conducive to experiment for the sake of it (Wharton, 2002: 165).

3.3   A summary of their relationship

How can we look at the relationship between language teaching and testing?

Davies (1968: 5) has said that "the good test is an obedient servant since it follows and apes the teaching", while in many situations, "testing is a baton and everything else dances to it". Is testing the servant or master to language teaching? Here we follow Hughes, who claims that the proper relationship between teaching and testing in surely that of partnership. It is true that there may be occasions when the teaching is good and appropriate and the testing is not; we are then likely to suffer from harmful backwash.... But equally there may be occasions when teaching is poor or inappropriate and when testing is able to exert a beneficial influence (Hughes, 2000).

4.   Suggestions on testing

4.1   A scrutiny of language testing practice in China

In China, the "homeland of testing" as dubbed by many, various problems exist in the present testing system.

4.1.1 Overdue focus on form, rather than on meaning

If we review some English testing syllabus statements in China, it is not difficult to find that most of them contain words like "focusing on the assessment of students' communicative ability in English". However, the test items are overwhelmingly designed on the basis of structuralism. Too much emphasis is put on accuracy, while too little on fluency. According to Xu Qiang, the drilling and testing of pronunciation, grammatical rules are much too common, especially in primary and secondary schools (2000: 114-115).

e.g. 1 Find out the one which has the different pronunciation.
    a. tea<u>ch</u>   b. <u>Ch</u>ina   c. s<u>ch</u>ool   d. lun<u>ch</u>
e.g. 2 Give the pronunciation of the underlined parts of the following words.
    <u>air</u>   h<u>air</u>   ch<u>air</u>   c<u>are</u>

These items have a high frequency of appearance in primary and secondary English tests in China. But why do teachers let students spend such a long time on written pronunciation practice? Isn't it enough for them to be able to read words correctly? Can't teachers check their students' pronunciation without appealing to pencil and paper?

e.g. 3 He is a _____.

a. China   b. Chinese   c. American   d. Englishman

e.g. 4 Angel _____ up very early every day that month.

a. get   b. had been getting   c. has got   d. has been getting

As we can see from examples three and four, the testing on grammatical knowledge has been very broad and detailed. Even a low-grade student with a very limited amount of vocabulary, has to know a lot of grammatical points. In the simulated tests or exercise books alike, directions like "Write down the simple past and past participle of the verbs" are rather common. In many high schools, students have to finish hundreds, even thousands of grammatical exercises, to prepare for the NMET (national matriculation English test). The same story goes for college students preparing for CET (college English test). Moreover, these test items require students more to discern, rather than to use language.

Although English courses in China are meant primarily to train students in the language skills necessary for communication, students have to take part in tests which do not test language skills directly. The tests are over-dominated with multiple choice items, checking students' discrete, segmented knowledge about language.

Besides, one of the most objectionable, though seldom remarked upon, features of formal testing is the intrinsic dullness of the materials. How often do test takers get excited about a test or a particular item on a test? This phenomenon is contrary to the "meaning-oriented" ideal: a good assessment instrument should be and can be a learning experience. Generally speaking, to meet the demand of major, high-stakes English tests in China, students are forced to pay much more attention on accuracy, and this often goes into extremity, which is quite undesirable.

4.1.2 Students and teachers misled by the forms of tests

In most language tests, when defining objectives in terms of test tasks, there has been a tendency to concentrate on knowledge and skills that are easy to test at the expense of skills and abilities that are not so easy to test. Worse than that, language skills that may be important for students to learn may even be left out of instructional objectives simply because it is not easy to test them. In Genesse and Johna's words, objectives may be chosen more because of their amenability to testing than because of their value to the language learners (1996: 161).

It is clear that paper-pencil, multiple-choice tests are convenient and efficient, but they have with them intrinsic problems. Hughes (2000) lists six weaknesses built into such items: **a.** The technique tests only recognition knowledge; **b.** Guessing may have considerable but unknowable effect on test scores; **c.** The technique severely restricts what can be tested; **d.** It is very difficult to write successful items; **e.** Backwash effect may be harmful; **f.** Cheating may be facilitated.

In addition, teachers and others concerned can obtain very limited information from the results of multiple-choice (MC) tests. Since the 1980s, some international tests like International English Language Testing System in Britain have begun to drop most or even all MC forms. However, in China, MC test forms are still strongly dominating the testing arena (Xu, 2000: 217).

A more lamentable aspect of formal, standardized testing is the influence of test scores on students' overall development. Individuals receive the scores, see their ranks in class or in school or in a wider range. And they draw a conclusion about their scholastic, if not their overall, merit. As Gardner (1993) says, psychologists and testers spend far too much time ranking individuals and not nearly enough time helping them. Take a consideration of those students whose academic record reveals a chronic history of failure. For them, it is a deflating, discouraging, and defeating experience. These students will regard the next step of learning and embracing more high-standard and high-stakes testing as another intimidation-driven and face-losing occasion once they lose. They will see the new higher standards as unattainable and will gradually give up in hopelessness.

4.2 Testing reform: an inevitable orientation

Due to considerations on cost and efficiency, many people in language teaching and testing field tend to reject the idea of testing reform towards a more natural and contextualized one. However, in the learning society of the twenty-first century, such conceptions as "cultural diversification", "self actualization", and "learner autonomy" are being rooted in more and more people.

With the development of various learning models and practices, it is time to adopt a multi-dimensional perspective in monitoring and assessing an individual's development. There has been a sizable body of evidence, according to Gardner (1993), which, by and large, points up problems with standard formal testing as an exclusive mode of assessment. Indeed, if one considers "formal testing" and "apprenticeship-style assessment" as two poles of assessment, it can safely be said that our society has gone too far along the route of formal testing and it is high time to consider changes.

Assessment should be undertaken primarily to aid students. It is incumbent upon the assessor to provide feedback to the student that will be helpful at the present time—identifying areas of strengths as well as weaknesses, giving suggestions of what to study or make up, pointing out which habits are productive and which are not, indicating what can be expected in the way of future assessments, and the like. It is especially important that some of the feedback takes the form of concrete suggestions and indicates relative strengths to build upon, independent of rank within a comparable group of students (Gardner, 1993).

But more to the point, it is desirable to have assessment occur in the processes of carrying out tasks—context of students working on problems, projects, or products that genuinely engage them, and that hold their interest and motivate them to do well. Such tasks may not be as easy to design as the standard multiple-choice entry, but they are far more likely to elicit a student's full repertoire of skills and to yield information that is useful for subsequent advice and development plans.

4.3   Construct a multi-faceted, multi-layer assessment system

In China, one striking feature of English teaching and learning culture is the dominating focus on language input. And correspondingly, one common mistake we have made at almost all levels of ELT assessment is to believe that once-a-year or twice-a-year standardized tests alone can provide sufficient information for the teaching and motivation to increase student learning. The adoption of communicative approaches, which emphasize language production through the process of language use and practice, can urge us to reflect on this phenomenon and help us improve this situation. To promote the efficiency of English language teaching in China, the primary work is to construct a multi-dimensional assessment system and reform the existing English tests.

4.3.1 Building a day-to-day English language assessment system

Generally speaking, the belief in the power of standardized testing has blinded many educational officials and school leaders to day-to-day classroom assessment. In this norm, assessment is made primarily to center on students' success, rather than failure. In the preceding section, various alternatives have been suggested to assess students in EFL classes. But for assessment to become truly useful in China, government officials, school leaders, and society in general must firstly come to understand the gross insufficiency of these tests as a basis for assessment for improvement of ELT and more importantly, those in the psychological and educational circles charged with the task of evaluation ought to facilitate such assessment—which can elicit information in the course of ordinary performance. Methods and measures should be devised to aid in regular, systematic, and useful assessment.

In modern language classes emphasizing more naturalistic, context-sensitive, and ecologically valid modes of assessment, the incorporation of test-type activities into a task-based classroom becomes very natural and particularly suitable (Willis, 1996). Students initially get exam practice by doing tasks in a private, non-threatening context. Their subsequent reflection on their performance, including peer and teacher feedback, serves a dual purpose. It provides a point of comparison with their current level of achievement. It also contributes to the planning stage which is an integral part of the task-based activities. This is, of course, a vision most people would like to see in the field of English education in China.

Moreover, this day-to-day, continuous assessment enables the teacher to assess over a period of weeks or months those aspects of a student's performance which cannot normally be assessed as satisfactorily by means of tests (Heaton, 1990). For example, the teacher can use continuous assessment to measure students' work in groups and their overall progress as shown in class. Continuous assessment enables teachers to take into account certain qualities which cannot be assessed in any other way: namely, effort, persistence and attitude. For Chinese students, this is especially important. Chinese students have long been said to be intelligent and diligent, but shy and introvert. A friendly, harmonious, and low-anxious atmosphere helps them to be more courageous, daring, and active.

Bear in mind that a positive attitude to learning is very important and should constantly be encouraged—either through some kind of formal grading or, preferably, by means of indirect and informal encouragement. Of course, the assessment must be of interest and instructive. To younger English learners, this is vitally important.

Bear in mind that the most reliable form of continuous assessment combines grades and comments from course work, observation of project and group work, homework assignments, oral questioning, peer evaluation, students' self-evaluation and progress tests.

Bear in mind that continuous assessment should be regarded as an integral part of the teaching and the students' learning. It should be designed and administered so that it forms a pleasant component of the teaching program. Thereupon, methods and measures ought to be devised that aid in regular, systematic, and useful assessment.

4.3.2 Suggestions on high-stakes English language tests

Formal tests can be an ally to the recognition of different cognitive features, but only if the tests are designed to elicit—rather than mask these differences (Cronbach & Snow, 1977, cited in Gardner, 1993: 170). It is particularly important that instruments used in "gate-keeping" niches like college admissions be designed to allow students to show their strengths and to perform optimally. Until now, little effort has been made in this regard and tests are more frequently used to point up weaknesses than to designate strengths (Gardner, 1993).

1) The purposes of the test should be made clear

According to Hughes (2000: 9-11), proficiency tests are designed to measure people's ability in a language regardless of any training they may have had in that language. The content of a proficiency test, therefore, is not based on the content or objectives of language courses which people taking the test may have followed. In contrast to proficiency tests, achievement tests are directly related to language courses, their purpose being to establish how successful individual students, groups of students, or the courses themselves have been in achieving objectives. Based on the definitions, CET4 should be an achievement test as it is related to college English courses and it is supposed to measure how efficient the courses have been or how much the students have learned. But all these years it has been designed more like a proficiency test, for it follows the early format of TOEFL and it is somewhat removed from the college English of any university, even more so in less competitive universities or highly specialized academies (drama, painting, physical education, etc.) where students start the course at a lower level of proficiency.

If the nationwide scale of CET is taken into consideration, such a test needs to be a proficiency one in that China is so big that the differences of English course in any university can be too noticeable to be ignored. For the same reason, an achievement test can not afford to be taken nationwide. This dubious status has landed the test in a dilemma which has earned much of its unpopularity (Liu & Dai, 2004). As a result, it is the first thing to think about the purpose of testing before developing it.

2) Multiple choice items must be largely reduced.

Multiple choice items are the dominating form of the paper-pencil tests in China, which put reliability and validity at the core of its score analysis. For test reform to happen, ways need to be sought out to increase the total usefulness of paper-pencil tests, rather than simply their reliability and validity.

In fact, paper-pencil techniques can be applied to lots of occasions. When test takers write down their responses to questions or problems, the technique is referred to as "paper and pencil". When pupils complete a written homework assignment, turn in a written report, draw a picture, or finish a worksheet, they are providing paper-pencil evidence to the teacher. Put it in Airasian's words, paper-pencil evidence-gathering techniques are of two general forms: selection and supply (1994: 13-14). Multiple-choice, true-false, and matching questions are called selection techniques because, as the name implies, the student responds to each question by selecting the answer from among a set of provided choices. Supply, or production, requires the test taker to construct a response in order to answer the question. A short-answer or "filling in the blank" question (without multiple choices provided) similarly requires that the test taker construct an answer. Book reports, journal entries, and class projects are all examples of supply-type, paper-pencil techniques.

Notice that a selection-type question provides the maximum degree of control for the person who writes the question, since that person specifies both the question and the choices. In supply-type questions, the person who writes the question has control only over the question itself; responsibility for supplying a response to the question resides with the students answering the question. As for test innovation in China, more supply-type tasks should be designed in major tests to reduce to the negative backwash effect brought by standardized tests, and to make our tests more interactive and authentic. This will naturally increase the amount of labor for marking. However, a true score exacts a price.

3) More weight should be given to speaking and listening skills.

If we have close scrutiny of English test papers, we can easily find that speaking and listening skills have long been left behind. In CET tests, they had a very limited and small "role" to play for years. In NMET, the situation is worse. Listening and speaking skills have long been out of the picture. Put aside other areas for the time being. In the metropolis of Shanghai, China's locomotive of economic development and innovation of policies to cope with its fast development, listening part did not make its debut until 1999 and its oral test began to be counted into the total score in 2001.

If we buy the concept that the four skills are equally important, they each ought to account for a quarter of the total test components and scores. The present format of large-scale, high-stakes tests in China betrays a very poor definition of language proficiency. If we only emphasize the importance of communicative or language use ability in English teaching, but do not highlight it in the components of English tests, the whole effort will end up in vain. And the backwash effect will definitely mislead teachers and learners to swerving to form-focused language teaching.

In addition, in some oral tests in China, the interpersonal or face-to-face environment is deprived. Take college entrance oral English test in Shanghai, the test taker talks to the computer—the "examiner", through the headphone while viewing the questions and requirements on the screen of the computer. To some extent, this relieves the burden of large amount of oral English test takers. The problem is that this is a one-way flow of information: the students get no feedback and the judges (when marking the students) can't evaluate the students' communicative strategies, for instance, body language. In others, it's common for examiners to ask students questions to which they already know the answer. Often an examiner is in a position of asking questions simply for the sake of asking questions. The whole situation is artificial; there is too much control and nothing spontaneous. As a result, information gap tasks, role playing, and opinion gap tasks can be helpful for oral tests.

4) Decisions should be made on student's overall quality.

To restate it, testing is a double-edged sword. If we don't use it carefully, it may hurt us. For decades, test scores of NMET have been "manipulating" the college-seekers lives' in China. As a compulsory part of NMET scores, it is extremely urgent for the decision makers to include more information and testimonies about the students' language capability into the final decisions.

The authors agree with Liu & Dai (2004) that nationwide tests should be discouraged and regional and university co-op tests should be encouraged. For one thing, as a monitoring device such as CET, a test has more supervisory power if administered every few years randomly than taken every semester by every university. For another, the smaller the scale, the better the test is geared to the actual needs of education in the modality.

As for CET4/6 reform, citing their words, "It would be more desirable if we make it a public test like TOEFL and IELTS. It can be administered by the Testing Center under the Ministry of Education and students can take it there if they wish to do so, just like they take an American or British test. Whether they fail or pass has nothing to do with the university from which the test takers come. Thereafter, college English teaching will return to normal: students will come back to their classroom and textbooks which are a hundred times better than collections of CET 4/6 Test papers". (Liu & Dai, 2004)

4.4   Consideration of other factors

In the whole system of ELT, assessment plays a key role. To make improvement of ELT by applying more effective teaching approaches like TBLT in China, testing system is the bottleneck and testing innovation is the trigger. Nevertheless, testing innovation alone cannot solve all the problems. Neither can it be launched without support from various aspects concerned.

4.4.1 Make more adaptations on teaching materials

Good language teaching hinges on good teaching materials. In China, as many non-native teachers are unsure about their command of English, they require not only excellent course books but also good supplementary source materials. With TBLT, the State Education Development Commission (SEDC), the official authority for setting educational policy, has made some efforts in this regard. Being the representative of the highly centralized Chinese system of education, SEDC introduced a teaching syllabus in 1992, and required that secondary school teachers teach English "for communication". At the same time the People's Education Press compiled a textbook series for secondary school English learners. The aims of the textbooks were to help students develop all-round ability in the four skills, and an ability to use English for communication. In 2001, SEDC required all secondary school teachers to use task-based language teaching and the relevant task-based textbooks have since been introduced in some schools (Li, 2004).

Although this is an encouraging signal, it is only an inaugural phase of ELT reform in China. We have too many primary and secondary schools, colleges and universities sticking to dull, grammar-centered and test-oriented teaching materials. At a time with a paradigm shift taking place in the field of ELT, more interactive, communicative and task-based textbooks need to be introduced and adapted to meet the requirement of Chinese students at different levels.

4.4.2 Give teachers more say in the process of syllabus design, teaching and assessment

There is an opinion against the adoption of communicative English teaching methods in China, which mainly argues that they are mostly imported and "brand-new"; appropriate methodologies should be developed by local English teachers to meet the context of China. The authors argue that firstly, it depends on the "room" enjoyed by teachers to create new methodologies. The concept of freedom for appropriate teaching methodologies by English teachers is a culturally relative one. In many developed countries in North America and Western Europe teachers are given a fair degree autonomy of choice. However, educational system in China is still highly centralized, with the government specifying both the content and methodology of teaching.

On the other hand, if teachers can be given more control in syllabus designing, in the teaching and assessment processes, English education in China can be expected to develop in a diverse and creative way. Indeed, English teaching needs creative and critical teachers but the present education system emphasizes categorical— true or false, or A or B answers in both teaching and testing.

Secondly, the choosing of communicative approaches like TBLT by SEDC, per se, reflects the legality of interactive, communicative approaches in China. Of course, it should be best for English teachers to trim and adapt both the teaching procedures and materials to make them more suited for their learners, since the situational constraints like large class size will certainly inhibit the adoption of TBLT. But with concerted efforts and willing hearts, difficulties can be overcome.

Meanwhile, more freedom in the hands of teachers can help to usher in a change to the view of education that Gardner has termed "uniform view of schooling" (1993), which calls for homogenized education in too many respects. According to the uniform view, as much as possible, students should study the same subject matter. Moreover, as much as possible, that subject ought to be conveyed in the same way to all students; progress in school ought to be assessed by standardized, formal tests. These tests should be administered under uniform conditions, and teachers and schools should be evaluated with nationally normed instruments, so that the maximum comparability is possible.

4.4.3 Top-down policy support

As mentioned above, official educational institutions have already felt that communicative language teaching and testing will be beneficial for China. By introducing communicative language teaching and testing as a whole, the government intends to make English education in China keep up with the step of English education in the world. The policy support from Chinese government in this respect is critical and fundamental at a time of paradigm shift of language teaching and testing approaches.

This is a time people hunger for success. But success can rarely be duplicated. Everybody has her/his unique character, living environment, IQ, opportunities, and learning style. Therefore, everybody has her/his own way to success. In the field of English teaching and testing, unless this is fully taken by education policy makers and measures are implemented in favor of constructive assessment, humanistic education, and all-round development, ELT in China cannot have a real leap forward.

5. Web-based language testing

In the above sections, we talked about the test development mainly based on the traditional mode: paper based mode. In this part we take a further look at CBT (computer-based language test) and CAT (computer-adapted language test), which have been studied in ELT for many years. In order to shed some light on this issue, we adapted an article on this study for those who might be interested in the relations of testing and internet.[1]

5.1 Introduction

Interest in Web-based testing is growing in the language testing community, as was obvious at recent language testing conferences, where it was the topic of a symposium (Alderson, 2001), a paper (Roever, 2000), and several reports (Wang et al., 2000). Web-based testing is also considered in Douglas' book (Douglas, 2000). It is the focus of research projects at the University of Hawaii, and a number of online tests for various purposes are available at this time.

Simply defined, a Web-based language test (WBT) is a computer-based language test which is delivered via the World Wide Web (WWW). WBTs share many characteristics of more traditional computer-based tests (CBTs), but using the Web as their delivery medium adds specific advantages while their delivery medium complicates matters.

5.2 Computer-based and web-based tests

The precursor to WBT is CBT, delivered on an individual computer or a closed network. CBTs have been used in second language testing since the early 80s (Brown, 1997). Computers as a testing medium attracted the attention of psychometricians because they allow the application of item response theory for delivering adaptive tests (Wainer, 1990), which can often pinpoint a test taker's ability level faster and with greater precision than paper-and-pencil tests. Based on the test taker's responses, the computer selects items of appropriate difficulty thereby avoiding delivering items that are too difficult or too easy for a test taker. But even for non-adaptive testing, computers, as the testing medium, feature significant advantages. CBTs can be offered at any time unlike mass paper-and-pencil administrations which are constrained by logistical considerations. In addition, CBTs consisting of dichotomously-scored items can provide feedback on the test results immediately upon completion of the test. They can also provide immediate feedback on each test taker's responses—a characteristic that is very useful for pedagogical purposes. The seamless integration

---

[1] Source: adapted from Carsten Roever. 2001. Language Learning & Technology. Vol. 5, No. 2, May, pp. 84-94.

of media enhances the testing process itself, and the tracing of a test taker's every move can provide valuable information about testing processes as part of overall test validation.

On the negative side, problems with CBTs include the introduction of construct-irrelevant variance due to test takers' differing familiarity with computers (Kirsch, Jamieson, Taylor, & Eignor, 1998), the high cost of establishing new testing centers, and the possibility of sudden and inexplicable computer breakdowns.

What to Test on the Web and How to Test It

The first step in any language testing effort is a definition of the construct for what is to be tested: Will the test results allow inferences about aspects of students' overall second language competence in speaking, reading, listening, and writing (Bachman, 1990; Bachman & Palmer, 1996); or will the test directly examine their performance on second language tasks from a pre-defined domain (McNamara, 1996; Shohamy, 1995), such as leaving a message for a business partner, writing an abstract, or giving a closing argument in a courtroom.

Whether a test focuses on aspects of second language competence or performance, its construct validity is the overriding concern in its development and validation. To that end, the test developer must be able to detect sources of construct irrelevant variance, assess whether the construct is adequately represented, in addition to considering the test's relevance, value implications, and social consequences (Messick, 1989). Also, they must examine the test's reliability, authenticity, interactiveness, impact, and practicality (Bachman & Palmer, 1996).

In the following section, appropriate content and item types for WBTs will be discussed and some WBT-specific validation challenges briefly described.

Item Types in WBTs

The Web is not automatically more suited for the testing of general second language competence or subject-specific second language performance than are other testing mediums. To the extent that the performance to be tested involves the Web itself (e.g., writing email, filling in forms), performance testing on the Web is highly authentic and very easy to do since testers only have to create an online environment that resembles the target one. However, a WBT or any computer-based test can never truly simulate situations like "dinner at the swanky Italian bistro" (Norris et al., 1998: 110-112). Rather than analyzing the possibilities of Web-based testing primarily along the lines of the competence-performance distinction, it is more useful to consider which item types are more and which ones are less appropriate for Web-based testing.

It is fairly easy to implement discrete-point grammar and vocabulary tests using radio buttons to create multiple choice items, cloze tests and C-tests with textfields for brief-response items, discourse completion tests or essays with large text areas, as well as reading comprehension tests with frames, where one frame displays the text and the other frame displays multiple-choice or brief-response questions. If the test items are dichotomous, they can be scored automatically with a scoring script. Such items can be contextualized with images. They can also include sound and video files, although the latter are problematic: These files are often rather large, which can lead to long download times, and they require an external player, a plug-in. This plug-in allows test takers to play a soundfile repeatedly simply by clicking the plug-in's "Play" button.

Probably the most serious drawback of WBTs in terms of item types is that, at this time, there is no easy way to record test-taker speech. Microphones are of course available for computers with soundcards, but recording and sending a sound file requires so much work on the part of the test taker that the error potential is unacceptably large.

Validation of WBTs

Quantitative and qualitative validation of WBTs does not differ in principle from validation of other types of tests. This is described in detail by Messick (1989) and Chapelle (1999). However, there are specific validity issues introduced by the testing medium that deserve attention in any WBT validation effort. E.g.:

Computer familiarity

It is well established that test takers' varying familiarity with computers can influence their scores and introduce construct-irrelevant variance (Kirsch et al., 1998). Tutorials to increase computer familiarity can eliminate this effect and the use of standard web-browsers in WBTs increases the likelihood that test takers are already acquainted with the testing environment. For example, Roever (2001) found no significant correlation between self-assessments of Web browser familiarity and scores on a Web-based test of second language pragmatics.

Delivery failures and speediness

One issue in the development phase of a Web-based test is to ensure that the test does not "skip" items during delivery due to technical problems. This can happen if the test taker accidentally double-clicks instead of single-clicking a button, or if there are errors in the algorithm that selects the next item in an adaptive or randomized test. It can be difficult to "tease apart" whether an item was not answered because the test taker ran out of time or because the computer did not deliver the item.

A Special Case: CATs on the Web

Computer-adaptive tests are possible on the Web and do not pose many technical problems beyond those encountered in linear tests but it cannot be emphasized enough that the design of a sophisticated CAT is a very complex undertaking that requires considerable expertise in item response theory.

Like general WBTs, CATs and WATs can be designed at various levels of sophistication. A very simple WAT could display sets of items of increasing difficulty and break off when a test-taker scores less than 50% on a set. The test-taker's ability would then roughly lie between the difficulty of the final and the preceding set. This is fairly easy to realize on the Web, since all that is required is a count of the number of correct responses. However, such a test does not save much time for high-ability test takers who would have to proceed through most difficulty levels. So instead of starting at the lowest difficulty level, initial items could be of mid-difficulty. Subsequent sets would be more or less difficult depending on a test taker's score until the 50% correctness criterion is met.

In the event that WAT used in a medium or high-stakes situation necessitates exposure control, the simplest way of limiting exposure is by means of a randomization function, which selects an item from a pool of equivalent items with the same parameters (Stocking & Lewis, 1995). However, this means that the item bank has to be quite large: Stocking (1994) recommends an item bank that is 12 times the test's length.

5.3 Why WBTs if we already have CBTs?

WBTs offer advantages over traditional CBTs with regard to their practicality (Bachman & Palmer, 1996), logistics, design, cost, and convenience.

"Anyplace, Anytime": The Asynchrony Principle

Probably the single biggest logistical advantage of a WBT is its flexibility in time and space. All that is required to take a WBT is a computer with a Web browser and an Internet connection (or the test on disk). Test takers can take the WBT whenever and wherever it is convenient, and test designers can share their test with colleagues all over the world and receive feedback. The use of scoring scripts for dichotomously-scored items can make the test completely independent of the tester and increases flexibility and convenience for test takers even further.

Testing Goes Grassroots

Whereas producing traditional CBTs requires a high degree of programming expertise and the use of specially-designed and non-portable delivery platforms, WBTs are comparatively easy to write and require only a free, standard browser for their display. In fact, anybody with a computer and an introductory HTML handbook can write a WBT without too much effort, and anybody with a computer and a browser can take the test—language testers do not have to be computer programmers to write a WBT. In addition, HTML contains elements that support the construction of common item types, such as radio buttons for multiple-choice items, input boxes for short response items, and text areas for extended response items (essays or dictations). Free or low-cost editing programs are available that further aid test design.

Of course, just because it is easy to write WBTs does not mean that it is easy to write good WBTs. Pretty pictures and animated images do not define test quality, and any test design and implementation must follow sound procedures (Alderson, Clapham & Wall, 1995) and include careful validation.

Testing Goes Affordable

A WBT is very inexpensive for all parties concerned. Testers can write the test by hand or with a free editor program without incurring any production costs except the time it takes to write the test. Once a test is written, it can be uploaded to a server provided by the tester's institution or to one of many commercial servers that offer several megabytes of free web space (for example, www.geocities.com, www. tripod.com, www.fortunecity.com). Since WBTs tend to be small files of no more than a few kilobytes, space on a free server is usually more than sufficient for a test. The use of images, sound, or video can enlarge the test considerably, however, and may require the simultaneous use of several servers or the purchase of more space.

For the test taker, the only expenses incurred are phone charges and charges for online time, but since many phone companies in the US offer flat rates for unlimited local calls and many Internet service providers have similar flat rate plans for unlimited web access, test takers may not incur any extra costs for a testing session. However, the situation can be markedly different outside North America, where phone companies still charge by the minute for local calls. In such cases, a version of the test that can be completed entirely offline should be provided and distributed via email or download.

5.4   Issues and limitations of using WBTs

The following are some issues that should be considered during the conceptualization and the early stages of WBT development.

Cheating and Item Exposure

The greatest limitation of WBTs is their lack of security with respect to cheating and item confidentiality. Obviously, any test that test takers can take without supervision is susceptible to cheating. It is impossible to ensure that nobody but the test taker is present at the testing session, or that it is even the test taker who is answering the test questions. That limits the possible applications of unsupervised WBTs to low-stakes testing situations.

Item confidentiality is also impossible to maintain, since test takers are not taking the test under controlled conditions, that is, they could just copy items off the screen. Also, items are downloaded into the web browser's cache on the test taker's computer, which means that they are temporarily stored on the test taker's hard drive, where they can be accessed. This is not a problem if items are created "on the fly" or if the item pool is constantly refreshed and each item is only used a few times.

Of course, cheating and item confidentiality are less relevant to low-stakes situations and can be prevented if the test is taken under supervision. This reduces the "anyplace, anytime" advantage of a Web-based test, but it may be a viable option for medium-stakes tests or tests taken only by few test takers, where the establishment of permanent testing centers would not be cost-effective and trustworthy supervisors can be found easily at appropriate facilities.

Self-Scoring Tests and Scripts

Using JavaScript to make tests self-scoring is an attractive approach because it can save a great deal of tedious scoring work, but there is a potential problem associated with this scoring approach: The script contains all the answers. In other words, the answers to all items are downloaded on the test taker's computer where a techno-savvy test taker can easily view them by looking at the test's source code. This can be made a bit more difficult by not integrating the script in the HTML code but instead embedding it as a separate script file, but with a little searching, even that can be found in the browser cache. Solutions to this problem are supervision, scoring by the tester (e.g., by means of SPSS syntax), or serverside scoring scripts which would have to be written in Java, Perl, or serverside JavaScript.

Data Storage

Requirements for secure data storage differ by the type and purpose of the WBT. If the test is taken clientside only, for example, as a self-assessment instrument without any involvement of the tester, test-taker entries should be stored for the duration of the test so that a browser crash does not wipe out a test taker's work (and score) up to that point. However, as a security feature, Web browsers are generally prevented from writing to the test taker's hard disk. The only file to which they can write is a cookie file, and the main content that can be written to each individual cookie is one string of up to 2,000 characters (about two double-spaced pages). This may not be enough to save a long essay, but plenty to save numerical responses, short answers, and biodata. A problem here is that cookies as a means of data backup work only in *Microsoft Internet Explorer*, which updates the cookie physically on the hard drive every time it is modified. *Netscape Navigator* holds the cookie in memory and only updates it when the browser window is closed, so that a system crash in the middle of a testing session irretrievably erases the cookie.

If the test involves the tester, that is, if test data are sent back to the tester's server, secure data storage is somewhat easier. The response to every item can be sent as a FORM email, so that a reconstruction of test taker responses is possible even after a browser or system crash. As an additional security feature to guard against server problems, sets of responses can be "harvested" by a JavaScript function and sent to a different server, so that in fact two or several records of each testing session exist.

5.5   The future of web-based language testing

It may seem premature to talk about the future when Web-based language testing is only now beginning to emerge as an approach to testing. However, some central issues that will have to be dealt with can already be identified:

- validation procedures for different types of media use, different types of delivery platforms and the equivalency of test-taking in different environments,
- the potential, limits, and most appropriate uses of low-tech WBTs and high-tech WBTs,
- oral testing over the web, as real-time one-on-one voice chat or computer-generated speech,
- the possibilities of virtual reality for near-perfect task authenticity and performance-based testing.

It should be abundantly clear that the Web itself does not make a good test, no matter how flashy the Web page, how sophisticated the script, or how beautiful the animations. But the Web greatly expands the availability of computer-based testing with all its advantages and will undoubtedly become a major medium of test delivery in the future.

Questions for further discussion:

1. What are the differences between assessment and testing? What is authentic assessment?
2. What is portfolio? What are the advantages and disadvantages of using a portfolio?
3. Explain Bachman's test usefulness theory.
4. What are the basic procedures for developing an effective language test?
5. What is communicative language test?
6. What is backwash effect? Think about TEM (Test for English Majors) and discuss the backwash effect of it.
7. How can teachers ensure good feedback on classroom tests?
8. Do you believe there exists the best test for every test situation and test developers have the magical power to develop such a test?

9. What problems are there with English language testing in China? In groups discuss how these problems can be tackled.
10. Do you like the current testing system in China? How should it be reformed?
11. What does high-stakes language test mean? Give some examples.
12. Do you have the experience of doing a test on a computer? What will computer and Internet bring to testing?

References:

Airasian, P. W. 1994. *Classroom Assessment*. McGraw-Hill, Inc.

Alderson, C. (Organizer). 2001. *Learning-centered Assessment Using Information Technology*. Symposium conducted at the 23rd Annual Language Testing Research Colloquium, St. Louis, MO.

Alderson, J. C., Clapham, C., & Wall, D. 1995. *Language Test Construction and Evaluation*. Cambridge University Press.

Bachman, L. 1990. *Fundamental Considerations in Language Testing*. Oxford University Press.

Bachman, L. F. & Palmer, A. 1996. *Language Testing in Practice*. Oxford University Press.

Brown, H. D. 2001. *Teaching by Principles: An Interactive Approach to Language Pedagogy*. Foreign Language Teaching and Research Press.

Brown, J. D. 1997. Computers in language testing: Present research and some future directions. *Language Learning & Technology*, 1(1): 44-59. Retrieved April 1, 2001 from http://llt.msu.edu/vol1num1/brown/default.html.

Chapelle, C. 1999. Validity in language assessment. *Annual Review of Applied Linguistics, 19*: 254-272.

Davies, A. (eds.) 1968. *Language Testing Symposium: A Psycholinguistic Perspective*. Oxford University Press.

Douglas, D. 2000. *Assessing Languages for Specific Purposes*. Cambridge University Press.

Fred, G. & Johna. A. 1996. *Classroom-based Evaluation in Second Language Education*. Cambridge University Press.

Gardner, H. 1993. *Multiple Intelligences: the Theory in Practice*. Basic Books.

Gardner, H. 1994. The Creators' Patterns. In M. Boden (Ed.), *Dimensions of Creativity*. Bradford Books/MIT Press.

Genesee, F. & Upsher, J. A. 1996. *Classroom-based Evaluation in Second Language Education*. Cambridge University Press.

Heaton, J. B. 1990. *Classroom Testing*. Longman Group.

Hughes, A. 2000. *Testing for Language Teachers*. Foreign Language Teaching and Research Press.

Hymes, D. H. 1971. *On Communicative Competence*. University of Pennsylvania Press.

Kirsch, I., Jamieson, J., Taylor, C. & Eignor, D. 1998. *Computer Familiarity Among TOEFL Examinees*. TOEFL Research Report No. 59. Educational Testing Service.

Li, X. Q. 2004. The need for Communicative Language Teaching in China. *ELT Journal* Vol. 58/3. Oxford University Press.

Liu, R. Q. & Dai, M. C. 2004. On the reform of college English teaching in China. *CELEA Journal, 27*/4: 3-8.

McNamara, T. 1996. *Measuring Second Language Performance*. Longman.

Messick, S. 1989. Validity. In R. L. Linn (Ed.), *Educational measurement*. Macmillan.

Norris, J. M., Hudson, T., Brown, J. D. & Yoshioka, J. (1998). *Designing Second Language Performance Assessments*. University of Hawaii at Manoa, Second Language Teaching and Curriculum Center.

Nunan, D. 1991. Communicative Tasks and the Language Curriculum. *TESOL Quarterly*, 25/2.

Roever, C. 2001. *Language Learning & Technology, 5* (2): 84-94. University of Hawaii.

Shohamy, E. 1995. Performance assessment in language testing. *Annual Review of Applied Linguistics, 15,* 188-211.

Skehan, P. 1998. *A Cognitive Approach to Language Learning*. Oxford University Press.

Stocking, M. L. 1994. *An alternative method for scoring adaptive tests* (Research Report). ETS.

Stocking, M. L. & Lewis, C. 1995. *Controlling item exposure conditional on ability in computerized adaptive testing* (Research Report) 95-24. ETS.

Wainer, H. 1990. Introduction and history. In H. Wainer (Ed.), *Computerized Adaptive Testing: A Primer*. Lawrence Earlbaum.

Wang, L., Bachman, L. F., Carr, N., Kamei, G., Kim, M., Llosa, L., Sawaki, Y., Shin, S., Vongpumivitch, V., Xi, X., Yessis, D. 2000. *A Cognitive-psychometric Approach to Construct Validation of Web-based Language Assessment*. Work-in-progress report presented at the 22nd Annual Language Testing Research Colloquium, Vancouver, BC, Canada.

Wharton, S. 2002. Testing Innovations. In *Challenge and Chance in Language Teaching*. Jane Willis & Dave Willis (eds.). Shanghai Foreign Languages Education Press.

Willis, J. 1996. *A Framework for Task-based Learning*. Longman.

Wood, R. 2001. *Assessment and Testing: A Survey of Research*. Foreign Language Teaching and Research Press.

Xu, Q. 2000. *The Communicative Approach to English Teaching and Testing*. Shanghai Foreign Languages Education Press.

CHAPTER 9

Teacher Training in English Language Teaching

Common sense and studies show that the quality of teachers is one of the most critical components of students' achievement. In most cases we even dare to say that teachers are the single biggest influence on how well students learn. So it's no surprise the discussion about enhancing and reforming education always zero in on the quality of teaching in the classroom. In many countries, teacher training has become an established network in the field of education. Take U.S. as a cornerstone of education reform, the historic No Child Left Behind Act that President Bush signed into law in January 2002, requires that by the end of the 2005-2006 school year there be a highly qualified teacher in every classroom.

The discussion in this chapter focuses on: Good teachers and good teaching; and teacher training approaches.

1. Good teachers and good teaching

1.1 Good teacher: teacher's quality

Palmer (1999: 27) makes the following comment concerning good teachers:

Good teaching isn't about technique. I've asked students around the country to describe their good teachers to me. Some of them describe people who lecture all the time, some of them describe people who do little other than facilitate group process, and others describe everything in between. But all of them describe people who have some sort of connective capacity, who connect themselves to their students, their students to each other, and everyone to the subject being studied.

Hassett (2000) believes that good teachers

- have a *sense of purpose*;
- have *expectations of success* for all students;
- tolerate *ambiguity*;
- demonstrate a *willingness to adapt and change* to meet student needs;
- are *comfortable with not knowing*;
- *reflect* on their work;
- learn from a *variety of models*;
- *enjoy* their work and their students.

Hu (2005)[1] studies four dimensions for developing qualities of good English teachers in Chinese secondary schools:

(a) the knowledge base for teaching;

(b) pedagogical effectiveness in fostering knowledge acquisition and intellectual qualities that support continuing professional development;

(c) professional development in the community of practice;

(d) the coherence of professional development work.

From his personal experience and observation, Beidler (1997) offers 10 suggestions on good teachers:

1) Good teachers really want to be good teachers.

2) Good teachers take risks.

3) Good teachers have a positive attitude.

4) Good teachers never have enough time: they are busy with their work.

---

[1] Hu, Guangwei. (2005). Professional Development of Secondary EFL Teachers: Lessons From China. Retrieved online 3 Apr. 2006 at http://www.blackwell-synergy.com/.

5) Good teachers think of teaching as a form of parenting.
6) Good teachers try to give their students confidence.
7) Good teachers try to keep students—and themselves—off balance.
8) Good teachers try to motivate students by working within their incentive system.
9) Good teachers do not trust student evaluations.
   Good teachers do tend to get very good evaluations, but they focus on the one or two erratic evaluations that say something negative about them. They ask themselves what they did wrong for those one or two students.
10) Good teachers listen to their students.

1.2   Good teaching

In the above we talked about the qualities of a good teacher. Brain (1998) summarizes four "core qualities" that make good teaching.

Knowledge

Sound field knowledge and broad knowledge system are what students consistently and clearly target as the number one quality of good teaching. You must be an expert in your field if you are going to be a good teacher. This is a prerequisite.

Communication

The second core quality that makes good teaching is the ability to communicate their knowledge and expertise to students.

It is a common misconception that knowledge of a subject is all that's required to be a good teacher; that the students should be willing and able to extract the meat from what you say regardless of how it is delivered.

Good teaching helps make a subject crystal clear to the students. A bad one makes it impenetrable, confusing and disorganized. Good teaching bespeaks the effort needed to find innovative and creative ways to make complicated ideas understandable to their students, and to fit new ideas into the context available to the student. There is a saying, "Give me a fish and I eat for a day; teach me to fish and I eat for a lifetime." This is the philosophy of good teaching.

Interest

Good teaching makes the material relevant to learners and maintains their interest. Good teaching shows students how the material will apply to their lives and their careers. Good teaching makes students *want* to learn the material by making it interesting.

Respect

A good teacher always possesses these three core qualities: knowledge, the ability to convey to students an understanding of that knowledge, and the ability to make the material interesting and relevant to students. Complementing these three is a fourth quality: good teaching consists of a deep-seated concern and respect from the teacher for the students in the classroom.

1.3   Tips on becoming a good teacher

Teaching is like no other profession. As a teacher, one will wear many hats. He/She will, to name but of a few of the roles teachers assume in carrying out their duties, be a communicator, a disciplinarian, a conveyor of information, an evaluator, a classroom manager, a counselor, a facilitator, a member of many teams and groups, a decision-maker, a role-model, and a surrogate parent. Each of these roles requires practice and skills that are often not taught in teacher preparation programs. Not all who want to be teachers should invest the time and resources in preparation programs if they do not have the appropriate temperament, skills, and personality. Teaching has a very high attrition rate. In the course of teaching, many teachers drift to other careers. It is obviously not what they thought it would be. One thing for sure, it's about more than loving students.

For instance, as a conscientious and responsible teacher, the day doesn't usually end when the school bell rings. He/She will be involved in after-school meetings, committees, assisting students, grading homework, assignments, projects, calling parents, and so on. All these demand some sacrifice of one's personal time. If one is committed to excellence as a teacher, it's a sacrifice he/she can and has to live with.

Teacher preparation/training programs exist in every country, and the requirements vary. One will have many options from which to choose. Our advice is:

Select programs that offer a rich and solid foundation of courses, regardless of whether one is intending to teach at the elementary, middle school, or high school level. Most experts in teacher training and development would agree that no teacher education program can actually teach one how to teach in the classroom. It is recommended to choose a program that offers a balance of subject matter content courses and pedagogy, including clinical experience in all its forms. And of course, the skills should be practiced as perfectly as possible, along with the deepening of understandings of the concepts, theories and generalizations that one encounters. By doing so, one can build a solid foundation for learning how to teach.

As mentioned above, "how to teach" is not something uniformly agreed on by teachers and experts in the field. Good teachers always weave into an effective personal style of teaching. However, in one's training process to be a teacher, one should bear in mind the following:

a. Learn to explain things efficiently and appropriately.
b. Learn to control feelings and keep cool.
c. Love students and develop a sense of humor.
d. Learn to be fair in dealing with people: set high expectations for all students.
e. Learn to build a balance between flexibility and strictness.
f. Have a command of the content to be taught.
g. Learn to be careful and detail-oriented.
h. Learn to be good managers of time.
i. Learn to be reflective and critical.

These qualities define some of the characteristics to be developed by to-be-teachers. If you like, more specific and detailed items can be added, especially when it comes to English language teaching. In the next section, we look at some suggestions on teacher training and development in China.

2. Teacher training approaches

2.1 An introduction

In China, teacher training is largely provided through teachers training colleges or universities. Most of the institutions that offer teacher training programs are publicly funded by the central and local governments. These training programs have been closely linked to the need to:

- meet increased demands for access to compulsory education,

- professionalize teaching for expanding education as a whole,
- ensure that professional development opportunities are available for upgrading the skills of quailed teachers,
- expand training modalities by utilizing a greater variety of options such as pre-service training and job-embedded training,
- reform/develop the curriculum in order to meet the new and emerging needs of education while at the same time, reflect current international trends.

The drive to improve quality in teacher education has been shown in the educational field; money spent on making teachers efficient is considered money well spent. Thus, complementary ways are more and more used to co-promote teachers' qualities, such as community colleges, privately-funded language training centers and so on. However, before we come to some complementary ways for traditional training, let's first look at the significance of teachers' self-development.

2.2   Reflective teaching in teachers' self-development

From teachers' training, teachers' education, to teachers' development and empowerment, what has been mostly discussed is the responsibility of some educational agencies and official bureaus. However, teachers' self-development is an inalienable and irreplaceable part of enhancing the overall teaching qualities.

For most teachers, "reflective teaching" is the most important means of self-development. Reflection is "active, persistent and careful consideration of any belief or practice in light of the reasons that support it and the further consequences to which it leads" (Zeichner & Liston, 1996: 9). Reflective teaching is not just thinking about teaching. It should involve "critical examination of our motivation, thinking, and practice" (Bailey, Curtis & Nunan, 2001).

2.2.1 Introduction to reflective teaching

In 1994, Richards and Lockhart, in their book *Reflective Teaching in Second Language Classrooms*, state that the interest in reflective practice (RP) has been growing in (second) language education for some time, as well as in education more generally. The book starts with around 24 questions including: "What are my beliefs about teaching and learning, and how do these beliefs influence my teaching?" (Richards

& Lockhart, 1994: 1) and "What patterns of language use occur when I teach" (Richards & Lockhart, 1994: 2). Richards and Lockhart set out five assumptions:

- An informed teacher has an extensive knowledge base about teaching.
- Much can be learned about teaching through self-inquiry.
- Much of what happens in teaching is unknown to the teacher.
- Experience is insufficient as a basis for development.
- Critical reflection can trigger a deeper understanding of teaching (Richards & Lockhart, 1994: 3-4).

Curtis dwells on such questions as "Does RP mean the same thing to different people?" "Would each of us define and describe it differently?" (1999a).

But what is reflective practice in teaching? Curtis (1999a) observes that one of the signs that topics such as RT and RP are becoming established as distinct entities, worthy of specialized study and consideration within the academic community, is the launch of an academic journal devoted to that topic: *Reflective Practice*, launched in February 2000.

In sum, there are five dimensions of reflective practice in teaching (Curtis, 1999a):

- Rapid reflection: Immediate and automatic (Reflection-in-action)
- Repair: Thoughtful (Reflection-in-action)
- Review: Less formal (Reflection-on-action at a particular point in time)
- Research: More systematic (Reflection-on-action over a period of time)
- Retheorizing and reformulating: Long-term (Reflection-on-action informed by public academic theories)

2.2.2 Teacher development as a self-activity

Within various definitions in the teacher development literature, many are based on the ideas of self-awareness and self-observation. Therefore, any attempt to fully understand the basis and principles of RP or RT must first start with the self.

Curtis (1999b) claims that teaching itself is a selfish activity. The basis for these claims, which appear to go against the accepted belief that teaching is in fact a very giving and unselfish teaching, is as follows.

Despite all of the recent and growing interest in collaborative language teaching, in most language classrooms in the world today, there is still only one teacher. This may be for a number of reasons, not least of which is the fact that having two teachers teach the same class at the same time, though potentially enriching the experience for all, does cost twice as much. Also, some teachers may feel face-threatened or that their classrooms are territorially occupied with another teacher in their classroom. Whatever the reasons, this leads to what Lortie has called the egg carton aspect of teaching (1975), referring to the enclosed and protected behind closed-doors spaces of the classrooms in which most teaching and learning takes place.

A key consequence of this enclosing or isolation is the development of necessary self-conducted traits, such as: self-assurance, self-confidence, self-discipline, self-reliance. Teacher development focused on the self/selves can result in the kind of professional growth that benefits learners. In this sense, learner-centered teaching may in fact be complemented by teacher-centered teacher development.

Self-awareness

Larsen-Freeman (1983) puts forward a four-part relationship in terms of what teachers need to make informed choices about their teaching: awareness, attitude, knowledge and skills, among which awareness is regarded as the foundation on which to base choosing from a number of possible options:

I cannot make an informed choice unless I am aware that one exists. Awareness requires that I give attention to some aspect of my behavior or the situation I find myself in. Once I give that aspect my attention, I must also view it with detachment, with objectivity, for only then will I become aware of alternative ways of behaving, or alternative ways of viewing the situation, and only then will I have a choice to make. (1983: 266)

It is worth noting that notion or even the possibility of being objective has been much questioned in the postmodernism that has grown since Larsen-Freeman's comments. Freeman (1989) defined awareness as "the capacity to recognize and monitor the attention one is giving or has given to something". Thus, one acts on or responds to the aspects of a situation of which one is aware. Freeman's model (1989: 36) of the constituents of teaching also links awareness with attitude, skills and knowledge, which he defines as follows:

Attitude: A stance toward self, activity, and others.

Skills: The how of teaching.

Knowledge: The what of teaching (Freeman, 1989).

Both of these sets of definitions and frameworks show that awareness is an essential starting point. Van Lier (1998: 131) goes a step further and identifies different types of awareness:

Level 1: Global: intransitive consciousness

Level 2: Awareness: transitive consciousness, involving perceptual activity of objects and events in the environment, including attention, focusing, and vigilance.

Level 3: Metaconsciousness: awareness of the activity of the mind.

Level 4: Voluntary action, reflective processes, and mindfulness: deliberate and purposeful engagement in actions.

All these contributions and discussions show that, for language teachers, awareness of what we are doing, why and how we are doing it, as well as awareness of our learners, actions and behaviors, are key elements in language teachers working as reflective practitioners.

Self-observation and self-monitoring

According to Richards (1990: 118), self-observation is a systematic approach to the observation, evaluation, and management of one's own behavior... for the purposes of achieving a better understanding and control over one's behavior. There are critical differences between open observation and focused observation with four particular outcomes in mind: evaluation, management, understanding and control.

Richards stresses that self-monitoring complements, rather than replaces, other forms of assessment, such as feedback from students, peers, or supervisors (Richards, 1990: 119). Even with limited time for professional development, self-observation can provide valuable feedback. Self-monitoring can also lead to critical reflection and can help us better understand the instructional process. Moreover, self-monitoring can help to give back the responsibility for professional development to individual teachers (Curtis, 1999b).

This could be one effective way of helping to counter the current top-down, market model, knowledge-as-product approach to educational management which appears to be increasingly prevalent in education in general, and perhaps even more so in language teaching centers tasked with generating institutional income (Curtis, 1999b).

When embracing the concept of reflective teaching, there is often a commitment by teachers to take responsibility for their own professional development. This assumption of responsibility is a central feature of the idea of the reflective teacher. In terms of methods of self-monitoring for language teachers, Richards recommends teachers making a record of a lesson, either in the form of a written account or an audio or video recording of a lesson as a way of getting feedback on their teaching (1990: 118).

Dewey (1933), generally credited as one of the earliest (western) proponents of RP in education, believed that three key attitudes are necessary for RP: open-mindedness, responsibility, and whole-heartedness. His definition of reflection was active, persistent and careful consideration of any belief or practice in light of the reasons that support it and the further consequences to which it leads.

According to Dewey, reflection "emancipates us from merely impulsive and routine activity...and enables us to direct our actions with foresight and to plan according to ends in view of purposes of which we are aware" (1933: 17). Admittedly, education does not occur in social vacuums, i.e. all institutionalized teaching and learning takes place within societies which organize, arrange, monitor and assess the teaching and learning that takes place within them. Foreign/second language education is no exception. Nevertheless, reflection is not just an individual, psychological process. It occurs within the social circumstances: it is an actionoriented, historically-embedded, social and political frame, to locate oneself in the history of a situation, to participate in a social activity, and to take sides on issues. In the process of enhancing teacher development, self-awareness, self-observation and self-monitoring does not have to be carried out in isolation. Quite contrary, self-conducted learning and teaching can be promoted and bettered in cooperation with partners. This individual-societal relationship in RP has also been identified and discussed by Bartlett (1990: 204), for whom reflection is: the relationship between an individual's thought and action and the relationship between an individual teacher and his or her membership in a larger collective called society. The intrapersonal-interpersonal connection is highlighted by Bartlett when he stresses the importance of this individual-societal interaction in RP: The first relationship involves the subjective meanings in teachers' heads. The second relationship explores consciously the relationship between individual teaching actions and the purposes of education in society (Bartlett, 1990: 204-205).

2.3   New technologies for on-site and distance teacher training

Almost all institutions delivering teacher education have recognized the critical importance of the inclusion of new technologies for on-site delivery and for distance teaching. A major thrust in the use of the new technologies in teacher education occurred in the 1990s. Since then many language teaching agencies and institutes have been making steady progress in integrating new technologies for delivery as well as in the actual teacher education program as a pedagogical proficiency requirement. This focus on new technologies has to some extent been driven by the comprehensive reform agendas for improving ELT in China.

Another noteworthy innovation in the use of new technologies in teacher education is that many colleges are in partnership with a number of primary and secondary schools. The colleges function to provide training and support to the schools and the colleges in turn benefit through opportunities to conduct action research and are facilitated by the schools with respect to practicum arrangements for trainee teachers.

Distance education programs can work as another alternative to enhance teacher's quality in ELT in China. This is another important and complementary way to strengthen language teacher training. Teacher education program offered by distance is relatively new and there is still much scope for expansion in relation to the use of distance technologies for program delivery. Distance education appears to be one of the critical areas which hold tremendous prospects for development in teacher education in the near future. Its advantages are obvious. The use of the newer technologies allows teacher education candidates, most of whom would be classified as adult students, to pursue studies with some degree of flexibility after working hours. The conferencing facility whether via the internet or by teleconference, exposes participants to a fascinating array of shared experiences centered on teaching and learning. Training support materials, if competently prepared and current, might considerably augment resources which are available in some institutional libraries. Such delivery could also be used to promote the professional development of teacher educators either on a short-term basis in specific areas, or for advanced qualifications at the Master in Education or Diploma levels.

Questions for further discussion:

1. Investigate among your classmates and find out the top five qualities of a good English teacher.

2. How can you make yourself a reflective teacher?
3. In what sense can we say teaching is a selfish activity?
4. How important is it for a teacher to be self-reflective? Why is reflection also a social behavior?

References:

Bailey, K., Curtis, A., & Nunan, D. 2001. *Pursuing Professional Development: Self as Source*. Teacher Source. Freeman, D., Series Editor.

Bartlett, L. 1990. Teacher development through reflective teaching. In J.C. Richards and Nunan, D. (Eds.), *Second Language Teacher Education*. Cambridge University Press.

Beidler, P. G. 1997. What makes a good teacher? In J. K. Roth (ed.) *Inspiring Teaching*, Anker, Bolton MA.

Brain, M. 1998. *Emphasis on Teaching*. BYG Publishing, Inc.

Curtis, A. 1999a. Re-visioning our roles: Teachers as experts, researchers and reflective practitioners. *Thai TESOL Bulletin,* 12(2): 24-32.

Curtis, A. 1999b. Collaboration as the key to excellence. In *ELT collaboration: Towards excellence in the new millennium: Selected papers from the 4th CULI international conference*. Chulalongkorn University Language Institute.

Dewey, J. 1933. *How We Think*. Henry Regnery.

Freeman, D. 1989. Teacher training, development and decision making: A model of teaching and related strategies for language teacher education. *TESOL Quarterly,* 23(1): 27-45.

Hassett, M. F. 2000. What Makes a Good Teacher. *Adventures in Assessment, 12*, SABES/ World Education, Boston, MA.

Hu, G. W. 2005. Professional Development of Secondary EFL Teachers: Lessons From China. http://www.blackwell-synergy.com/.

Larsen-Freeman, D. 1983. Expanding roles of learners and teachers in learner-centered instruction. In W. A. Renandya & G. M. Jacobs (Eds.), *Learners and Language Learning Anthology Series*. 39: 207-226. SEAMEO Regional Language Centre.

Lortie, D. 1975. *Schoolteacher: A Sociological Study*. University of Chicago Press.

Palmer, P. 1999. The Grace of Great Things: Reclaiming the Sacred in Knowing, Teaching, and Learning. In *The Heart of Knowing: Spirituality in Education*. Ed. Stephen Glazer. Jeremy P. Tarcher/Putnam.

Richards, J. C. 1990. The teacher as self-observer: Self-monitoring in teacher development. In J.C. Richards, *The Language Teaching Matrix*. Cambridge University Press.

Richards, J. & Lockhart, C. 1994. *Reflective Teaching in Second Language Classrooms*. Cambridge University Press.

Zeichner, K.M. & Liston, D.P. 1996. *Reflective Teaching: An Introduction*. Lawrence Erlbaum Associates, Inc.